Joe Wilson
and the
Creation
of Xerox

Joe Wilson and the Creation of Xerox

CHARLES D. ELLIS

WILEY

John Wiley & Sons, Inc.

Published by John Wiley & Sons, Inc., Hoboken, New Jersey
Published simultaneously in Canada

For general information on our other products and services or for technical support, please contact our Customer Care Department within the United States at (800) 762-2974, outside the United States at (317) 572-3993, or fax (317) 572-4002.

Wiley also publishes its books in a variety of electronic formats. Some content that appears in print may not be available in electronic books. For more information about Wiley products, visit our web site at www.wiley.com .

Library of Congress Cataloging-in-Publication Data:

Ellis, Charles D.
  Joe Wilson and the creation of Xerox / Charles D. Ellis.
    p. cm.
  Includes index.
  ISBN-13: 978-0-471-99835-8 (cloth)
  ISBN-10: 0-471-99835-4 (cloth)
    1. Wilson, Joseph C. (Joseph Chamberlain), 1909–1971. 2. Xerox Corporation—History. 3. Copying machine industry—United States—History. I. Title.
  HD9802.3.U64X474 2006
  338.7'68165092—dc22   2006007379

Printed in the United States of America

10   9   8   7   6   5   4   3   2   1

To those many mentors outside my family who disproportionately and favorably influenced my life by their guidance and examples: Marion Casey, Nellie Walsh at Gerry School, Al Gross in Boy Scouts, Dick Mayo-Smith at Exeter, Chris Argyris at Yale and beyond, the team at WYBC, John McArthur and Jay Light at HBS, Dick Dilworth at Rockefeller Brothers, Joe Lasser at Wertheim, Joe Reich and Dick Jenrette at DLJ, Bob Lindsay at NYU, Fred Mayer at Exeter, Ev Smith and Don Jacobs at Greenwich Associates, Peter Drucker in Claremont, and David Swensen at Yale.

CONTENTS

INTRODUCTION

Stories about Joe Wilson abound in the Xerox culture—his vision, his values, his entrepreneurism, his risk-taking, his acumen, his intellect, his leadership. But the stories you hear the most are about the man.

Long after it was practical, Joe tried to know everyone in his company on a first-name basis. He was more apt to ask you how the family was than how the business was. Everyone who knew him—and that was just about everyone in the company—has a personal story to tell about Joe Wilson, a story about how he touched or inspired them personally. He was that kind of person.

When he died in 1971, he had a little card in his wallet. It was frayed, suggesting it had been there for years. Here's what it said:

> To be a whole man; to attain serenity: Through the creation
> of a family life of uncommon richness; through leadership of
> a business which brings happiness to its workers, serves well
> its customers and brings prosperity to its owners; by aiding a
> society threatened by fratricidal division to gain unity.

What a beautiful and succinct statement of a life's goals—family, work, and community. And from everything I know about Joe Wilson, he achieved all three with stunning and remarkable success. His family, his company, and his community can all attest to the power and the endurance of his legacy.

Protecting and enhancing that legacy is very important to those of us at Xerox who carry his mantle. I believe it's what galvanized Xerox people to turn the company around over the past few difficult years. Many of you will recall that when I was named President and later Chief Executive Officer of Xerox in 2001, the company had its back against the wall. We were teetering on the brink of bankruptcy. Some wise analysts said we couldn't save Xerox. The pundits were writing our obituary. Industry analysts wrote that time had passed us by. Many said that Xerox was doomed.

But this generation of Xerox people would not allow that to happen. They said, Not on our watch! Xerox cannot and will not fail. I hope the historians will record that Xerox people banded together and willed Xerox back to success because they believed in the company that Joe Wilson founded and the values he instilled.

Leading Xerox these past few years has been the opportunity of a lifetime. And in what may be the understatement of all time, I've learned a lot along the way:

- I've learned about the power of communications. You can't do enough of it.
- I've learned about the power of culture. You need to change the bad and leverage the good.
- I've learned about the need to articulate a vision of where you are taking the company. Employees especially need to know what they are signing on for.
- I've learned a lot about the power of leadership. Bad leadership can ruin a company overnight. Good leadership can move mountains over time.

But mostly I learned three lessons from Joe Wilson.

Lesson 1: Invest in innovation even when you can't afford it.

When Joe Wilson saw that Haloid was in a declining market in a postwar economy, he bet money he didn't have on the innovative idea of Chester Carlson. And when Xerox was on the ropes a few years ago, we invested money some said we could ill afford on creating innovative ideas to secure our future.

Even as we dramatically reduced our cost base, we maintained research and development spending in our core business. In fact, we didn't take a single dollar out of R&D in our core business—not one.

As a result, the last few years have been our biggest new product years in our history.

Joe Wilson taught us a lesson we will never forget: Creating customer value is the key to the success of Xerox and innovation is the key to creating customer value. It's a lesson and a legacy that has become part of the DNA of Xerox: Invest in innovation or perish.

Lesson 2: Recognize the importance of values. Joe gave us a set of six. They are perhaps more ingrained in Xerox today than when he first promulgated them in the early 1960s. They form our North Star. Take any one away and Xerox would cease to be Xerox. They are:

- We succeed through satisfied customers.
- We value and empower our employees.
- We deliver quality and excellence in all we do.
- We require premium return on assets.
- We use technology to deliver market leadership.
- We behave responsibly as a corporate citizen.

During the decade of the sixties when Xerox came to prominence and was growing rapidly, the Rochester community—like so may others across the nation—was torn apart by race riots and the struggle for social justice. Corporate citizenship was in its infancy. There were no books to tell CEOs how to behave or what to do.

Joe Wilson didn't need a book to tell him what to do. He understood that a healthy community was good for Xerox, that a corporation has a moral obligation to give back, and that no company can operate independent of the community in which its people live and work.

Through Joe's leadership, Xerox did not turn its back on the problems of the midsixties. We embraced them by donating human and financial resources to the community, helping start organizations to spur economic growth in the inner city, providing job opportunities and training, and launching a diversity program within Xerox that is still a point of corporate pride.

Joe's involvement in the civil rights struggles of the mid-sixties forever changed the face of Xerox and set us on a course of social involvement that has become part and parcel of the way we have done business ever since.

Lesson 3: Joe's next lesson is perhaps the most profound: The genius of any organization resides in the hearts and minds of its people.

I keep an old videotape of Joe Wilson in my office. It captures him informally welcoming a new group of employees to Xerox in 1962. Here's part of what he has to say:

> Welcome to Xerox. You are the key to our success. Andrew Carnegie once said people are all important to any business. "Take away my money and my customers and my products and my equipment and leave me my people," Carnegie said, "and within a few years I'll have my steel plants operating at full capacity." That's the way we feel about people at Xerox. Your imagination and your perseverance are central to the company's success.

Joe's counsel was brought into sharp focus over the past few years as Xerox struggled to right its ship. When people ask me how we made so much progress in such a short period of time, I don't have to think about the answer. I tell them you have to have a good strategy, but it can be roughly right. And you have to have a good implementation plan, but it too can be roughly right. The critical component is the alignment of a talented and motivated people around a common set of objectives.

Joe was a man of many paradoxes. He was as comfortable in the corridors of power as on the factory floor. He was an entrepreneur and risk-taker who felt a strong obligation to protect jobs and pay good wages. He was fascinated by the power of science and technology but insisted that it be harnessed to make us more human. And he was a leader who set high goals but was rooted in the art of the possible.

He was also an amazingly literate man who quoted Plato and

Shakespeare with ease. One of his favorite verses was from Robert Browning:

> That low man seeks a little thing to do,
> Sees it and does it:
> This high man, with a great thing to pursue,
> Dies ere he knows it.
> That low man goes on adding one to one,
> His hundred's soon hit:
> This high man, aiming at a million,
> Misses by a unit.

Like everything about Joe Wilson, that strikes me as wise counsel. This generation of Xerox people is committed to reach for the stars. But we're also committed to do so in a way that honors the legacy of our founder and our inspiration: the man I never met. After reading Charley Ellis's wonderful ode, you'll know why Joe Wilson is still with us in profound and important ways. Someone once said that few people leave footsteps in the sands of time. Joe Wilson is one of these few.

Anne M. Mulcahy
Chairman and Chief Executive Officer
Xerox Corporation
Stamford, Connecticut

FOREWORD

"**W**here have you gone, Joe Wilson?"

If Simon and Garfunkel had decided to write their signature song lyric about a business leader instead of a baseball player, they would have written about Joe Wilson. Just as DiMaggio elevated the game of baseball by infusing his values and character into the way he played the game, so Wilson elevated the profession of management by infusing his values and character into the way he led his company. As Charley Ellis's wonderful biography shows, Joe Wilson valued many things: the promise of technology, the economic development of his community, the fair treatment of his workers, racial equality, and so on.

What Joe Wilson personally valued had an impact on how Joe Wilson led, and as a consequence, Joe Wilson's legacy speaks to a profound anxiety that I, in my capacity as business school dean, observe among those who are in or entering the business world. This anxiety does not arise out of the difficulty of satisfying fickle, demanding consumers. It does not arise from the uncertainty that comes with competing in a fragile, complicated global economy. Nor does it arise out of the concern with mollifying shareholders who respond to extraordinary performance with ratcheted expectations of higher performance.

Rather, this new anxiety has its origins in the belief that the experience of business leadership is supposed to be something more than satisfying consumers, meeting strategic challenges, and creating shareholder value. The experience of leadership is supposed to be something more than a daily obsession with how to maximize profits. Yet, when I interact with current business leaders or when I

talk with MBAs about their hopes and fears regarding future opportunities, both groups seem troubled in the way that *The Graduate's*
young Benjamin Braddock was troubled. Both business leaders and
newly minted MBAs seem worried that a relentless focus on profits
today simply leaves them "in the game" so that they can maintain
that same exhausting focus tomorrow. They worry that the game—
even when played skillfully—is just not as fulfilling as it was supposed to be.

The story of Joe Wilson is an inspiring story for those who are
looking to believe that the experience of business leadership can be
something more. Joe Wilson shows that for the truly great leader
of a business enterprise, the commitment to the shareholder and
the relentless demands of competition do not require the sacrifice
of deeply held values or the suppression of self. On the contrary,
the leader's unwavering commitment to values can be one of the
bedrocks of economic value creation; this unwavering commitment
infuses an energy and passion that is essential if an organization is to
rank among the highest performing.

Stated somewhat differently, Joe Wilson shows that successful
leadership can be based on a strong connection between the positive
values that define the leader's self and the values that define the
organization's culture. A position of leadership is an opportunity to
elevate those core values and, in the process, infuse meaning into
the organization for which the leader is responsible.

Of course, it has been 25 years since Joe Wilson's death. One
might wonder why it is necessary to look back so far to make this
important point. Aren't there any Joe Wilsons today? Of course
there are; there are many: BP's John Browne, Costco's Jim Senegal,
eBay's Meg Whitman, FedEx's Fred Smith, Goldman Sachs's John
Whitehead, and Xerox's Anne Mulcahy are among others known
and not yet known. We don't see them as often as we should; their
stories are often lost amid the newspaper articles focused on ethical
violations or compensation contracts that allow CEOs to be rewarded
in a way that is completely incommensurate with their performance.

But even if there are modern-day Joe Wilsons, there is value in looking to history. The passing of time affords a perspective that allows
for the careful and patient reconstruction of the connection between
the details of a leader's life and the indelible impression that the
leader leaves on an organization.

In undertaking this careful and patient reconstruction, Charley
Ellis gives us the opportunity to think about leadership in a different
way. Rather than think about leadership as a formula that someone
else has discovered and that the rest of us must follow, one can
instead begin to think about leadership as the paving of the connections from what is deeply personal to what is highly professional.
So, as you read this book, enjoy and reflect on that connection.

Joel Podolny
Dean, Yale School of Management

1

EARLY YEARS

Rochester is a river town, founded on the Genesee River where the falls drop 90 feet, providing power for the grain mills that were the first real business of the Flour City. Milling brought prosperity to Rochester in the early 19th century as the Erie Canal—on an ingeniously designed aqueduct bridge—crossed *over* the Genesee River. With the canal's waterway crossroads established in 1824, Rochester's population multiplied a hundredfold in just 10 years.

Before this surge, development had been slow, and for good reason. Ebenezer "Indian" Allen, the first settler in the mosquito-infested swamps south of Lake Ontario, where the insects caused what was called "Genesee Fever," made a treaty with the Seneca Indians and built a mill in 1789. Then in 1803, Colonel Nathaniel Rochester and two partners in Maryland invested $17.50 in 100 acres they later described as "a god forsaken place, inhabited by muskrats, visited only by struggling trappers, and through which neither man nor beast could go without fear of starvation or fever or ague." Hamlet Scranton was the first log cabin resident: He came in 1812. During the next dozen years, water power and grain milling supported a small town.

With the Erie Canal crossing *over* the Genesee River and creating a "water crossroads," the small town became a small city. As water power lost prominence, Rochester's climate, moderated by the Great Lakes, made the region ideal for growing hardy plants. In a few years, the Flour City became the Flower City, as more than 100 parks of various sizes attracted 200,000 visitors each May, who flocked to the area to see 540 different varieties of lilacs in bloom.

Half a century later, technology transformed Rochester when George Eastman popularized amateur photography by making it easy: "You push the button and we do the rest!" On the steady profits that flowed from one of the great consumer businesses of all time, he built the largest corporation in the Empire State: Eastman Kodak. Still known reverently as Mr. Eastman, he financed the Eastman School of Music, which holds 500 concerts annually, and joined with John D. Rockefeller to build the original University of Rochester.

Kodak was based on a technology and an innovative marketing concept that were just as new in the late 1800s as xerography and charging by the copy would be in the 1960s. Eastman Kodak headquarters remained in Rochester and Kodak was Rochester's largest employer. Kodak was the major corporate citizen, and George Eastman was the major individual citizen of Rochester, providing a bar by which Joe Wilson could measure himself and his company.

Social activism became a celebrated tradition in Rochester. In addition to the philanthropy of Eastman, it was the home of former slave Frederick Douglass and the Abolitionist movement and is where Susan B. Anthony began the Women's Suffrage movement. This may explain why taking responsibility for social improvement would have such special meaning for Joe Wilson.

The Wilsons came to Rochester in stages. Joe Wilson's great-great-grandfather, William Wilson, emigrated from England to Binghamton, New York, in the early 1800s. His great grandparents, Harry and Ann Wilson, grew up in New York City and soon after their marriage moved to Syracuse where their son, Joseph C. "JC"

Wilson was born in 1854. A muskrat trapper along the Chenango River as a boy, JC Wilson left school after the eighth grade, apprenticed to a jeweler, and soon became his leading traveling salesman. In 1878, JC Wilson moved to Rochester to become the partner of a pawnbroker-jeweler. He married Alice Hutton of Syracuse in 1881, and they had two daughters and one son. In 1885, JC acquired full ownership of the pawnshop and renamed it JC Wilson & Company. Later, he invested in a used clothes retailer, Acme Sales Company, and became the equivalent of a community banker by lending moderate amounts to help finance local businesses. In addition to earning good profits on his loans (and on street railway contracts), JC Wilson developed a network of grateful friends and the sort of influence that would fit well with his increasing interest in politics.

JC Wilson's son, Joseph Robert Wilson, was born in 1882 and graduated from the University of Rochester in 1903. Since the affable father was always known as "JC", the son—who was known as Dick to his family and friends—was often called "JR." The nickname stuck, and later in life he became Mr. JR. While assisting his father in the pawnshop, JR Wilson met Katharine M. Upton, the daughter of a railroad engineer, when she came to pick up the gold watch her father had left for repair. They married in 1903.

The year 1906 was significant—just by coincidence—for each of four very different business beginnings in very different regions that would be important to Joe Wilson's life for very different reasons. In 1906, Chester Carlson, the future inventor of xerography, was born in Seattle. In 1906, George Beidler started the Rectigraph Company in Oklahoma City to produce copies *without* requiring a photographic negative. And in 1906, John Gordon Battelle gambled successfully on a newly patented process for upgrading low-grade zinc ore mined from properties owned by his family in Joplin, Missouri, and made the fortune with which he would endow a great industrial research organization: Battelle Memorial Institute.

Also in 1906, JC Wilson and three partners incorporated in

Rochester the tiny Haloid Corporation. Most of Haloid's employees had been working for the M.H. Kuhn Company, a small paper coating shop located in an eighth-floor loft of the CP Ford Shoe Company building on Commercial Street at the upper falls of the Genesee River. M.H. Kuhn had been started in 1902 by the son of a German immigrant emulsion maker and a few others who had worked at Eastman Kodak. JC Wilson had arranged for JR Wilson to join M.H. Kuhn after graduating from the University of Rochester in 1903. But before he could get started with Kuhn, young Wilson suffered a serious kidney ailment that kept him out of work for two years. By then, M.H. Kuhn had failed. JC Wilson, believing his son's best prospects were to grow with a small business, provided most of the start-up financing for Haloid. The new little company hired most of Kuhn's employees and set up shop in the same eighth floor loft, enabling JR Wilson to join Haloid. He would later joke, "We started at the top!"

The scrappy little start-up enterprise certainly did not use sophisticated technology: The "air conditioning" needed to set the emulsions was provided by huge cakes of ice, with fans blowing the cooled air over the coated paper. Haloid's coating alley was so short that the sensitized paper had to go down one side of the loft, make a U-turn, and go back up the other side. Primitive as it was, the small company developed a modest business making photographic paper that was sold directly to commercial photographers at a lower price than Kodak's. Product irregularities had hurt the Kuhn Company badly, so Haloid recruited a skilled emulsions expert, Homer H. Reichenbach, who strongly recommended building a new plant where conditions could be controlled (he also suggested the name Haloid would suit a business based on Halogen salts).[1]

[1]*A History of Haloid*, in the Rochester Commerce, by William O'Toole, October 1956. Facts and quotations from documents are often given citations. However, facts and quotations may also come from the numerous interviews given by the individuals identified in the Afterword and in the draft biography prepared by the company. Interviewees include Blake McKelvey and Rochester's historians. When interviews were done by other interviewers, they are individually cited.

In 1907, Haloid and its 12 employees were ready to move out of the loft and into a new plant. But to make the move it needed money—a lot of money for such a small business—$50,000 (or nearly $1 million in current dollars). Finding that much equity capital for a small business was hard. No institutional investors made venture capital investments in those days, so the money would have had to come from wealthy individuals. JR Wilson turned to Gilbert E. Mosher, an acquaintance who was a successful Rochester businessman who had recently become wealthy when his company, Century Camera Company, sold out to Eastman Kodak. As JR Wilson had surmised, Mosher was looking for opportunities to invest.

Mosher was in a strong negotiating position; Wilson was not. So Mosher drove a hard bargain and insisted on being in charge of business operations and having, with his associate J. Millner Walmsley, effective ownership control through a voting trust that would hold the stock of JC Wilson and others. In addition to providing the needed capital, Mosher was a capable and experienced executive with good judgment who wanted to apply his management capabilities. "He might drive a hard bargain, but he gave you a dollar's worth of value for every dollar you paid. What he was offering the Haloid Company was executive ability, financial astuteness, and strong leadership. Any company in Rochester would have welcomed this man's help."[2] Mosher took a disciplined approach to business that differed considerably from Wilson's.

JR Wilson liked to play the mandolin and the piano, and he liked to play loudly. At the company, he developed a reputation for being gregarious with customers and outside visitors, but having an explosive temper in the office, scolding employees he felt made mistakes and frowning sternly while muttering to himself. JR was often out late at night drinking with the boys and then back at work early the next morning, being just as hard as nails on the very same men. At home, JR's grumbling about his frustrations at the company and his

[2]Dessauer, page 2.

bragging about what he would have done or could have said—usually to Gilbert Mosher—so dominated family dinnertime that his young son quietly promised himself never to let that sort of thing happen when he was grown up and had his own family.

Joseph Chamberlain Wilson—always known as Joe Wilson—was born on December 13, 1909. He and his brother Dick, who was six years younger, were never particularly close. Nor was Joe emotionally close to his parents. Joe's mother, Kate, was reserved and formal—certainly not "cuddly"—but invariably gracious and polite to others, a characteristic she passed on to her devoted and conscientious son. Recognizing his particular interest in books, she helped Joe learn to read and write at an early age. Despite his poor eyesight, he often spent time in bed reading with a flashlight under the blanket he had pulled up over his head, alone in his own private world of adventures and ideas.

As a boy, Joe often played alone in his room, constructing little buildings with ceramic poker chips. He had schoolboy friends, but was always quite shy, never good at sports, and something of a loner. When the Wilson family moved to Rugby Street, Joe changed elementary schools from No. 7 to No. 16, where he enrolled in a special program for gifted children. Changing schools changed his circle of friends and must have added to a feeling that he was on his own. He went to special classes for gifted students at Madison Junior High for two years and then on to West High School where, given his poor eyesight, he chose to be assistant manager of the basketball team and then, as a senior, became manager. Joe liked school, studied hard, earned good grades, enjoyed discussing books and ideas, and developed a lifelong appetite for knowledge and understanding. He began to realize that he could make his life more interesting, more useful to others, and more personally rewarding.

As a teenager, he also did conventionally unconventional things. He marked the racy passages of library books such as the *Canterbury*

Tales, Don Juan, and *Don Quixote.* Readily accepted as the leader among his circle of friends, he assigned different days to each of his pals and gave explicit directions on how to approach the shelves holding the selected books indirectly and casually so they could all read the racy sections at the library without crowding together in ways that might attract the librarian's attention.

Before completing high school, Joe paid a few surreptitious visits to the burlesque shows at Corinthian Hall located near Rattlesnake Pete's Saloon. He also did his first back flip off the diving board at Keuka Lake and served as a counselor at the YMCA's Camp Cory. He became skilled at shooting pool, learned the batting averages of all the great baseball players, and developed a major crush on Marilyn Miller, the Broadway star.[3]

Joe's shy manner and intellectual inclinations made it hard for him to feel comfortable with his father, a volatile man who had strong convictions and was often gruff. Joe was much closer to his affable, knowledgeable, and patient grandfather, with whom he developed a special one-on-one relationship. This established a recurring, lifelong pattern of developing close counseling relationships with different men. Over the years, three individuals served as his principal personal advisors. With each, he discussed a wide range of topics to gain their perspectives and independent views, as well as to enjoy the pleasures of close friendship and trust: first, his grandfather, JC Wilson; then his classmate, Jack Hartnett; and later, his business colleague, Sol Linowitz.

During Joe's formative years, the widely admired, respected, and well-liked JC Wilson was the greatest single influence on the development of his namesake grandson. They spent many hours talking about every subject under the sun. Joe was indelibly impressed with the self-control and willpower of his grandfather, whose motto was "Never make a promise you cannot keep and say nothing rather than

[3]Recollections of Lincoln V. Burrows, May 19, 1979.

something if you are in doubt." Joe and his grandfather often discussed the City Manager movement, which was gaining momentum with the support of George Eastman. In the spring of 1927, this was the subject of Joe's valedictory oration at West High School's graduation.

Growing up in Rochester, Joe Wilson looked forward to becoming part of the community and, eventually, a leader within the city. Rochester, which would always be central in Joe's world, was very clearly separated from such major centers of government, finance, culture, and recreation as New York, Boston, and Chicago, especially in winter when snowdrifts were deep. The minimum travel time to reach New York City was nine hours by train or twelve hours by automobile. There was no way to fly. Rochestarians may not have considered themselves isolated, but clearly their city was "geographically independent."

At the same time, Rochester enjoyed many local strengths: The University of Rochester had the Eastman School of Music; the region had easy access to many types of outdoor recreation; and the greater Rochester community provided a good climate for raising families. In addition, Rochester was blessed by the absence of most of the problems that plagued America's big cities: traffic congestion, slums, and divisive politics. Rochester was a peaceful place to grow up, and the Wilsons had become part of Rochester's establishment. In Rochester, Joe enjoyed a strong and secure sense of place.

While Joe was growing up, Haloid was also progressing under the strict direction of Gilbert Mosher, who became general manager and then, taking over from JC Wilson, became president in 1917. He substantially expanded the sales organization and opened new sales offices. Mosher's strength was finance and he dressed the part of a big-time financier: he wore spats, a homburg, and gloves—with a flower in his buttonhole—and carried a cane. Mosher lived in style, riding in a chauffeured Cadillac limousine, wintering in Boca Raton, and summering at a fishing camp in the Catskills. In business management, Mosher was from the old school. He expected employees to stand up when he entered the Haloid office and barely tolerated such follies as a coffee break. A stickler for neatness, Mosher liked to make unexpected visits to the plant, where he would check for dust in corners and on high shelves and then berate employees— including JR Wilson—for any discovered negligence. In his office, there were no chairs for visitors and smoking was not allowed. Mosher once ordered a subordinate to clear off the benches near the employee parking lot and to "fire the damned malingerers" who were lounging on them. They might get a 10-minute break, but "many of those lazy good-for-nothings had been goofing off for a full 20 minutes!" Mosher was right on the 20 minutes, but what he didn't know was that the men were not stretching a 10-minute break, they'd come 20 minutes ahead of the start of the second shift. (Joe Wilson's thoughtful discipline included choices of what *not* to do as well as what to do. He surely learned selective lessons about behaviors to avoid from both his father and Mr. Mosher.)

As John Dessauer, who led research at Wilson's company for many years and produced a book about the company (*My Years at Xerox*), reported: "Mosher did not marry until he was well on in middle age, and during this bachelorhood he had an incredibly lengthy succession of housekeepers. If no one remained in his service very long, it was because he pursued the same tests in his house: He would conceal a match or a slip of paper on top of a cupboard. If it was still there a few days later, the housekeeper would icily be charged with negligence." For many years he lived as a bachelor. Then, after his mother's death, he married Miss Helen Halloran, a Catholic whose picture he had kept on his filing cabinet for many years, but did not marry until the death of his Baptist mother.

Since Haloid could not compete in research and development with Eastman Kodak, General Aniline & Film, or DuPont, its strategy was to have a resourceful group of direct salesmen ferreting out small niche markets where brand names and a consumer franchise didn't much matter, but where selling, service, and lower prices

could develop a meaningful comparative advantage. Sales and business expansion had JR Wilson on the road a good deal of the time,
as sales offices were established in New York, Chicago, and Boston.
Production space was doubled in 1923. But even with that expansion, demand was so strong that employees were working overtime
within six months. (Haloid expanded facilities again in 1926, but for
the next 20 years, sales would not surpass the 1923 record.)

Joe Wilson went to the University of Rochester. His father and
uncle were both graduates of the University. His father had
served as a member of the board of managers, and his beloved
grandfather had been active in the major capital campaign that
helped finance the University's move to its new River campus. So,
with all of his best friends staying home in Rochester and going to
the U of R, it was not hard for Joe to set aside his thoughts of an
Eastern college and accept his father's offer of a new Buick Cabrolet
roadster if he would stay home and enroll with the 114 other students in his class at the University. Joe pledged DKE, his father's fraternity, where he later served as treasurer. He also managed the
football team, wore a raccoon skin coat, was junior prom chairman,
and served on the Y council. In his junior year, he received another
Buick roadster from his father. Always very studious, he was
observed by his classmates to be the one who was the most self-
disciplined, who asked the most questions, and who was always the
most thoroughly prepared.[4] This set another lifelong pattern of
deliberately planned behavior.

Joe demonstrated a keen appetite for knowledge and a thirst not
only to understand what he was reading, but also to know what was
behind everything he read.[5] This pursuit of understanding in what
he read was matched by his keen interest in understanding other
people as individuals and knowing what they were doing and why.

[4] McKelvey, page I-186.
[5] Jack Hartnett interview with Blake McKelvey.

Majoring in economics, Joe earned high grades (with the one glaring exception of physical education), was elected to Phi Beta Kappa and graduated summa cum laude. Wilson was also learning a major life lesson: He had considerable talent, and with concentrated, disciplined effort, he realized he could achieve results that were important to him and to his community.

Even more important for his life in leadership, he would become deeply engaged, through books, in a rich intellectual life that would enhance his private time while informing and empowering him during his years at the company and in public service. He developed an appreciation for the interrelationship of capitalism and democracy. Through Shakespeare, he learned lessons that he applied when formulating company policies for retired workers. As an adult, Wilson made time to read two or three serious books a week, searching for ideas and insights to integrate into his own thinking, which he could easily and regularly reference in his many speeches. The books he read—and carefully marked and annotated—were kept in his extensive library at home. His love of continuous study and learning was not only unusual for a business executive it was, in an unusually warm and close marriage, one of the few interests not shared by his wife.

2

PEGGY

Joe Wilson met Peggy Curran when both were doing a good deed for a friend. Lincoln Burrows, Joe's classmate and fraternity brother, had caught pneumonia and was in bed for several weeks. Joe and Peggy both happened to call on him during the same afternoon. They came separately, but Joe gave Peggy a ride home in his new Buick. A few days later, Peggy went to a fraternity party with Joe and that night reported: "Mom, I've met the man I'm going to marry."

Both knew they were very different from one another when they started dating. Joe was Establishment and well-off. Peggy's father was a local hotel manager and clearly not well off. Joe was a conscientious student, considering an academic career; Peggy did not plan to go to college. Peggy was the eldest of eight children; Joe had only one brother. She was a devout Catholic with a sister who was a nun; he was a "lapsed" Presbyterian. Their religious differences were, for Joe, particular cause for concern and became the topic of several thoughtful discussions with his friends. But Peggy and Joe enjoyed each other greatly and felt comfortable together, and Joe always preferred very few, really close relationships. His increasingly special romantic relationship with Peggy harmonized with Joe's warm relationship with his grandfather, which continued to be particularly important to his sense of self and his place in Rochester.

A high-ranking 32nd degree Mason, JC Wilson began his political career in 1895 as an insurgent candidate for alderman with the support of the Good Government Club. When he won decisively, he was quickly brought into the regular Republican organization by George W. Aldridge, the master of the GOP in Monroe County. For 34 years, JC Wilson was a political leader who "loved to distribute patronage and extend many helping hands."[1] As the Republican leader of the 19th Ward, with a population of 60,000, JC Wilson rose steadily up the ranks in Rochester's political offices. Over more than three decades, he served continuously and sequentially as Alderman (1895–1900); City Assessor (1900–1917); Treasurer (1917–1919); and Comptroller (1919–1928).

In 1928, during a battle to adopt the City Manager form of municipal government—which JC had endorsed in 1925 and which had strong support in his 19th Ward—Wilson split with the regular GOP organization. He joined the Citizens' Republican Committee, ran for councilman-at-large, and won the largest vote. With the change to the City Manager structure of government, the position of Mayor of Rochester became just a ceremonial job of presiding at routine meetings and signing routine papers. Political leaders saw a match: JC Wilson was popular and gregarious; he had served Rochester for 35 years in public offices; he knew everyone, and he was familiar with both financial and organizational details of the city. Because they believed his well-established reputation in financial circles would enhance the city's creditworthiness, JC Wilson was the unanimous choice of the councilmen to fill the ceremonial office of Mayor.

Then in his mid-seventies, JC Wilson took to his new job as Mayor of Rochester with enthusiasm, never minding its having been

[1]*Rochester Evening Journal*, Nov. 18, 1927.

stripped of any real power and being clearly subordinated to the role of City Manager. Neither did he mind that the impressive suite of offices formerly used by the Mayor had been taken over by the City Manager nor that the new Mayor's office was consigned to just one part of what had been the old Mayor's anteroom. Wilson loved being Mayor and performed his role with enthusiasm.

Two years later at the age of 78, JC Wilson was convalescing from an illness. He expressed a desire to retire, but was persuaded to run again for the post of councilman-at-large. The regular Republicans, confident they could bring Wilson around to their side after the election, also nominated him. This obliged the City Manager League either to reject Wilson or to endorse a Republican. Although confined to bed and unable to campaign, he was hailed in the newspapers as "the most popular office holder in the last two generations," and after 35 years of service to Rochester, JC Wilson was re-elected. Too weak to put on the clothes lain out for him, he was unable to attend the organizational meeting held downtown after the election. He would live only a few weeks longer.

When his beloved grandfather died in 1930, Joe was deeply upset and needed to talk.[2] Riding in his new car, Joe and Peggy talked together for several hours. In the weeks that followed, their already comfortable relationship grew stronger. They continued dating through his senior year at the university and at the invitation of Joe's parents, Peggy made several visits to the Wilson's summer cottage at Point Pleasant on Lake Ontario.

Then, following a major argument, they broke up. Almost simultaneously, Peggy's family moved away to Buffalo where Mr. Curran would manage the Ford Hotel and work as a local builder. In addition to those emotional and geographic separations, their personal directions were also diverging. For Joe, it was time to decide what he would do after graduation.

[2]Wilson inherited $250,000 from his grandfather. In purchasing power, this would be about $4 million in current dollars.

Joe was uncertain about his career, particularly given the Depression. He decided against studying at Julliard to become a concert pianist. An academic life still had some appeal, but since he was determined to earn more money than a professor could, he was considering a career in business or banking. (In one of his courses, each student had been asked what he or she planned to do. Joe Wilson's direct answer, "Make a million dollars," while glib, was a clear signal that he intended to accomplish something in business that was significant.) One of his professors suggested that two years at Harvard Business School would not only help prepare him for any career he might choose, but would also give him the time and detachment to ponder his alternatives. Even though he was both shy and quiet, the Harvard Business School's lively, give-and-take case discussion method of instruction and learning suited Joe well; he graduated near the top of his class with High Distinction.

The deepening Depression, which caused one-fifth of the class to drop out of the business school after their first year, made getting a job the major concern for most students.[3] Fortunately, Joe always had Haloid. He worked at Haloid's New York City sales office in the summer between his first and second years at Harvard, and even better, had an assured position waiting for him after graduation. Following an interview with Gilbert Mosher, Joe's job was agreed upon: He would be paid $20 a week, begin as an assistant in bookkeeping and serve as a management apprentice—with his father providing most of the instruction. (Politics provided a basis for Joe to show his independence: Attracted by the substance of Franklin D. Roosevelt's 1932 presidential campaign, Joe had several heated arguments with his father, a traditionally staunch Republican and a strong Hoover man. These arguments were repeated in 1936, and in that election, Joe broke from family custom and voted Democratic for FDR.)

[3]McKelvey, page II-5.

Seriously shy and all too conscious of his getting a job largely because Haloid was his family's company, Joe was quite deferential to other workers, particularly to those who were older—and older employees apparently agreed that he should defer to them. Striving to be helpful, Joe made some suggestions based on his business school studies, but his suggestions were quickly labeled presumptuous, so he pulled back. As time passed, however, Mr. JR began to recognize Joe's talent and the benefits of his formal training, so he more and more often deferred to Joe's analysis and judgment—including evaluations that increasingly differed from Gilbert Mosher's.

Joe would make even better progress in romance. Visiting Foran's Saloon, the speakeasy on Spring Street he and Peggy had frequented with their college friends, he was promptly escorted to a back room where Jack Foran bluntly asked him where was his wonderful girl. Foran had advice to give—and he gave it in what Wilson later recalled as "an hour's harsh talk." Blow-ups were opportunities for make-ups. Buffalo was not all that far. Besides, rumor had it that she was being courted by a Buffalonian, so Joe had better get with it, or he was going to lose a real prize!

Joe drove to Buffalo to call on Peggy. She too had grown in the two years he'd been away at Harvard. She saw herself as more independent and self-sufficient; Joe saw her as more attractive than ever and, with both a strong will and a sense of social responsibility, even more interesting. After that first visit, Joe drove to Buffalo every weekend and soon declared his commitment to Peggy—but she held back for several months.

Luckily, the Curran family moved back to Rochester in late 1934. By the following spring, Joe's prospects at Haloid were accelerating and his relationship with Peggy was again strong. For one of Joe's trips to New York City, Peggy and a friend took Joe to the railroad station. As the train pulled away from the station, Joe turned to wave goodbye from the open doorway. He could hear Peggy call out as the train pulled away, "Yes! I'll marry you!"

By agreeing in writing that their children would be raised as Catholics, Joe got approval from Father John B. Sullivan, the Rector of St. John the Evangelist Church, to marry Peggy Curran in a ceremony performed right after the early morning mass on October 12, 1935. Marriage was one of several changes in Joe Wilson's relationships during the thirties.

3

THE THIRTIES

aloid had a most unusual experience during the Depression: After taking a small loss in 1929, it *prospered*. The two engines of Haloid's prosperity were a demonstrably superior photocopy paper, Haloid Record, and the Rectigraph Company, which it acquired in 1935. Haloid Record, introduced just as the decade began, represented two-thirds of the company's $1.5 million in sales in 1931. It was developed over five years by a Haloid chemist named Homer Piper. Haloid Record gave the company and its sales force a clearly superior product to sell at such a good profit that, unlike most companies, Haloid's earnings increased through the hard years of the Depression, and while other companies were laying off workers and going part-time, Haloid employees were working overtime.

During the 1930s, as Wilson later observed: "The old products would have bankrupted the company. Fortunately, Haloid Record met strong demand and taught us all a lesson: The greatest strength against adversity is to have a stream of new innovations all the time." As Wilson repeatedly reminded his associates, the only reason any of them were at Xerox in the glory days of the 1960s was due to the creative work of unique individuals—Chet Carlson with xerography and Homer Piper with Haloid Record—who had the strong motivation to create innovative new products or new ways of doing business, often after overcoming daunting adversities. In future years, when emphasizing the vital importance of innovation and new products, Wilson often remarked, "These two cannot be overestimated. Without Homer Piper's invention of Haloid Record—an invention by one man—we might not have survived the Depression. We learned a lesson which was never forgotten: The best way to fight recession is to be ready to introduce new products."[1]

Haloid Record was a vital advance, but it surely would not be very long before competitors—perhaps even mighty Eastman Kodak—developed comparable competitive products. Wilson clearly recognized that, over the long haul, as a me-too maker of photographic paper, Haloid was in an increasingly untenable strategic position. Little Haloid could never win over the long haul, in direct competition against such formidable giants as DuPont, Agfa, and Kodak. Haloid was the classic polar bear on an iceberg heading toward the equator. Wilson saw Piper's success as an object lesson. He would often recall with respect: "Homer Piper showed those of us who later worked on xerography that you can lick *any* technical problem—provided you *never* give up!"[2]

Wilson persistently looked for new products—partly because he understood the grave risks of standing still and letting others take the initiative in technology, and partly because he understood the reciprocal value of gaining a technological advantage for his company. To achieve substantial success, Haloid would have to get into a different and *better* business. As Wilson succinctly put it to his co-workers, "We're going nowhere—fast!"

In addition to learning that Haloid was in an increasingly dangerously weak strategic position, Wilson also learned about operations and, in particular, about sales and developed a keen, lifelong interest in this part of the business. He learned about the life of a salesman, the

[1]Speech to Boston Security Analysts, December 8, 1958.
[2]Dessauer, page 4.

role of compensation, and how much a salesman depended on having good products to sell. He absorbed a first-hand lesson he often repeated: "It is the customer and the customer alone who will ultimately determine whether we succeed or fail as a company."

Competing with Eastman Kodak, one of America's technology and marketing giants—and setting up shop in Rochester, which was where Kodak's headquarters were located—would have been absurd presumption for Haloid except for one vital irony: Kodak was so *very* strong that it was *too* strong. Kodak was an obvious monopoly, and antitrust initiatives had been good, popular politics ever since the days of Teddy Roosevelt and Woodrow Wilson. Any lawyer would have advised Eastman Kodak to allow, even encourage—and if necessary, make certain—that at least a few companies could be cited as competition. It was preferable that they be direct competition and, ideally, in Kodak's own backyard. As a small firm, Haloid was perfect for this role: Its very existence was ideal legal evidence that Eastman Kodak was not really a monopoly. And for community relations in Rochester, it would certainly do no harm to have good relations with a popular local politician like JC Wilson.

Another lucky break for Haloid had been forming in an Oklahoma City abstract office where George Beidler worked as a clerk. Dissatisfied with the tedium of copying documents by hand, he conceived of producing them by photography. Since Rochester was the center of photography, Beidler went there to construct the first photocopying machine in 1906. He then returned to Oklahoma City where he incorporated the Rectigraph Company. (The name Rectigraph came from the process of a mirror reversing the image so right-reading copies could be made without needing an intermediate negative.) Three years later, Beidler returned to Rochester and incorporated his business in New York State. Beidler's only competitor was Photostat, which had strong links to Eastman Kodak. Photostat and Kodak nearly drove Rectigraph out of business, but luckily Rectigraph was saved by a court ruling that a copy produced by a process that required a negative was not admissible evidence because it could be tampered with and changed. Since Photostat's process required an intermediate negative, its copies could not be used as legal copies, but Rectigraph's direct—and tamper-proof—photostatic copier made copies that were legally valid. This was great for Rectigraph. By 1920, Beidler had a new plant located in Rochester, and in 1927, he expanded into Canada.

A gifted inventor completely devoted to his business, Beidler was a colorful individualist. Not trusting anyone, he memorized his emulsion formulas so they need not be written down—where someone might steal them. In a ragged sweater with the sleeves cut off, he did all the mixing himself. Then, after 30 years of being totally engrossed in his inventions and every aspect of his business, Beidler's interests suddenly changed. As his impatience with government regulations grew, he simply lost all interest in business and developed an even greater devotion to the game of golf. Playing every weekend and increasingly during the week, Beidler brought golf to work as well, constructing a putting green in the orchard behind his company's plant and an indoor driving range on the second floor. He also insisted that his new employee, a chemist, play golf with him. (After one golf ball broke a 15-gallon container of dangerous, concentrated ammonia, he switched to cotton practice balls.)

By 1935, George Beidler was ready to concentrate entirely on golf and sell Rectigraph. JR Wilson heard about this and proposed an acquisition to Gilbert Mosher. Combining the Rectigraph machine with Haloid Record paper would give Haloid an important advantage in the market, because it was common practice that those who bought equipment also bought supplies from the same company—particularly, as Joe Wilson later observed, "if the machine requires reliable, prompt service."[3]

JR Wilson got Mosher's agreement to go ahead, and soon negotiated an option to buy Rectigraph. To raise the money needed

[3]Speech to Boston Security Analysts, December 8, 1958.

to exercise the option—and to enable Mosher to sell some stock—
Haloid would need to go public.[4] So, in 1936, with profits for
the combined companies just under $250,000, a small public sale
of Haloid stock was arranged with two regional securities firms:
Donoho, Moore & Company and Mitchell, Harrick & Company.
Haloid sold 40,000 shares out of a total capitalization of 200,000
shares at $17.25 per share and Gilbert Mosher sold 15,000 shares.
Mosher collected $258,000 and Haloid collected $690,000. (The
underwriters received $102,000 and the 7% cumulative preferred
stock was retired.) The common shares were listed on the New York
Curb Exchange, the precursor to the American Stock Exchange.

Acquiring Rectigraph would prove to be far more important
than anyone realized in 1935—for two reasons. First, Rectigraph
sustained Haloid's viability as a business just long enough to give it
time to acquire the rights to what became xerography and develop a
completely new line of products. Second, Haloid gained a crucial
asset that was not even recorded on the company's books on the
date of purchase. That asset was a new employee who was initially
quite upset by the sale and very nearly quit.

J ohn Dessauer, a highly trained German chemist, had left Germany
in 1929 to avoid being drafted into the Nazi army. Born in
Aschaffenburgh, Germany, in 1905 into a family that for five generations had made and sold specialty papers, he studied at Albertus
Magnus University in Frieburg and at Munich's Institute of Technology, and then earned a doctorate at Achen. On his father's advice
that America was the land of opportunity, Dessauer emigrated to the
United States, arriving just after the stock market crash and the start
of the Depression—and before he had learned much English. After
several weeks of unsuccessful job hunting, Dessauer got a tip from a
fellow German, an organ builder working for Wurlitzer on an organ
at Binghamton's St. Patrick's Church. Agfa was building a new plant

---

[4]Haloid and Rectigraph operated separately until operations were merged in 1937.

in Binghamton and might be hiring. Luckily for Dessauer, his job interview was with a chemist who spoke only German: He was hired immediately to work with a team of experienced German technicians. Dessauer worked for Agfa for six years and then, on just 24 hours notice, he was fired because, Dessauer always believed, "the long arm of Hitler called the shots, even in America."[5]

Dessauer again needed a job, hopefully one linked to photography, but not directly competitive with Agfa, because his contract had included a two-year noncompete provision. A family friend suggested Rectigraph, where Dessauer was hired partly to play golf with the owner, but primarily to develop new photographic papers so Rectigraph would not be as dependent on Kodak for supplies. (Kodak clearly favored Beidler's rival, Photostat Corporation, with which it had a major supplier contract.) The new paper Dessauer was assigned to develop was expected to meet or beat the then market standard: Haloid Record.

Soon after joining Rectigraph, Dessauer was surprised to learn that his new employer was being sold to Haloid. Even though he had no job alternative and the Depression had no visible end, Dessauer very nearly quit. Then he met Mr. JR and Joe Wilson. Quite taken with Joe Wilson and the leadership he could give Haloid, Dessauer decided to stay. Joe Wilson was put in charge of Rectigraph and quickly found that he was good at the work and liked the responsibilities of leadership. He set up a sales and service organization, which was considered highly unusual at the time, but proved to be very effective.

Meanwhile, Wilson was learning more about Haloid. With his office door closed, Mr. JR regularly sat with Joe to explain various aspects of Haloid's operations and discuss business decisions. Wilson was getting more and more deeply involved in the business and finding it increasingly interesting and enjoyable. While Joe may

[5]Pell, page 44.

have joined Haloid initially out of a sense of responsibility to his family for the family firm and partly because he had no real alternative, he was now becoming increasingly committed to Haloid and was quietly resolving to stay with the company and make of it what he could. This sense of commitment would broaden, particularly after a soon-to-be-experienced corporate confrontation with Gilbert Mosher.

In 1936, Joe Wilson was named Secretary of the Corporation. Commissioned by Mosher and Mr. JR to recruit two other young men to work in advertising and accounting, he showed a real talent for recruiting able men to the company. Haloid hired his recruits, John B. Hartnett and Harold S. Kuhns, on August 31, 1936. Hartnett, a graduate of Cornell, had 10 years' experience in sales. Kuhns, with an MBA from Harvard, had five years' experience. In 1940, Kuhns was elected Controller (and then Executive Vice President in 1953). Hartnett would build a sales force of 100 men and Kuhns would integrate the accounting of Haloid and Rectigraph. (When it was decided not to bring Joe's brother, Richard Wilson, into the company, Mr. JR built for him the first Howard Johnson's Restaurant in the region. Located at Brighton's Twelve Corners, the restaurant was run for many years by Peggy Wilson's brother, Jack Curran.)

Wilson focused on building the sales and service organization with Hartnett, saying again and again: "The customer is Number One. And Two *and* Three! We never want to let a customer get hurt." Wilson and Hartnett drove together to work each day; ate the lunches they brought from home together; took long walks for exercise; and played squash together at the YMCA. Far more important, Hartnett became Wilson's regular sounding board on every aspect of the company as Wilson became increasingly determined to find ways to improve operations and develop an effective forward strategy for his family's business.

In 1937, after two years of increased dividends to stockholders but no improvements in wages, Haloid's workers petitioned for an increase. Mr. JR recommended acceptance, but Mosher flatly refused.

Some of the workers staged the nation's first sit-down strike and called in the Amalgamated Clothing Workers, the strongest labor union in Rochester, for help in organizing Haloid. Mosher opposed unionization. He dictated a memo instructing that no concessions be made, and left Rochester by train for his winter residence in Boca Raton, Florida.

The Wilsons, seeing unfilled orders accumulate while a dozen workers kept the doors barricaded and had their food passed in through the window, decided by week's end to meet with union representatives. Kenneth Keating, later a U.S. Senator, served as counsel to Haloid. Abraham D. Chatman, of the Rochester Joint Board, and Gus Stebeck, a national organizer for the Amalgamated Clothing Workers, participated in the negotiations. (For a company as small as Haloid, the senior talent involved was impressive, particularly for someone as open-minded and anxious to learn as Joe Wilson.) Fearing a long strike and sure that they would be right to recognize what they believed were fair and legitimate labor demands, the Wilsons decided not to follow Mosher's instructions. Instead, they agreed to make moderate concessions: an increase in wages plus one week's vacation. While Mosher was affronted by what he saw as deliberate disobedience, he was in Florida for the season, so the personal confrontation would have to wait until he returned to Rochester.

Wilson's integrity and ability to understand the needs of others helped him make another leader-to-leader connection that would matter greatly to the company's future in constructive labor relations. When Haloid acquired Rectigraph, a nonunion shop, Abe Chatman, the union leader at Haloid, went to Wilson: "Joe, you've made us vulnerable now. You can shift work from Haloid to Rectigraph. In fact, you could even close Haloid and shift *all* the work to Rectigraph." To this Wilson responded: "If you want to organize Rectigraph *and* the workers there will have you, be my guest." Wilson made it clear that, as a matter of policy, there would be no management opposition.

Over the years, as the company opened plants around the country, it would eventually have 35 different contracts with the union.

While the Wilsons worked long hours year-round, Mosher was away more and more. Spending winters in Florida and summers at his camp in the Adirondacks, Mosher was at Haloid less than half the time. As the Wilsons got closer and closer to the business and its operations, Mosher got more and more removed and out of touch. Still, he insisted on the perquisites of management, particularly when making major decisions such as negotiating labor contracts. As a result, the backlog of deferred decisions kept growing, causing small matters to balloon with frustration into major problems. Finally, having already realized a five-fold return on his original investment, Mosher decided to move on.

Saying he desired "to step aside in favor of a younger man who, by training and experience in the service of the Company, is eminently qualified to discharge with honor to himself and with advantages to The Haloid Company the important duties appertaining to the honored office of President," Mosher announced by a letter to the 1938 stockholders' meeting that he would not stand for re-election as President of Haloid and went on to state that he desired "to relax somewhat from the pressure of routine business; to save more time for the enjoyment of other interests; to have the opportunity to assist those who are taking up the major responsibilities which I lay down."

JR Wilson was again named President of Haloid, as he had been 20 years before, and Joe Wilson became Secretary-Treasurer. Business improved in 1939, and the Wilsons instituted weekly meetings of the half-dozen managers, with Joe often chairing the meetings. Morale was improving and new paper products were being developed. Haloid's future prospects looked increasingly hopeful. At the 1940 annual meeting, Joe Wilson was elected to the Board of Directors.

However, underneath the outwardly calm appearance of business as usual—buoyed by Haloid's unusual successes during the Depression years—major tensions were building between JR Wilson and Gilbert Mosher. While acknowledging Mosher's success in improving the company's financial condition, Mr. JR increasingly complained about the way he was treated by Mosher, and described him as a "dominant, and at times an extremely arrogant character. He plays a lone hand and is utterly intolerant of any and all opposition, and does not ordinarily welcome advice from his associates on important matters.

"I have studied his nature and disposition and have always endeavored to accommodate myself to his whims and peculiarities. At times this has been difficult, for I have not always agreed with his policies and purposes and have, I regret to state, submerged my own personality rather than enter into arguments which, on the few occasions when arguments have occurred, invariably eventuate in stained relations. In which atmosphere and environment, I function to extremely poor advantage."[6] JR Wilson may have avoided specific arguments, but he and his son could not avoid their emerging confrontation with Gilbert Mosher.

[6]JR Wilson memorandum to shareholders, 1940.

4

YEARS OF STRUGGLE

The exercise of power can surprise those who are not even thinking about power and how to use It. While war raged around the world, Joe Wilson and his father would face their own major battle at Haloid.

The Wilsons' focus was on operations and they were committed, hands-on managers, but real corporate power centers on ownership and control. The Wilsons had paid little attention to Gilbert Mosher's apparently off-hand comment that he might someday sell Haloid, but they certainly should have: Mosher had once tried to merge Haloid with the American subsidiary of Belgium's Gavaert Photo Production, and he had made his own fortune a few years before joining Haloid by selling Century Camera to Eastman Kodak.

In March 1940, the Wilsons were surprised to learn that Mosher had unilaterally agreed on an acquisition valuation for Haloid (with continued employment for current management) by General Aniline and Film Corporation, the international unit of I.G. Farben, the giant German chemical organization. When its president returned from vacation, General Aniline's acquisition of Haloid was to become final.

The Wilsons had no interest in Haloid being sold. (Less than two years later, in the conduct of World War II, General Aniline's U.S. properties—which would have included Haloid—were seized by the U.S. Government.) After intense discussions, the Wilsons decided to buy out Mosher's remaining 10,000 shares at $25—up significantly from the $17.75 he had received in the 1936 public offering. With the promise of a $250,000 loan from Lincoln Alliance Bank and Eastman Kodak's promise to continue supplying essential photographic paper to Haloid, the Wilsons made their offer. But Mosher refused to give it any consideration, bitterly accusing the Wilsons of violating his confidence and putting his General Aniline deal in jeopardy.

When, for other reasons, the agreement with General Aniline fell through, Mosher, who wanted to complete the liquidation of his 1920s investment, spoke with bitter determination: "I'm still full of fight. I mean to control and run this Company as I always have and will not brook any interference so long as I stay in that front office. If this organization won't work with me, I'll build a new one."

During the next year, serious sparring developed between the Wilsons and Mosher on such varied topics as membership of the Board of Directors, the Board's authority, the minutes of meetings, their respective job responsibilities, Mosher's abrupt deferral of a promised pay increase for Homer Piper, and proxy voting at the coming annual meeting. Mosher presented Piper with a proxy to sign that would have greatly changed Mosher's power as a director and insisted that it be kept secret. Piper refused, so Mosher immediately fired him. JR Wilson rehired Piper and, after a time, Mosher relented. For several months, communication between Haloid's Chairman and Haloid's President—Gilbert Mosher and JR Wilson, respectively— was strictly in writing and many decisions were not discussed. For example, Mosher authorized a $100,000 plant improvement without even mentioning it to JR Wilson.

Mosher tried in 1941 to change the composition of the Board of Directors. Blocked, he agreed on a compromise and accepted an amendment of the by-laws that temporarily gave him extraordinary powers. Then, in a surprise departure from what others had understood was the agreement, he named a New York City lawyer to vote his proxy for three new directors and oust Homer Piper, Eugene Nicks (Assistant Treasurer and a 25-year employee) *and* Joe Wilson.

JR Wilson, who was presiding over the Board meeting, declared the proxy vote in violation of the previous agreement and therefore out of order.[1] With lawyers advising both sides on procedure, the Wilsons and Mosher soon had two overlapping Boards of Directors that, curiously, met simultaneously and in the same room. Mosher was actually Chairman of both boards, but the Wilsons had the votes on one and Mosher had the votes on the other, so the two boards sparred legally for official legitimacy. Somehow both sides agreed to avoid drawing public attention to their impasse by cooperating on such matters as dividends, approval of the labor agreement with the Amalgamated, and the election of corporate officers.

In preparation for the annual meeting in 1942, the Wilsons actively solicited the proxies of Haloid shareholders. Visiting with many individual shareholders in the area around Rochester,[2] usually in groups at one of the city's saloons, they emphasized the effectiveness shown by their full-time executive group over the past three years; explained that the competitive complexities were beyond any one man; and said that all they wanted of Mosher was that he give up his extraordinary powers and serve as counselor-advisor and as Chairman of the Board—as he himself had offered to do back in 1938.

The Wilsons' proxy solicitation was very successful: They obtained the support of 85% of the outside shares. With this secure majority, the Wilsons proposed a slate of recognized Rochester business leaders—including Mosher and several of the current directors.[3] (Kenneth Keating, later a U.S. Senator, informed the Wilsons by telegram that he had just learned from a friend that Mosher had

---

[1] All but one of the 18 shareholders present agreed with this ruling. (One who did not, W.H. Salmon, was known to be "obedient" to Mosher.)
[2] Of 900 shareholders, 700 lived in Rochester.
[3] Raymond Lienen, Vice President of Lincoln Alliance Bank; Herman Cohn, President of Superba Cravats; and F. Ritter Shumway, President of the Ritter Company.

approached that friend about becoming a director of Haloid and that therefore he, Keating, would no longer be representing the Wilsons because, "I have to resign as your attorney—or I'll lose my best fee-paying clients!" Joe Wilson never could understand a professional man having such shallow values.) At the stockholders' meeting, the Wilson slate received more than double the votes won by the Mosher slate.[4] A three-man Executive Committee of the Board was established, but its views sometimes conflicted with Mosher's authority as Chairman and General Manager. To avoid risking harm to the company in a visible dispute, both sides agreed to show restraint and find ways to cooperate. At the 1943 annual meeting, the voting split was almost 19 to 1 in favor of the Wilsons,[5] so the controversy was clearly over and the Executive Committee was firmly in control. In 1944, Mosher was kicked upstairs to Honorary Chairman, Mr. JR was elected President and Joe Wilson became, at 36, Vice President and General Manager of Haloid with full authority over all operations.

Joe Wilson was determined to come into his own as a business manager: Even if Haloid was small and family-owned, it was a public company in a dynamic industry with interesting potential. Wilson was determined to perform his new responsibilities effectively and to fulfill his family's expectations. Young as he was, Wilson was actually at the age when most entrepreneurs achieve lift-off. There were things to do, skills to learn, people to meet, speeches to give, and relationships to develop as the leader of a small—but increasingly important—business organization in Rochester. And, before he could lead others, Wilson recognized, he would first need to make himself the kind of leader others would want to follow.

Likeability and his position as the new young Vice President of Haloid naturally led to invitations to join in more and more community service organizations. This was already important to Joe Wilson

[4] 91,480 vs. 40,961.
[5] 95,723 vs. 5,150.

in 1942. Carefully and conservatively dressed, Joe Wilson certainly did not present an imposing figure that stood out in a crowd, but his infectious smile, attentive manner, and unfailing memory for names and faces combined to make Wilson unusually likeable. He took the lead in organizing a campaign by the Junior Chamber to raise funds for a series of outdoor concerts by the Civic Music Association in Highland Park. With 5,000 people attending the first Starlight Symphony on July 5, press coverage gave him his first taste of public recognition. He enjoyed it, realizing that public service could be personally satisfying. Joe Wilson had begun a lifetime of work for a better and better Rochester.

Most people do what they personally like to do and what they think they do best, but Joe Wilson always believed in doing what responsibility demanded, and quite deliberately made himself learn to become what he thought others thought he ought to be. Wilson had been too shy to speak in public, so now he was determined to learn to speak well. Once too shy to speak to older women who passed him in the halls at Haloid, Wilson knew he *had* to become a good speaker. Public speaking would be an important part of making himself over and creating a new Joe Wilson. His opportunity came when he was made a team captain for the Community Chest (a group similar to the United Way), where Rochester had a long record of having both high rates of participation and high *per capita* gifts. Because he was named team captain in the early spring, he had until the fall to practice the public speaking expected when team captains reported their results. He felt he needed those six months to gather the stories he would tell at each week's reporting meeting.

When he began his weekly reporting talks, he had a story for each one—saving the best, of course, for last. The early stories went well. Joe got laughs and applause. So he was feeling confident as he rose at the last weekly session to tell his story and make his report. He told his joke—a slightly off-color one—and was surprised to get no audience reaction. He was even more surprised when he turned around to go back to his seat. While he'd been speaking, two more guests had slipped into the room and taken their seats—just behind Joe, but plainly visible to everyone else—the Catholic archbishop and the Episcopal bishop! After that experience, Wilson knew he could never have a *worse* experience in public speaking, so he began to relax and soon found his voice.

Eastman Kodak, the research and development giant in photography was the dominant company in Rochester. Not only was it the worldwide industry leader in both marketing and technology, it was the direct competitor for tiny Haloid. Kodak produced more than 90% of the world's supply of sensitized paper, while Haloid, selling largely to professional portrait photographers, was a very distant Number Two. (Kodak paid out more dollars on its annual Bonus Day than Haloid's total sales for a full year.) Eastman Kodak was not only Haloid's major competitor, but also Haloid's major supplier. Haloid purchased more than half of the base paper for its photocopy and photographic paper from Eastman Kodak plus all of its silver nitrate, Haloid's second most important raw material.[6] Wilson understood it would be very hard for Haloid to sustain even its distant #2 position once the War was over because DuPont and other chemical giants were sure to come into the photo supplies market with far greater financial, manufacturing, and technical capabilities. And after the war, Eastman Kodak would be free to concentrate its vast resources on developing new photocopy products, and the informed talk around Rochester was already about several exciting, innovative new products being in the works. As Peter McColough, who rose through sales to be CEO, later observed: "Haloid's business was like living off the leftovers from Eastman Kodak. And with the World War over, competition would surely get tougher and tougher. And it would be led by Kodak."

[6]Remington Rand indicated an interest in possibly acquiring Haloid, but this was quickly rejected. (One reason for the speed in rejecting a possible deal was worry that if there were an open discussion at the Board, Gilbert Mosher might try to force a sale.)

During World War II, military priorities had meant that Haloid, as a military contractor, was assured of having its necessary base materials supplied consistently by Eastman Kodak. But when the war ended, there would be no such guaranteed supply. Haloid would be exposed to the obviously major risk of being cut off, as a competitor, by Eastman Kodak. Wilson had always been deeply impressed by Eastman Kodak, once recalling: "I was born in a humble little house near Kodak Park, and I remember as a kid the two great smokestacks kind of dominated my life. I felt about them almost like the Egyptians felt about the pyramids." He understood how forceful a competitor his giant neighbor could be and that Haloid was very small and facing grave risks. And if he were a bit intimidated by his new managerial responsibilities, Wilson had reasons beyond the looming presence of Eastman Kodak. Only in his thirties and with little managerial experience, Wilson must have felt uncomfortable knowing he was a Founder's grandson *and* the President's son in a small firm on which he and his family all depended economically— and had not yet proven himself capable of doing his job.

The 1940s were very difficult years for Haloid, even with the war-related demand for photographic products adding to overall sales. The decade began with a protracted fight for corporate control; continued through the hard, uncertain war years; and ended with such a poor profit year that it required eliminating the dividend the Wilson family and other shareholders expected to receive. Financially, Haloid was in real trouble: Sales may have more than doubled from $3.9 million in 1940 to $9.7 million in 1949, but earnings, even with postwar inflation, increased only 30 percent because profit margins had been cut in half.

Wilson understood that Haloid's troubles were certain to get worse because Haloid's products were out of date. He knew he would need to reinvent the company and redefine its business. His concerns were confirmed when, with the war over, military demand fell off sharply as the government made drastic reductions in wartime orders. Simultaneously, silver prices and wage rates were increasing rapidly.

As a realist, Wilson understood that Haloid was in grave danger with no place or time to stand around waiting to see what might happen. While Haloid Record Paper had been a "money spinner" during the Depression, other much larger companies were striving to develop improvements and would soon be producing better products. Haloid was standing still—and it was standing in the shadow of Eastman Kodak. If the external threat to Haloid was epitomized by the strength of Eastman Kodak, the apathy within the little company and by the widespread view that "everything has gone OK in the past, so why try to change things now?" were even more dangerous.

Determined to move Haloid forward and make it a better, stronger company, and also recognizing that Haloid's current managers were suited only to maintaining the status quo, Wilson knew he needed outside help. So he hired several consultants, a managerial practice he would use over and over in the years ahead: Booz, Allen & Hamilton to advise on the overall management structure; Van Doren, Knowland, Schloder to redesign the Rectigraph camera; Stewart Brown & Associates to survey every aspect of the marketing organization; and the George S. May Company of industrial engineers to evaluate and make recommendations for improving the production and sales activities of Haloid.

When the May Company report came in, Wilson took charge of implementing the consultant's recommendations. As Wilson explained in that year's annual report to the shareholders, "The cost was, of course, substantial, but your Board and officers believe it was the wisest expenditure they have made to bring expert and professional viewpoints, completely unbiased by the tradition of the business, to bear upon the problems which your company faces in this vastly complex postwar economy. Our basic policy will be to push forward urgently and courageously our program of improvement and development." Such balanced wording and clear commitment to action would become familiar to many company people in the years ahead.

What would *not* become familiar was soon obvious: Accepting the recommendations of Booz, Allen was a big mistake. It would be one of the few serious management mistakes Wilson would make, but with all the other difficulties Haloid was then facing, it was a major blow. Booz, Allen proposed new functions in production control, cost control, and quality control *and* a reorganization of Rectigraph in order to reduce costs. But, this reorganization didn't reduce costs as was needed, it significantly increased them. As his friend Jack Hartnett said: "Joe didn't make many mistakes, but this one was a big blooper."

Two years later, Wilson reversed the whole management reorganization and took Haloid back to its original design. Chagrined, he had learned how important it was to be an active, in-control client with a consultant and would never have another serious problem working with consultants. Simultaneously, Wilson was gaining experience with the value of accurate information; the wisdom of sharing responsibilities, learning how to balance one objective with another, and knowing when to sacrifice near-term results to achieve long-term gains. Much more important, while working on labor negotiations, implementing the May Company report and, particularly, joining in the struggle for corporate control, Joe Wilson developed a strong personal commitment to Haloid and its future.[7]

Joe Wilson resolved to stay with the company and develop his career by continuing to build Haloid. He was already coming into his own, particularly in his father's view. As Joe's friend Lincoln Burrows recalled: "For Mr. JR, the sun rose and set on his son Joe." Even though Mr. JR never fully understood what was later done to transform little Haloid into Xerox—and never really tried to understand—he said he knew all he needed to know. As he would say at Board meetings, "If Joe tells me it's so, that's all I need."[8] In April 1944, JR Wilson was suffering from angina and decided to retire at the age of 63. So at 36, Joe Wilson was elected President and moved into his father's former office on the first floor, quietly ambitious both personally and for his company.

Recognizing that Haloid needed to get out of the strategic box

[7]Recollections of Lincoln V. Burrows, May 19, 1979.
[8]Linowitz, page 39.

it was in, Joe Wilson was determined to find a technology that fit in with Haloid's overall business in photocopying documents. As he said so solemnly to his associates, "We owe it to ourselves." Wilson began reaching for ways to make Haloid much better and much stronger. He developed a vision of pioneering a virgin technological territory that was separate from chemistry, where Eastman Kodak would always dominate, and instructed John Dessauer to look for such an opportunity and to conduct the search with urgency.

As Wilson explained 20 years later, "We were in the field of copying or 'photostatting,' as it was then called . . . [so] we were extremely conscious of the tremendous potential *if* a process could ever be found with the attributes of [what we now call] xerography—dry, convenient, simple, etc. We knew the great disadvantages of the process that we were in and we had, I think, enough experience to make some intuitive, but reasonably good judgments that if you could accomplish some things, the market would then be very, very much larger than it was then. The things that were emerging at that time—the diffusion transfer process, the Verifax process and the Thermofax process—were pretty crude and did not have the attributes that seemed to us as ideal. So we created an image in our own minds of something that we would like to have if we could ever find a technology to produce it—and happily we found the technology. We were in very serious straits after the war with our old photostat process competing against the giants like Kodak. The company's future was really quite bleak. We had very little research power of our own and no particular invention in sight, so we were searching the world over for literature or something to latch onto."[9]

Joe Wilson's bleak future—unless he could find a new technology—was matched by the bleak experiences over many past years of a remarkable inventor.

[9]Interview with Allen Fenton in Rochester on June 8, 1966.

5

CHET CARLSON

Joe Wilson might have been doomed to become nothing more than the very fine man who lived a useful, but unexceptional life in one of New York's nice upstate cities—passing through and leaving no lasting marks—but circumstances and events can present opportunities enabling people who have the vision, drive, and capability to live exceptional lives and make major contributions. The circumstances and events that would present such an opportunity—in the form of an extraordinary new technology—to Joe Wilson began in a conspicuously inconspicuous way with a boy born truly with nothing.

Chester Carlson's early years were dominated by deprivation. Born on February 8, 1906, he grew up as an only child because his older brother and younger sister had both died at birth. (Carlson's four grandparents had emigrated to the United States from Sweden in search of religious freedom, and settled in Minnesota where they were farmers.) Carlson's father, Olaf, became an itinerant barber, worked in various parts of the American West, and settled in Seattle, where he married and where Chet was born. Olaf Carlson later developed tuberculosis and spinal arthritis so bad that he could not work, so his small family lived in poverty and depended on support from relatives. It got worse.

In 1910, Chet's father lost their small savings by speculating on the purchase—sight unseen—of a "farm" in Aruba, Mexico. When the Carlsons arrived, the "farm" was "nothing but dry adobe clay and cactus—and totally unproductive." Then Carlson's mother Ellen got malaria; the Mexican government confiscated their land; and the Carlsons returned, flat broke, to San Bernardino, California, where they were allowed to stay in the unused rooms of a large house in exchange for Mrs. Carlson's doing all the housekeeping.

When Chet was 12, he would get up each day at five in the morning to earn money to help support his parents. He did odd jobs, washed windows, and cleaned up the office of a local newspaper. The newspaper experience, he would later recall, "impressed me with the difficulty of getting words into hard copy and, in turn, started me thinking about duplicating processes." Chet also started recording his several and varied inventive ideas, including possibilities for a ballpoint pen, disposable facial tissues, a new system of automotive hydraulics, and filter cigarettes. One day, Chet grandly told his cousin, who rode his bike seven miles to play with the younger boy, "I'm going to invent something *big* one day—and then I'll buy myself . . . a . . . typewriter!"

At 16, Chet was the principal provider for the Carlson family. Then, in yet another loss, his mother died of tuberculosis. Staying for an extra year in high school, Chet got a job in the chemical lab at a cement plant two miles away. Nursing his crippled father and working nights and weekends, he saved some money, which his father then squandered trying to launch a health food business.

Chet and his father were living in a single room with a concrete floor when his Uncle Oscar, a high school principal, came to visit. Chet said he wanted to go to college, but felt he couldn't afford it until after a few more years of hard work. Fortunately, Uncle Oscar disagreed. Bluntly, he urged Chet to continue his education as quickly as possible or risk never going to college. Taking that advice, Carlson soon enrolled at nearby Riverside Junior College, a cooperative work-study institution, and worked in the nearby Riverside

Portland Cement plant as a sample grabber, cement tester, and mix chemist.

At Riverside, Professor H.H. Bliss taught physics and inspired in Chet a strong interest in the subject that came to dominate his intellectual world. By taking extra courses, he completed the two-year junior college course—expected on the cooperative work-study schedule to take four years—in just three years and managed to save a few hundred dollars. Carlson hoped to complete his education at the California Institute of Technology. After taking an extra summer course in mathematics, he passed Cal Tech's tough qualifying examinations in physics, chemistry, and mathematics, and was accepted as a junior, majoring in physics. So Chet could concentrate on his studies, he and his father moved near the campus. Engrossed in his studies, Carlson found himself socially isolated, as he had been so frequently before and would be so often in future years. All his life, Carlson was persistent and stoic, writing in his journal, "I am given a hand: I will play it out," and asking a recurring, central question: "Where is my place?"

In 1930, Carlson graduated from Cal Tech in the top quartile of his class, but was again without: He had no job and was $1,400 in debt. Sending 82 letters asking about work, Carlson got only two replies, only one interview and no offers—until Bell Labs finally hired him to test materials in New York City. A year later, he transferred to Bell Labs' patent department, but with the Depression deepening, he was laid off in 1933. Starting with the As in the phone book, he called each law firm alphabetically and ended up working for a year in the patent law firm of Austin & Dix. He was about to be laid off again when he got a job in the patent department at P.R. Mallory and Company. Over the next seven years, he studied nights at New York Law School, earned his law degree, and rose to be head of Mallory's patent department.

Since he could not afford to buy law books, Carlson spent many hours in the library tediously copying long passages from textbooks for law school. Frustrated by the cost and mindless time taken to make copies of important drawings and charts, Carlson became convinced that the world needed a way to make accurate copies by a process that was cheaper and faster than the slow photostat process then available at 25¢ a page.

In 1934, he was still employed at Mallory. Often a dozen or more copies of patent specifications were needed. They always required laborious typing with multiple carbons and were often plagued by errors. Seeing this situation, Carlson began thinking seriously about low-cost copying. He wasn't interested in duplicating, which required a stencil or master; he focused on *copying*. Carlson reasoned that the originals to be copied would come in very different forms—typed, drawn with India ink, written with pen or pencil—so they would have no common solvent that might be used to transfer part of the image.

Once, as he and a Mallory colleague worked late into the night over a photostat machine, Carlson said: "There *must* be a better way of making these copies!"

"Sure," came the reply, "but nobody has ever found it."

"Maybe nobody has ever tried."

As Carlson later described his own thinking: "I recognized a very great need then for a machine that would be right in an office where you could bring a document to it, push it in a slot, press a button, and get a copy out. I set for myself a spare-time project of trying to fill that need. I wanted a *copying* process, not a *duplicating* process."

Light would have to be the active agent, but Carlson would need something different from conventional photography which was, and probably always would be, dominated by Eastman Kodak. "It was obvious," Carlson recalls, "to start experimenting with photoelectric and photoconductive materials. But I went down an awful lot of blind alleys." Photoconductive material becomes a better electric conductor when struck by light. It had been known that certain non-metals like sulfur, normally considered an insulating material, might conduct electricity a million times more readily in the light than in the dark. Carlson decided that photoconductivity looked promising for his purpose.

Carlson was 28 when he decided to see if his background in electricity might enable him to make copies with electrostatics. At the Science and Technology Division of the New York Public Library, he read, in evenings and on weekends over six months, all the available books and articles on printing and duplicating, particularly where light caused electrical effects, and very particularly photoconductivity. His reading included reports by a Hungarian physicist, Paul Seleny,[1] who had made photoelectric pictures by dusting an insulated surface that had been charged electrostatically with the outline of an image. Instead of using electricity to cause a chemical reaction, electricity could be used to lay down an electrostatic charge. This reminded Carlson of George Lichtenberg, a genius from the 1700s who had held a high-voltage conductor against a sheet of insulating material dusted with powder and found the lines of the sparks coming from the conductor reproduced in the powder. Carlson believed he was onto something with real promise. He was.

In an extraordinary intuitive leap, Carlson decided to try combining electrostatics and photoconductivity, using an electrostatic charge on a surface that was dusted with fine powder to create an observable image. With this approach, an entire page could be exposed at once—a major advantage over relying on slow line-by-line production of an image via facsimile. "It was so clear to me at the very beginning that here was a wonderful idea. I was convinced, even before testing, that it was pretty sure to work and that if it did, it would be a tremendous thing."[2] At 31, Carlson had made the classic leap of invention: combining two phenomena that had until then

[1]Interview with Professor Joseph J. Ermanc of Dartmouth College in 1965. Seleny worked for the Tungsram Corporation in Hungary and published in *Zeitschiff für Technischer Physik* and others. He and Carlson exchanged some correspondence.
[2]Ermanc interview, pages 24 and 25.

been left unconnected. The combination was scientifically brilliant and extraordinarily original.

Brilliant in concept as it was, Carlson's 1937 invention had one great and obvious problem: It didn't work.

Joe Wilson and Chet Carlson had one important characteristic in common: Both developed their thoughts through total immersion and both studied every aspect of any problem they were working on. Here's the way Carlson described his creative leap. "Of course, I don't think inventions of this kind come just overnight as a sudden flash. I think there's got to be a long incubation period. First one has to recognize the problem, saturate himself with the problem and the field of technology or the field of science where a solution might be found. He must let his subconscious mind work on it for a long period, perhaps years, until the right elements eventually fit together in his thinking."[3]

Carlson devoted the three years from 1935 to 1938 to searching for clues to a successful process. He spent many evenings and weekends in the New York Public Library tracking down odd chemical and physical phenomena which might offer the vital clue. "It is difficult for me now to think back to the exact point in time when the idea was born. It must have been sometime in 1937 that I finally hit upon the key," by realizing that the photoelectric currents gave only a very feeble effect in the electrolytic processes with which he had been experimenting. Racking his brain for a way to make the currents stronger, "It dawned on me: If I couldn't make the current stronger why not try to raise the voltage, so a few photons can control a lot of energy? To raise the voltage, I had to change from a conductor to an insulator. Then I could use plenty of voltage. Electrostatics was the answer.

"I knew instantly that I had a very big idea by the tail, but could I tame it?"[4]

---

[3]Ermanc interview, page 64.
[4]*Haloid-O-Scope*, Volume No. 4, March 1954.

While Carlson had done his inventing on his own time, he felt that as an employee of P.R. Mallory, he should secure a release for his invention. He wrote to make such a request of Mr. Mallory and got it on October 2, 1937. He filed for patent protection on October 18. In order to create a continuous train of thought and effort, documenting failures was as important for patent records as documenting what worked, and so was the signature of a witness who understood what was being done to reduce the concept to practice.

But a paper patent wouldn't do. To demonstrate practicality—and earn future profits—Carlson needed a working model, so he worked on this in the kitchen of his apartment during nights and weekends. Sulfur seemed particularly promising: An excellent insulator, it is also photoconductive. But it smells awful and this brought complaints from neighbors, including a woman who later became his friend and in 1934, his wife: Elsa von Mallen. To stop annoying neighbors, Carlson moved his experiments to a spare apartment behind a beauty shop in Astoria.

Carlson still needed help in reducing his invention to practice. He was working full time and going to law school at night, so he had almost no time. Even worse, he had very little skill with his hands. Accepting this reality, he concluded: "I needed someone more experienced in laboratory work to give me help."[5] In 1938, a young immigrant craftsman looking for work placed an ad in *Electronics*, offering the skills of an electrical engineer with strong experimental capabilities. Carlson invited the advertiser to come for an interview. Otto Kornei came, but he was not impressed. Still, since he had no other work and was responsible for a wife and child, Kornei reluctantly agreed to work part-time for six months while looking for a better position. Kornei's job was to build a working model of Carlson's invention with a budget of just $10 a month for materials. His pay would be $90 a week—which came out of Carlson's paycheck at Mallory. If successful, Kornei would receive 20 percent of revenues

[5]Ermanc interview, page 68.

up to a total of $10,000 and 10% thereafter. Kornei doubted Carlson would ever have revenues to share.

One Saturday, after a few weeks of lonely work, Kornei was joined by Carlson as he coated a 2" × 3" zinc plate with sulfur, a readily available photoconductive insulating element that took a positive charge when rubbed with cloth. With Carlson watching, Kornei rubbed the sulfur-coated surface and wrote 10.22.38 *Astoria* on a glass microscope slide with a grease pencil, shined a light for a few seconds through the glass and onto the sulfur-coated zinc plate, and then dusted that plate lightly with lycopodium powder. Blowing the loose powder away, the numbers and letters written were reproduced in the powder that remained electrostatically stuck on the plate. "It was fuzzy and the print made by pressing wax paper on the plate was fuzzier still, but it was what Carlson's theory had predicted. It worked and he had proved his point."[6]

Trying to improve each step in the process, Kornei and Carlson experimented with all sorts of changes and modifications and found that anthracene worked better than sulfur as a photoconductor. They also tried numerous fusible resins, including copal, dragons blood, gum damar, and many others, mixing each with carbon and dyes, melting them, and then grinding the resulting mass into fine powders. But these improvements were minor details compared to the extraordinary core intentions.

At the age of 32, Chet Carlson had produced the first new technology for putting words and pictures on paper in 150 years—the first since the late 1700s.[7]

So what? Nobody cared. Even Elsa had no interest. And at the end of his six-month commitment, after making several practical advances but becoming discouraged over prospects, Kornei quit

---

[6]Linowitz, page 61.
[7]Historians rank Carlson's invention with Senefelder's invention of lithography in 1798 and with the Niepee-Daguerre invention of silver-halide photography in the 1830s.

when he got a real job in Cleveland.[8] Carlson and Kornei met in New York City to discuss ending their agreement: Kornei was offered the rights to one idea he originated and gave up his right to 10% of revenues from electrophotography (originally called electronphotography). Determined to carry on, Carlson sent letters to 34 companies, including IBM, RCA and AB Dick, describing his invention and asking for an opportunity to demonstrate. All 34 had little or no interest. Some never replied; some wrote to decline; a few allowed a demonstration—and then sent Carlson away, saying they were just too busy with other things.

"After talking to a number of people in the industry," said Carlson, "I found that my crude little demonstration did not impress them. A technical person could usually understand it, but few of them saw the potential in it. Businessmen were not very impressed. It was hard to find anyone who could visualize what could be done toward the engineering development of the process."[9] He commented in an article for *Newsweek*, "I did give up a few times and I tried to forget it. . . . But I was so convinced it was important, I couldn't let it rest. It was just hard to put over because the materials were so crude. It wasn't likely to excite a businessman."[10]

The lack of excitement was understandable. The process was slow and cumbersome. Results were crude. Six steps were required

[8]Many years later, Carlson surprised Kornei with a gift of 100 Xerox shares after the 914 made XRX one of the highest priced stocks on the New York Stock Exchange, saying "without your help, I might never have had all this." Kornei was delighted. If Kornei had held these shares, they would have been worth $1 million in 1972. In 1960, ironically, Kornei wrote to complain bitterly about getting such a small share of the bonanza. Carlson was surprised. Lawyers said he had no obligation. Chet wrote: "I have your letter of July 26. Specifically what is it you want?" Kornei asked for 600 shares. Carlson sent 500—and a detailed explanation of why 600 shares would exceed the agreement dissolved in 1939. Kornei was understandably thrilled. (David Owens, *Copies in Seconds*, page 262.)
[9]Ermanc, pages 3 and 31.
[10]*Newsweek*, Nov. 8, 1965, page 86.

to make xerographic copies in Carlson's original experiment. First, a photoconductive surface was given a positive charge. Second, the material to be copied was placed over the surface and exposed to a number 2 photofloodlight for several seconds. The positive charge dissipated wherever light hit it, leaving the photoconductive surface positively charged wherever ink was on the original. Third, since opposites attract, negatively charged particles carrying powder were then spread onto the surface to adhere to the areas of positive charge.[11] Fourth, a sheet of paper was placed over the photoconductive surface and received positive charge. Then the paper was removed from the photocondutive surface, carrying with it the negatively charged toner. Finally, the powder was fused onto the paper by heat to fix the image, and the process was complete. But it was so complex and took so long that it was easy for most people to pass over. Fortunately, not everyone passed it by.

In 1940, a column in the *New York Times* featured a story on Carlson's new patent. An IBM junior executive read it, was interested, and arranged an introduction that led to 18 months of discussions and correspondence. Ultimately, Carlson offered IBM an exclusive license for a 5 percent royalty and a $10,000 annual minimum. IBM considered this—for several years—but never took action. When Carlson finally arranged to put on a demonstration, IBM's executives agreed the idea was interesting, but then turned him down.

For six long years, Carlson worked alone and spent all of his money and time working to improve and promote his invention. For his efforts, he received a daunting series of negative reactions. It's not really surprising that nobody picked up electrophotography: Carlson's demonstrations of the potential power of what would become xerography were not very convincing. And with world war coming, companies were sensibly concentrating on other priorities. Eastman Kodak, for example, focused on perfecting color film—

---

[11]Lycopodium, graphite, gum sandarac, among others.

immediately for military purposes—and for future use by amateur photographers.

In 1940, Carlson received the first of his four basic patents on the process he called electrophotography. That same year, he got his law degree and was admitted to the New York Bar. He also developed a severe case of spinal arthritis that threatened to doom him to repeat his father's painful struggle.

Carlson's second patent was based on the principle of photoconductivity and his focus was on photoconductivity, the process used in Astoria for "10–22–38," freeing Carlson from the constraints of prior patents based on photoemission. This second patent specified the process of forming the powdered image on a plate and then transferring the image to any type of paper, cloth, or other material (while competitors' copying processes had to use specially coated papers). Kornei's 1938 experiments encouraged Carlson to make several changes. Abandoning his own original patent, he filed a new patent application on April 4, 1939. The definitions in Carlson's patents are all in words—with no numbers—and are so broad they dominate all other patents in the field. Carlson's basic patent was later described as "maybe the best patent ever written in the U.S."[12] Carlson's best patent combined with what it needed now: good luck.

[12]By Frank Steinhilper, Haloid's head of patents.

6

BATTELLE

A lucky break—so very usual in Chester Carlson's life—would be critical in the next phase of his confluence with Joe Wilson, a confluence that would bring enormous, favorable change to both men's lives. Carlson's basic patent on electroradiography was issued on October 6, 1942 (as U.S. Patent 2,297,691), and the machine patent was issued in 1944. That year, Dr. Russell W. Dayton of the Battelle Memorial Institute of Columbus, Ohio, visited P.R. Mallory, where he and Carlson discussed various Mallory patents. As their discussions were ending somewhat earlier than the time scheduled for Dayton's return to Columbus, Carlson filled the extra time by mentioning his own work on electrophotography and his six-year-old patent. Dayton seemed interested, so Carlson showed him the copies he had produced. Seeing the copies, Dayton was intrigued and decided to arrange for Carlson to visit with John Crout at Battelle in Columbus and to give a demonstration.

After Carlson had completed his demonstration in Columbus, Dayton made a short statement to his colleagues: "Gentlemen, however crude this may seem, this is the first time any of you has seen a reproduction made without any chemical reaction and by a dry process." Crout was intrigued by the opportunity to apply Battelle's expertise in physics, so he asked Dr. Roland M. Schaeffert, the head of Battelle's new graphic arts division, for an opinion and got this encouraging reply on April 6, 1944:

> Mr. Carlson's invention of electro-photography appears to have possibilities, and if it can be made to work in a usable manner, broad commercial application can be expected.
>
> The success of the process, it would seem, depends primarily upon the attainment of sharp definition of the electrical image, and secondarily upon the development of some workable technique for transforming this image into a printable substance.
>
> It is suggested that the first approach in the development of this process should be an investigation of photoconductive materials, and the requirements for obtaining a well-defined electrical image on such material. If this is successful, the next step would be the development of means for fixing the image in the form of a transferable or printable substance. (It may be that ionized ink particles could be attracted to the electrical image as well as powder.)
>
> When, and if, the development of the process reaches the point where a well-defined transferable or fixed image can be obtained, consideration may be given to the following:
>
> 1. Application to duplicating to replace such things as carbon copying, mimeographing, photostatting, etc.
> 2. Applications to lithographic or photo-effect printing.
> 3. Applications to photoengraving and the production of relief or intaglio printing surfaces.
> 4. Applications to copy preparation and to the production of original text matter or photocomposition.

This process looks like a good research gamble. It would seem that the success or failure of the process might be determined during the early stages of the research work.[1]

After Schaeffert's promising report, Crout told Carlson that Battelle was ready to negotiate terms. But if Chet Carlson's invention had finally gained acceptance, it was certainly still a very limited and restrained kind of acceptance.[2] After further discussion, Battelle offered Carlson this modest proposition: Battelle would spend $3,000 a year on electrophotography research and pay Carlson an honorarium of $1,000 a year so long as Battelle kept the rights as exclusive agent under Carlson's patents, particularly the patents granted between 1942 and 1944. And if Battelle received any income from licensing the process, Carlson would get 25%. Moreover, if Carlson reimbursed Battelle for its research expenses at any time within the following five years, his share of the income would rise to 40%. Carlson accepted. He had no alternatives.[3]

Meanwhile, Carlson resigned from P.R. Mallory in 1945. After eight years, he had been promoted to manager of the company's patent department and had remained there for three years. His plan was to become a patent law attorney in his own tiny firm, Kneisner, Hoag and Carlson—and develop his invention on the side. A year later, times were still so tough for Carlson that he wrote to numerous companies looking for work for his new firm *and* to the

[1]Dessauer, pages 34 and 35.
[2]And in his personal life, Carlson was experiencing another kind of disappointment. He and Elsa separated in 1943 and divorced in 1945.
[3]Carlson's favorite joke was about the circus clown who threatened to quit because he was fed up with being banged around as a human cannon ball. "Please don't quit!" protested the circus manager. "You *can't* quit. We'll pay you more. We'll give you top billing with your name in lights. We *need* you!" "Why do you need me?" "Where else can we find a man of your caliber?"

New York Patent Law Association, seeking part-time work for himself as a patent attorney.[4]

Carlson and Battelle tried again and again to interest companies in using electrophotography to produce small volume copiers. They contacted dozens of companies, including such giants as General Electric, Eastman Kodak, Addressograph-Multigraph and RCA. They got several nibbles, but no bites. These companies made no great mistake when they passed on electrophotography. Not only was the technology little more than a dream in Chet Carlson's soaring imagination—with years of essential, but very uncertain and risky development work lying ahead—but the business potential also seemed very seriously limited since Battelle kept for itself the rights to all offset applications and to anything approaching duplicating: 20 copies or more.

The demand for less than 20 copies—which with hindsight we now know would become enormous—was very small in those days. Making fewer than 20 copies was assumed to be a wasteland between high volume and low volume. If many copies of an original were wanted, a master would be typed—a painstaking process because it had to be error-free—and the copies would be run off cheaply on a duplicating machine. If only a few copies were wanted, carbon paper would be used. The border between duplicating and carbon paper was unspecified, but it was certainly well below 20 copies. Today the great majority of copying is in the range of 10 to 25 copies—right where the *least* copying was done before xerography.

Battelle's Dr. Harold E. Clark later put Carlson's work into perspective: "Electrophotography had practically no foundation in previous scientific work. Chet put together a rather odd lot of phenomena, each of which was obscure in itself and none of which had previously been related in anyone's thinking. The result was the biggest thing in imaging since the coming of photography itself. Furthermore, he did it entirely without the help of a favor-

4Pell, page 21.

able scientific climate. There are dozens of instances of simultaneous discovery down through scientific history, but no one came anywhere near being simultaneous with Chet. I'm as amazed by his discovery now as I was when I first heard of it. As an invention, it was magnificent. . . . The only trouble was that as a product it wasn't any good."[5]

To make Carlson's magnificent invention into a successful product, an extraordinary entrepreneur was essential, and only the thinnest threads of connection brought Carlson's patents into Joe Wilson's awareness.

Usually quite formal in his demeanor, John Dessauer was in the very informal position of sitting on the toilet in the men's bathroom on a hot July day in 1945, scanning the April issue of the *Kodak Monthly Abstract Bulletin*, Eastman Kodak's internal journal on technical developments. His attention focused on a 200-word summary abstract of a report on electrophotography—a report that might never have been written and might never have been published and was only read by Dessauer because it was summarized in a special supplement.

[5]John Brooks, "Xerox Xerox Xerox Xerox." *New Yorker*, April 1, 1967.

7

CONTACT—JUST BARELY

Nicholas Langer, a patent attorney who had recently mustered out of the Army Signal Corps and was earning money by writing technical articles for popular magazines while looking for a permanent job, wrote an article about Carlson's patent in a special supplement available only to subscribers of *Radio Electronic Engineering News* in the August 1944 issue. Without Carlson's linkage to Battelle, Langer would probably not have written his *Radio News* article that Kodak abstracted eight months later and Dessauer read and then showed to Wilson. "It was as if lightning struck when I read that abstract," Dessauer recalled years later. As a chemist, it would not be surprising that Dessauer had never before read the *Kodak Bulletin*, but he was paying attention to this particular article because it had been recommended to him by Robert Schuman, one of the best scientists on his staff.[1]

[1]Merritt Chandler understood from Harold Clark that the article had instead been identified by Eugene Feurst. Bob Gundlach recalled it was Steve Hurst. Clyde Williams of Battelle, in a 1964 letter to Chester Carlson, said he recalled John Dessauer's visiting Battelle for a different reason and being shown a development with the comment, "I'd like to show you a development that will put Haloid out of business." Schuman retired in the early 1950s on a modest pension equal to 40% of final pay. Given the tight economics of Haloid in those years, retirement benefits were low so he moved to a trailer park in Florida. In 1960, Schuman wrote

Both men knew that Joe Wilson, as Vice President, was looking for a new technology that could enable Haloid to "hitch its wagon to a star" and lift itself up and out of its dependance on chemistry, because in chemistry, there were only two probable scenarios: Either Kodak was way ahead or Kodak would catch up and surpass anything Haloid could do. That's why Joe Wilson had been looking for some method of copying documents that was fast and did not depend on wet chemicals.

The abstract Dessauer was reading that July day was very short and began as follows:

> It consists in rubbing in the dark the surface of a photoconductive insulating material, such as sulfur or anthracene, about 1 mil thick, coated on a metal plate, until a static electric charge is developed, and then exposing the electrically charged coating in a camera to light. The parts of the coating illuminated will become more highly conductive than they were in the dark . . .

Electrophotography was clearly related to Haloid's business of photocopying and just as clearly came from a different technology: It was based on *physics*, not Kodak's realm of *chemistry*. While Dessauer was a chemist, not a physicist, he thought the process looked interesting, and possibly *very* interesting to Haloid. He

---

plaintively to Joe Wilson: "I can't keep quiet any longer about my receiving no recognition and no reward for finding and bringing to management's attention the original article in *Radio News*. Wilson sent the letter to Dave Raub, who saw it as a "crock" and recommended that nothing be done that might risk giving claimants a free ride because it would only encourage others, perhaps many others. Fortunately, Bill Asher heard about the letter and told Joe Wilson: "Bob told me that same story years ago. There's a good chance it's true." Horace Becker spoke with Eugene Feurst at John Hyashi's funeral, and Feurst confirmed that it was Schuman who had tipped off Dessauer.

requested the original article, read it, and decided to show it to Joe
Wilson (but neglected to say who had tipped him to it.)

When Dessauer showed him the article, Wilson's response was,
as usual, cautious and deliberate. Reading carefully, he said, "It does
sound interesting, but before we get involved, I'd like the opinion of
outside experts to advise on the merits of the idea." Wilson turned to
Microtronics, Inc., a two-man engineering laboratory in New York
City that specialized in camera design and had been studying a possible photostat camera for Haloid. He asked them to meet Chester
Carlson and evaluate his process—and *not* to mention Haloid.

George Cameron of Microtronics wrote to Carlson, who then
visited Microtronics and explained that the arrangements he had
made just a few months before gave Battelle Memorial Institute control of the development of electrophotography. (Battelle's expenditures were modest but rising: $702 in 1944 and nearly $7,000 in
1945.) So Cameron and Ernest Taubes of Microtronics went to visit
Battelle in Columbus in the fall of 1945. They reported to Wilson
that Carlson had great hopes for the usefulness of his process, but
that there was no evidence yet of its practical feasibility. Still,
Carlson had development support from Battelle, and the process was
truly innovative. Their report to Wilson concluded with this favorable judgment: "This process has tremendous possibilities and
should definitely not be overlooked."[2] They strongly recommended
that Joe Wilson go to Columbus. His visit led to Haloid's involvement with Battelle and eventually to Wilson's decision to commit
Haloid to this nascent technology. Their meeting would mark the
turning point for both Joe Wilson and Chet Carlson.

Wilson made his initial visit to Columbus with Dessauer in May
1946. Favorably impressed, he wrote to his father: "Suffice it to say,
I believe the nucleus of a basic new discovery is here in this process."
He recommended Haloid's securing a license under the patent. "Of

[2]Cameron to Wilson, April 26, 1946.

course, it's got a million miles to go before it will be marketable," he acknowledged. "But when it does become marketable, we've got to be in the picture!"[3] A month later, Battelle's John Crout assured Wilson that Haloid would get first consideration. Wilson and Dessauer were soon traveling to Columbus twice a month with Wilson exhorting and encouraging the technical people at both Battelle and Haloid to continue pressing ahead.

In September, Battelle engineers went to Rochester to meet with Wilson and Dessauer to advance negotiations with Haloid. Over dinner at the Genessee Valley Club, where Joe Wilson played host, using his father's membership, they discussed ways to work together. Wilson knew other, larger companies might compete for a license, but he persuasively capitalized on Haloid's small size: "We *are* small, but that's really an advantage for Battelle because we *need* to make this technology work commercially. We'll give it everything we've got!"

B attelle's representatives had good reason to be skeptical. Joe Wilson was only 36 and had just been elected president of a family business that had depended for several years on wartime sales to the military—plus one civilian product, Haloid Record, that now faced competitive obsolescence. With the war over, a postwar depression was widely anticipated: It would be a tough environment for Haloid. So why should Battelle become dependent on little Haloid? Fortunately, Battelle had no real alternatives. So, as Wilson later explained, "We were able to convince Battelle that we would work with it and not put it on the back burner. They were soured on big companies and had about decided to give it to a smaller company."[4] Wilson's case was persuasive. Haloid did need new technology, Wilson was clearly very bright and articulate, and Wilson's

[3]Dessauer, page 42.
[4]*Fortune*, July, 1963, page 208.

personal commitment was both obvious and convincing—and he inspired trust and confidence.

If Battelle's representatives felt they had no alternatives, Wilson knew Haloid certainly had none: Carlson's electrophotography was Wilson's and Haloid's last, best hope. When challenged by Haloid directors who were understandably concerned about Haloid's diminishing profits, Wilson bravely assured them of the remarkable nature of the investment opportunity: "As soon as the process is perfected, it will be worth every cent we pay."[5] The full significance of the phrase "as soon as perfected" was, in fact, very great, but the long series of frustrations and disappointments and cumulative costs that lay ahead would only be known *after* 12 long years of struggle had passed.

The first disappointment came very soon. Battelle produced a long report on all the work it had done to develop Carlson's invention. To dramatize the quality of electrophotographic copies, Battelle cleverly inserted such a copy as page 142 of the report. Wilson was delighted by the idea and asked Battelle to make more copies of page 142 so he could show them to his directors. This simple request caused a crisis that might have resulted in both Haloid and Battelle giving up entirely.

Battelle's Roland Schaffert explained: "We tried and tried, but were unable to produce the same good copy of page 142. It was just one of those things: The old plates had become used up or damaged, and we were having difficulty making new plates. We had insufficient information on what had caused the trouble, so we didn't yet know how to remedy it. Some of Haloid's people became very disturbed. Our department was under suspicion of having faked the results in our previous work and we were seriously criticized by everybody. . . . At this critical time, it took a lot of persuasion to prevent both Haloid and Battelle from withdrawing support from the project. As it was, we

---

[5]McKelvey, IV-5.

succeeded in getting a stay of execution long enough to make further studies. A great morale booster for us was the fact that Joe Wilson consistently refrained from admonishing or blaming anyone, and took the stand that mistakes were made and that they were honest mistakes. Joe was obviously disappointed by our results, but he was never bitter. If he had to take it on the chin from the Haloid directors, he was ready."[6]

Dessauer was asked to give his considered recommendation about the possibilities of using the process to produce marketable hardware. "When I look back now," Dessauer said in the mid 1960s, "I wonder how I had the courage to recommend going ahead. The photoconductors then used were sulfur and anthracene. Both were too slow for commercial use. It was not until later that Battelle found that selenium would work as a photoconductor.[7] Luckily, Battelle was soon making good, clear copies—including copies of the notorious page 142—which were rushed to Rochester for Joe Wilson's demonstration to his directors.

In October 1946, Wilson returned to Columbus where he finally met Chester Carlson. Wilson was impressed. Behind Carlson's modest manner, Wilson recognized a scientist with a solid understanding of the properties he was explaining *and* real imagination. But Wilson, like Christopher Columbus before him, was making a major "enabling error"—he significantly underestimated how large a task was before him. (By the late 1400s, most educated people understood that the earth was a sphere. Columbus thought it was a relatively *small* sphere. He was wrong, but the error "enabled" him to believe he could successfully make the voyage. Fortunately, like Wilson, he had the tenacity to "sail on and on until reaching a continent he had never anticipated finding.") While his associates at Haloid were quite skeptical, Wilson believed electrophotographic

[6]Dessauer, page 44.
[7]*Xerox Pioneer*, page 13.

machines could be developed and brought to market reasonably easily. He soon would learn otherwise.

Meanwhile, Battelle scientists developed a series of salient solutions to significant problems. Converting to selenium illustrates the process of defining and solving numerous problems. Discovering that vacuum-coated selenium was much more sensitive than anything that had been tried before, a Battelle scientist named William E. Bixby performed enhancing experiments at the lab at night with the aid of his wife. He found that temperature control was critical: If it was too warm, the charge did not hold; if it was too cool, adhesion was poor. He also learned that selenium was almost 1,000 times more sensitive than sulfur or anthracene had been. Drawing on his photographic experience, he adjusted the red "safelights" and found that a low level of safelight was also important. Finally, Bixby tried increasing the proportion of selenium relative to anthracene and found that pure selenium worked best. Even better, multiple copies could be made without recoating the plate. Most importantly, high sensitivity enabled projection imaging, which made it possible to copy two-sided originals.[8] (Using selenium as a photoconductor in copying machines was patented in 1955 and became a crucial competitive advantage because no substitutes were discovered.) In another example of clever engineering, it was found that toner, made largely from carbon black, worked much better if blended with a carrier of small beads that held the tiny toner particles electrostatically until surrendering them to the photoreceptor surface.

Corona charging was another illustration of combining tinkering and theory—and a major advance from rubbing the plate with a cloth. Battelle technicians were on the verge of giving up on using needles when Carlson said, "I think you've been holding them too close to the plate. Try increasing the distance."

One of the technicians protested that a greater distance between the needles and the plate would surely weaken the charge. Carlson

[8]Pell, page 32.

gently persisted, "You may be right, but please try it my way. You've got nothing to lose." A greater distance was tried. To the surprise of those relying on "common knowledge," it worked.[9,10] One of the observing technicians muttered in appreciative wonder: "Well, I'll be God damned!"

"It all sounds pretty obvious today," said Schaffert years later, "but we worked a year before we thought of using static electricity to pull the image off the plate and onto the paper. Before that we tried all sorts of adhesives."[11] Particularly important was Battelle's learning how to keep the background clear. Tiny residual bits of powder held onto the plate by a slight electrical charge caused un-wanted dark spots to show up in what should have been white space on the final copy. As one possible solution, Schaffert's team tried mixing salt into the developing powder. It worked, sweeping the background clear.

While Carlson's creative genius and Battelle's remarkable develop-ment skills were crucial, Joe Wilson's vision, disciplined persistence, and organizational leadership were essential. If the development of Carlson's technology had been left in the hands of Battelle, it would probably have languished and died there. The process was too com-plex and required too many steps, and the cost to develop a commer-cially successful product would have been prohibitive for a nonprofit research organization like Battelle that had no particular interest in developing commercial products. What was needed was an entrepre-neur with vision who could appreciate the commercial possibilities and recognize the profit potential that would justify the large financial

---

[9]Dessauer, page 47.

[10]As Erik Pell explains, "The current depends upon the maximum electrostatic field. Between two parallel plates, the field is uniform and equal to the voltage divided by the plate separation. But with a sharp point and a plate, the field is its maximum right at the point and is strongly dependent upon the radius of the point. It depends only slightly upon the distance from point to plate. Dimensionally, the field must be a voltage divided by distance—in the point geometry, the distance is the radius of curvature of the point."

[11]*Fortune*, July 1963, page 119.

commitments required. It required a visionary who had the personality and leadership style needed to organize and sustain a long-term development effort by his whole organization, which had to be on a scale beyond Battelle's reach and beyond the imagination of other corporations. That indispensable entrepreneur and organization leader was Joe Wilson.

8

SOL LINOWITZ

In the summer of 1946, Joe Wilson first met Sol Linowitz, who would perform a useful supporting role in Wilson's career. They met at the home of Frederick Mulhauser, president of the Rochester City Club, the leading civic organization in Rochester and the place where many remarkably prominent people—senators, authors, diplomats, and visitors from abroad—came to speak to audiences of up to 1,000 serious-minded people. Joe and Sol were, at 37 and 32, new young members of a program committee to select nationally prominent speakers for a stimulating series of eighteen Saturday luncheons during the coming year.

Both men were chosen to serve on the program committee because they were seen as rising young stars. Wilson had just become president of Haloid; Linowitz was trying to rebuild the practice of a once-prominent law firm in which he was now a named partner. Wilson was already well positioned within Rochester's establishment; Linowitz contemplated possibly running for public office and had been approached about the Democratic nomination for Congress. Both men were active in the Rochester Association of the United Nations, and both were determined to make something special of their lives, their talents, and themselves. Wilson was mastering his shyness, developing his skills as a public speaker, and learning to be more assertive; Linowitz had already mastered the genial, self-deprecating humor that would lead others to see him as being really quite special and all too modest.

The formative learning experiences of Sol Linowitz's childhood were three. First, he realized that he was endowed with several useful advantages: He was a good student, he had real musical talent; and he made connections quickly because people found him unusually engaging. Second, being Jewish, he was surrounded by visible and invisible prejudices that would constrict him unless he managed to be clearly different. Third, during the Depression, his father lost his prosperous business as a fruit wholesaler, which meant that Sol had to struggle to earn his own way through college, law school, and the early years of his profession.

Linowitz went to Hamilton College on the advice of an alumnus who was his high school English teacher, even though the scholarship offered there was less than one from the University of Virginia. He was one of only two Jewish freshmen, so they were assigned as roommates, until the other boy dropped out after only one semester. Linowitz then roomed with a Mormon. Both studied hard and graduated at the top of their class: Linowitz was Valedictorian, and his roommate, Salutatorian. (Linowitz liked to relate that his mother, attending her first college graduation, was justly concerned that his address—traditionally given in Latin—was "hard to understand" way back where she was sitting.) Christian chapel was compulsory every weekday; church was compulsory on Sunday. Ironically, Linowitz's high academic standing earned him the honor of taking attendance at services, but as a reminder of his Jewishness, Linowitz was not invited to join a fraternity. For a man as talented and proud as Sol Linowitz, such slights must have hurt deeply, but he never let it show.

In addition to waiting on tables, working in the library, and selling Christmas cards, Linowitz also earned money by reading for Elihu Root, the former Secretary of State and winner of the Nobel Peace Prize in 1912. His great public stature made an impression on young Linowitz, awakening aspirations in his own mind. When

Linowitz acknowledged that he might study to become a rabbi, Root advised him to become a lawyer: "A lawyer needs twice as much religion as a minister or a rabbi!"[1]

Linowitz joined the college dramatic society and played violin in the Utica Symphony, both requiring a proficiency in following a script or score written by others that would enable him to play in later years in a quartet and continue to act in community theater. In another instance of performing according to script vs. reality, he created for himself a summer job as a bandleader, hiding his heritage by taking the assumed name of Chick Lynn. More significantly, Linowitz became so skillful at performing that he was *always* on stage— as a lawyer, as a diplomat, and in every other role that came his way.

At Cornell Law School, Linowitz met and fell in love with an undergraduate, Toni Zimmerman. To be closer to Ithaca so as to continue courting his future wife, Linowitz joined a Rochester law firm instead of going to New York City, even though many people in the Rochester community would not welcome Catholics, and many more did not welcome Jews. With war coming, Linowitz was classified 3-A because by then he was married. He joined the Office of Price Administration (OPA), where he met on favorable terms with people who later became prominent, such as John Kenneth Galbraith, Ben Heinmann, Chester Bowles, and a series of lawyers and judges. Finally getting into the Navy, he continued working in Washington as a lawyer and met James Forrestall's young assistant, Adlai Stevenson. At Chester Bowles's special request, he was released from the Navy to rejoin OPA so he could argue in court the case for rent control of apartments in New York City.

In part because of this publicity, he was offered the Democratic nomination for a seat in Congress in his early 30s. However, Linowitz decided to return to practice law in Rochester. The law firm he had worked in before the war was badly weakened. Recognizing opportunity, Linowitz and a colleague agreed to take

[1]Linowitz, page 41.

over the firm, which they renamed Sutherland, Linowitz and Williams.[2] The firm was so weak that, to save on costs, no new stationery was ordered with the firm's new name. To buy a home, Linowitz took a $10,000 mortgage and borrowed $2,500 for the equity from his wife's aunt. It wasn't much of a law practice or law firm, but it was a start.

Linowitz was ambitious and classically upwardly mobile. Joining the Rochester Association for the United Nations gained him access to Rochester's social elite. It was there that he met Joe Wilson several times, as well as through the chamber of commerce and The Rochester City Club.

Serving as Program Chairman of The City Club—when Wilson was President—enabled Linowitz to get closer to Wilson and to begin becoming something of a public figure. He had a strong appetite for public recognition and was skillful at getting it. When he later became the club's president, he approached the local television station, suggesting that he could conduct a televised interview with each week's speaker. The show gained a good audience for a simple reason: It was followed by Sid Caesar's popular *Show of Shows*. Linowitz's skill with self-deprecating humor was shown in his repetitively reciting the comment of his daughter on his first TV appearance: "I loved it, Daddy, except two things: the way you looked and the way you talked!"

Similar in age and similar in public interests, both Linowitz and Wilson were bright, both were voracious readers interested in books and ideas, both were noticeably articulate and particularly enjoyed thoughtful discussion, and both were musical and enjoyed playing classical music (Sol on violin and Joe on piano). And while both young men were engaging and good-looking, both men were loners, and both had many good reasons to be looking for companionship, so their friendship developed rapidly to a closeness that is unusual among men.

[2]Linowitz, page 48.

In 1950, Wilson was looking for a lawyer to negotiate an agreement with Battelle. Haloid's usual lawyer was retiring,[3] so Wilson needed someone new. And in this case—an agreement involving a new process for copying—he had a particular reason for looking beyond Haloid's traditional law firm: Eastman Kodak used the same firm. Wilson made an appointment to meet Linowitz at his law office and asked: "Sol, how would you like to handle a one-shot for Haloid?"

"What do you mean by 'one-shot'?"

"The renegotiation of a contract. It would mean your going to Columbus, Ohio."

Smiling, Linowitz looked at his watch. "When do I leave?"

Both men laughed and shook hands. They made the trip by train to Columbus together. It was a grim experience: bitterly cold outside with no heating in the passenger cars. The two men huddled in overcoats after sharing a compartment on a sleeper and having no breakfast because there was no dining car—and then the train got stuck for several hours in heavy snow. Fortunately, out of such experiences come the strong bonds of friendship. (Years later, Wilson and Linowitz were in Europe crossing the English Channel. As their ferry boat rolled in the heavy seas during a stormy crossing, Wilson shouted out to Linowitz through a howling wind: "At least this beats Columbus!")

Finally arriving in Columbus, they went to Battelle for a demonstration of Carlson's invention. It was *not* the greatest show on earth. The Battelle team took from a shoe box a piece of cat fur, a transparent plastic ruler, a metal plate, and a bright light.[4] After rubbing the plate with the fur and shining the light through the ruler and onto the plate, some off-white lines showed up on the dark surface. Then the plate was dusted with dark powder and, after brushing it clean, was pressed against some paper—and there, somewhat blurred, were

[3]Percival Oviatt of Nixon, Hargraves.
[4]Linowitz, page 56.

the lines of the ruler. As Joe Wilson looked closely at the plate through his bifocals, one of the Battelle demonstrators said proudly: "That's it!"

Wilson said one word: "Magnificent!"

Linowitz said two words, asking incredulously: "That's it?"

"Yes," came the reply. "That's *it*."

Wilson wanted to draw up an agreement quickly, but Linowitz thought that it was ridiculous. A process that required so many more steps than other copying processes to produce such a crude and unpromising reproduction didn't make much sense to him, so he tried to talk Wilson entirely out of going forward with electrophotography. But Wilson was determined to go ahead, and he was the client.

That autumn, Wilson chaired a meeting with Battelle representatives in Rochester, where the central terms of an agreement—explicitly excluding fingerprinting, toys, and electron microscope shadowgraphic—were worked out with Linowitz's advice and counsel. Haloid would get an exclusive license for making copies with limited volume—under 20 copies per original. Haloid would pay $10,000 immediately and $25,000 annually, equal to nearly 20% of Haloid's current profits, plus an 8% royalty on any commercial sales. Wilson saw the $25,000 annual payment as an investment rather than an expense because Battelle agreed it would spend the money from Haloid on further research to develop Carlson's process. Battelle gave Haloid exclusive rights to most applications while Haloid took responsibility for increased research support, for seeking sublicensees who would do research in the field, and for paying Battelle large royalties.

During the fall of 1953, Joe Wilson and Sol Linowitz drew closer together. Joe was recovering from his first heart attack, and Sol made a point of visiting often for long talks. The connection between Joe and Sol developed rapidly as they discussed everything from amusing anecdotes and gossip to the most important questions of strategy and corporate policy. Sol shared his confidential worries about the shaky financial situation at his law firm, while Joe spoke openly about his concerns for Haloid. "We came from such very different backgrounds," said Linowitz of Wilson. "He was establishment and accepted and Republican and local. I was an outsider, a Jew, and a Democrat. But we had so very much in common: our dreams, our search for what was new and would work, our curiosity and love of learning, our youthfulness, and our aspirations. We quoted great thinkers to each other: They became integral to our dialogue." As Wilson and Linowitz got to know each other better and better, they liked each other more and more and developed great respect for each other's capabilities. As they grew closer, Jack Hartnett, who had been Joe's daily companion, was simply squeezed out. Joe and Sol developed a practice of taking long walks together on weekends, sometimes around the local reservoir and sometimes around Mendon Pond. The walks became regular Sunday events while Peggy and the children were at church. Wilson would bring a typed list of topics he wanted to discuss before making final decisions and would cross each item off with a pencil after it was resolved.[5] In time, these regular walks became part of the informal management structure Wilson used to transform Haloid.

On their Sunday walks, Wilson and Linowitz commiserated over the many frustrations they each experienced, and Wilson expressed bemused recognition that the only justification for his continued optimism was his lack of technical training that prevented him from understanding how devastating the many technological failures really were. Yet both young men sensed that Carlson's invention was Haloid's and Wilson's one big chance for major success.

During all of this time, technological leap-frogging by competitors was a constant concern. Strategically, Wilson was clearly contending with the continuing risk that somewhere, someone would re-enact the pursuit of innovation that he was sponsoring and some-

---

[5] Linowitz, page 52. Wilson kept the lists. They later resurfaced during discovery procedures and the SCM antitrust case.

how create an unbeatable nightmare for Haloid. That's why Linowitz was asked to check into the companies that had inquired at the patent office about Carlson's patents. He worked through a trademark expert, Walter Derenberg, who encouragingly reported that there was no evidence of anyone ever having asked about Carlson's patents.

In Wilson, Carlson, and Linowitz, three very different minds, personalities, and approaches to questions were again and again in evidence. All three men were brilliant, hard-working, and long-term in their thinking. Linowitz was skeptical, incremental, and self-protective. Carlson was introverted, stubborn, reclusive, and a visionary. Wilson was conceptual, disciplined, determined, and an engaging enthusiast who inspired and worked well with others.

Linowitz had great ability to sense accurately and adapt swiftly to the significance of each situation and to position himself advantageously. As one of his colleagues explained, "Sol could quickly see an opportunity to advance—and he *always* took it. When a photographer was present, Sol would position himself next to a prominent person and then, when the photographer was ready, turn to the prominent person and point at just the right moment. As a result, his picture was often in the paper the next day. Even if served mud pies as hors d'ouevres, Sol would show that he loved them. He is a chameleon to the situation, always adapting and optimizing his position." Time and again, Linowitz would, with great personal charm, make the person he was speaking with feel very confidently that he was *the* most important and interesting person in the world, but minutes later, Linowitz, who had become accustomed to using his relationships with other people to advance his own standing, would have moved on and would not even be aware of the person he had just been speaking with.

As an associate in his law firm, Al Swett worked for Linowitz and was on call seven days a week from 7:00 AM to 11:00 PM. According to Swett, "Sol would sometimes call me at the office at seven or later in the evening and want me to drive over to his house with certain papers. When I rang the doorbell, it was always answered by the housekeeper—never by Sol." Linowitz kept two secretaries busy full time and Swett wrote virtually all the memos Linowitz then signed, including one memo that was revised seventeen different times in one very long day. "I once worked on a memorandum and its many, many revisions from noon until six one evening," recounts Swett, "Half an hour later, I was getting ready to go home when Sol's secretary came into my office with a wry smile on her face: 'Try *again!*'"

Law is a vicarious profession. A good lawyer will never take unto himself the problems and feelings that belong to his client. As an advisor, a lawyer does his best work while remaining emotionally detached and rational. Linowitz, explained Swett in an interview, "was a master of detached, rational analysis and advice who even took a very detached, front-row view of his own life. He had no heroes, and no one was ever explicitly admired by him. He never gave much of himself to anyone because he couldn't." Trust and love involve vulnerability and, after his difficult experiences growing up, Linowitz would never again put himself in the position of being vulnerable or dependent on others. He was—in law courts, on tennis courts, or in conversation—an accomplished defensive player, and he always played singles, even if others were in or on the court.

Linowitz would not—and probably could not—commit fully to Joe Wilson's company, so he was never an employee. While Wilson provided Linowitz with a fully outfitted office, Linowitz always preserved the self-protective independence of maintaining a significant private law practice and his own real office at Sutherland, Linowitz and Williams. Although Linowitz was never an employee of the company, Wilson rewarded him with substantial stock ownership and options that made him wealthy. He also honored him with a sequence of corporate titles. In the mid-1950s, he was made Vice President in charge of licensing and patent development. He later became Chairman of the Executive Committee, Chairman of the Board, and eventually, Chairman of the Board of Xerox International.

Wilson always positioned this unusual arrangement as quite natural, saying matter-of-factly when announcing another Linowitz promotion in corporate title: "Of course, Sol will continue his law practice." In addition to being Linowitz's largest and most regular client, Wilson made sure his company was Linowitz's most *profitable* client, once refusing to pay a bill until it was increased by at least 20%. Wilson was trusting and giving in many ways that Linowitz could not be. This difference did not matter in the early years of their friendship, when Joe Wilson had so much to give and was the client. But as the years went by, their differences in values and ways would matter greatly.

As a lawyer developing an important relationship with a potentially major client, Linowitz's primary task was clear to him: More important than advising Wilson on policy matters or strategies, Linowitz's priority was to understand Joe Wilson as a human being and to know every aspect of what made him tick. He needed to know what moved him, what his private and personal motivations and anxieties were and would be, and how he would react to any situation. As an associate in Linowitz's law firm observed, "Sol saw Joe through a magnifying glass." This detached scrutiny enabled Linowitz to anticipate Wilson's thinking, and to be unusually helpful to him. Increasingly, it also enabled him to manage the development of their relationship. As a lawyer paid by the hour, initially Linowitz was entirely dependent upon and subordinate to Wilson. But over time, in a series of imperceptible stages, their relationship gradually changed until they became virtual equals. And then, at least in some aspects of their relationship, Linowitz would grow from junior partner, to partner, to senior partner, quite frequently giving Wilson guidance that was closer to instruction than to advice. One subtle, but visible, manifestation: In his numerous "Dear Joe" letters, Sol typically signed them with his full name: "Sol M. Linowitz."

For all of their similarities and compatibilities as they worked together over many challenging years, Wilson and Linowitz were very different people. Wilson was centered on and deeply rooted in

Rochester. Except for his two school years at Harvard, he had spent all his past years and expected to spend all his future years in Rochester. People always knew he was a local Rochestarian when, as a true native, he pronounced the city's name, *Rah-chester* (putting strong emphasis on the first syllable). Linowitz was *in* Rochester, but not *of* Rochester. As it would eventually turn out, he was just passing through. In time, Sol Linowitz would decide he had outgrown the role he had been performing for the company and for Joe Wilson. But in the late 1940s and through the 1950s, Linowitz was one of Wilson's key lieutenants and close friends during his era of extreme entrepreneurship.

9

TOWARD XEROX

For Joe Wilson, 1946 was the year to "concentrate the mind wonderfully."[1] With 100 salesmen working out of seventeen branch offices, most of Haloid's sales and earnings were coming from Haloid Record and from Rectigraph machines and supplies. However, both lines were experiencing declining profits because both were near the end of their product life cycles. Haloid's annual report that year was blunt: "The prospects for earnings are unfavorable" due to an almost 30% surge in higher wages and increased costs for silver. The 1946 jump in costs was $500,000, a large amount for a company reporting earning of only $150,000, a full third of which was due to a tax rebate.

Years later, Wilson would give this realistic, retrospective description of Haloid's true position: "a little company just breaking even after the war—a company with meager financial resources, without much research and engineering competence, with a small thinly spread sales force and obviously without specialized plants because xerographic products had not been made before by any man anywhere.

---

[1] Dr. Johnson once said this to explain the sudden brilliance of a condemned man's articulation in an appeal for clemency, which Johnson had actually ghostwritten himself: "A sure appointment with the gallows concentrates the mind wonderfully."

I must confess that if we had fully foreseen the magnitude of the job, the millions needed for research and new capital, the marketing complexities, the manufacturing problems involved in making new things work right and reliably all over the world in all temperatures and humidities, we probably would not have had the fortitude to go ahead. But we did."

Joe Wilson didn't look back: He looked forward—far, far forward. With limited financial or managerial resources, little experience in manufacturing, marketing, or technology, and no experience in managing a large international business, Wilson set out quite deliberately with the people and resources he had at hand to realize the unknown commercial potential of an underdeveloped technology with the inconvenient name of electrophotography. If the best definition of entrepreneurship is to commit to achievements beyond the capacity of currently available resources, Joe Wilson's chosen commitment was an adventure in extreme entrepreneurship.

Entrepreneurs differ greatly from promoters who swing for the fences: The entrepreneur's persistent priority is a disciplined, managed minimization of risk. While casual observers may celebrate Wilson's ultimately astounding financial success, his real achievement as a leader and manager were in his rigorous financial discipline, his focus on developing a new technology, and his remarkable capacity to keep his organization committed to his vision for many long, lean years while going through the uncertainties of deliberate transformational change.

Very few leaders have so successfully undertaken such enormous change. During the later 1940s, Joe Wilson plunged into the struggle, knowing only the general direction of his quest. Believing that Carlson's invention could be developed into the solution to Haloid's daunting strategic dilemma, Wilson boldly committed to achieving the necessary technological advances, raising the needed money, creating new markets for new products based on the new technology and reorganizing his company on every dimension. Without Joe Wilson's remarkable skills, personal strength of character, and disciplined commitment, Haloid could never have become Xerox.

W hile the prospect of developing an office copier had real attraction for several companies, no one expected the huge demand that would develop. Copying demand had been growing slowly for well over a half century. Thomas Alva Edison invented the basic mimeograph machine, but seeing little demand for this early copier, he sold the rights to Alfred Black Dick of Chicago, who improved the basic process. According to his grandson C. Matthews Dick Jr., when the AB Dick mimeograph machines came to market in 1887, "People didn't *want* to make lots of copies of office documents." By and large, the first users of mimeograph machines were nonbusiness organizations such as churches, schools, and Boy Scout troops. Office duplicating by machine was a new and unsettling idea that upset long-established office patterns.[2] To attract companies and professionals, Dick undertook an enormous missionary effort. In 1887, the typewriter had been on the market for little more than a decade and wasn't yet in widespread use.[3] Neither was carbon paper, although it had originated in 1807. If a businessman or a lawyer, for any reason, wanted copies of a document, he would have five separate copies typed or made by hand. Gradually, typewriters and carbon paper gained popularity at the end of the 19th century, and mimeographing early in the 20th century. By 1910, some 200,000 mimeograph machines were in use. By 1940, there were nearly 500,000.

Offset duplicating, which produced higher quality copies, was introduced in the 1930s and soon dominated the high-volume end of the market. Wilson had originally hoped to succeed in the duplicator segment of the market, which was effectively limited to copy volumes greater than 20 copies because duplicators required that a master be made first—a relatively costly and time-consuming process.

[2]The negative connotations of copying—"Copycat!" "He copied *my* work!" "It's not *nice* to copy!" "Aw, that's just a *copy!*"—are deeply rooted in our language and our values. Today's complex of laws to protect intellectual property go back to the copyright laws that have protected authors and publishers since the seventeenth century. Forgery copies of papal indulgences date back to the Middle Ages.

[3]The first typewriters were produced by the Remington Arms Company of New Haven, Connecticut.

Copiers, which would eventually become Haloid's target market, were expected to produce only smaller numbers of copies, mostly much smaller numbers.

As his focus turned increasingly to developing the new technology and his company's future, Wilson faced serious challenges with Haloid's traditional business. In 1947, Wilson's second year as President, Haloid's sales were just over $7 million and profits declined to just under $140,000—because the pressure of rising materials costs and wages became acute, and Haloid could not pass along these higher costs by raising prices because it was not a strong enough competitor. Dividends were cut by one-third, from 90¢ to 60¢ with none paid in the fourth quarter. Caught in a serious cash squeeze, Haloid had to borrow from banks just to finance its higher-cost inventories.

For the next two decades, Haloid would always be short on cash, continuously struggling to minimize costs that were not essential to the development of electrophotography, and needing to obtain external financing for investments in this potentially promising but still unproven technology. It was in this grim context that Wilson contracted with Battelle, to spend $25,000 on rights to an undeveloped technology that had been rejected by many companies and might never earn a commercial profit.

On January 20, 1948, Wilson wrote a six-page letter to Haloid's directors about his recent meeting at Battelle, including a 15-page analysis of the electrophotography process and its commercial prospects. The analysis was packed with specific information and balanced in tone. In reading it, his father could see how very intrigued Joe Wilson was. (Wilson, typically careful to evaluate all risks, also asked a patent attorney to verify the validity of the four Carlson patents.) However, for most of the senior people at Haloid, response to Wilson's memo was not enthusiastic. It was very restrained.

A month later, Wilson was back in Columbus. John Dessauer and Ernst Taubes of Microtronics were with him for a full-scale demonstration. Wilson's report on this meeting was again replete with detailed information and, leaving the specific terms open for further discussion, he urged seeking an exclusive license. In May, Wilson initiated discussion of how Haloid might produce a copying machine by using electrophotography: It would require well over a decade to go from idea to reality, a very long entrepreneurial gauntlet for anyone to run.

In July, John Crout phoned Wilson: Battelle was ready to grant a license to Haloid. After months of negotiations, Wilson would get the exclusive license he wanted on the use of electrophotography, effective September 30. Haloid agreed to find at least three sublicensees who would also invest in electrophotography research, expanding the breadth and depth of the search for new applications.

Taking a great but calculated risk, Wilson committed his company to a new technology that had never been used effectively and might never turn a profit. Over the next five years, Wilson would invest twice as much in research and development as Haloid earned over the same period. Wilson personally mortgaged everything he owned; twenty years later he would remark, "I would have to be psychoanalyzed to tell you if I would take the same risk again. It's when you're young and naïve that you have the courage to make the right decisions."[1]

Wilson and Dessauer, wanting a freer hand than allowed by the initial Battelle accords, returned to Columbus and pointed out that if any of the other licensees made major advances, significant disagreements could develop. (Dessauer made another contribution: He did some checking and concluded that the Carlson process was at least scientifically feasible *and* that it was an "unsponsored orphan" at Battelle.[5] This insight gave Wilson an important advantage in deciding his negotiating strategy.) After some thought, Battelle proposed granting Haloid exclusive rights to all developments, volunteering exactly what Wilson had been hoping to achieve. On the train ride home that night, Wilson and Dessauer "celebrated exuberantly."[6]

[4]Harvard Business School, Directory of Named Chairs.
[5]Linowitz, page 55.
[6]Dessauer, page 126.

Getting other companies interested in doing research in the new technology was never easy. For example, Linowitz sent out 126 identical letters to a list of corporations considered the most likely to be interested, welcoming inquiries. Not one replied. The only consolation was that such systematic lack of interest among larger companies was the only reason Haloid had won Battelle's support.[7]

Explaining how he and others at Battelle were feeling during this period, Lew Walkrup, the project manager there, said, "It is hard to believe our utter naïvete in electrostatics when we started this thing. [The technology] went through many stages in its development at which any sane management committee would have been justified in turning it down. There always had to be something *extralogical* about continuing."

And why would a pragmatic engineer be swayed by extralogical factors? Walkrup continues: "Several reasons. First, this was a brand new process. It led us to a vacant field of technology, which in itself was a magnet and challenge to any research scientist. Second, I suspected there would be a much larger market for this invention than anyone guessed—though I'll admit I never dreamed it would become as fabulous as it did. Finally, I was hoping it would yield enough profits to allow us to come back for more and more research, since I felt we were truly entering a new area of human knowledge."[8]

Developing the new technology would still require large sums— perhaps as much as $1 million—a lot more than Battelle and Haloid could provide. (One million dollars was seven times Haloid's current annual earnings, and those earnings were going down.) In the spring of 1947, Battelle called Wilson with a beautiful question. The Army Signal Corps was interested in a bid to develop a dry photography

[7]Linowitz, page 73.
[8]Dessauer, page 63.

process. Would Haloid be willing to submit a bid with Battelle? Haloid had sold lots of photocopying gear to the Army Signal Corps during the war, so Wilson and Haloid were known suppliers. If Haloid would join with Battelle, the Signal Corps might finance all or most of the necessary research on electroradiography.

Less than a week later, Wilson, Linowitz, and Dessauer were on their way to Fort Monmouth. Waiting at Penn Station for the train to Monmouth, Linowitz recalled, "We became so engrossed in conversation that we missed the train. My advice, which Joe and John Crout accepted, was that we should claim delay in New York because of other important business we had to do that day, rather than admit negligence: It was better to look arrogant than stupid." A skeptical team from the Signal Corps was startled by Wilson's handing out examples of electroradiography and his explaining how quickly they'd been made. A demonstration was quickly arranged and a research grant of $120,000 was made[9]—and later increased to $200,000.

Even with others' blatant lack of interest in electrophotography, Wilson was not only determined in his entrepreneurial commitment, he was already expanding the scope of his strategic vision for his company. For his overall strategy to succeed, Wilson knew he needed to create a franchise for Haloid comparable to IBM's. Wilson's objective was not *product*-centered; it was *corporate*. As important as it was to promote major new products, the strategic priority for a technology company that would create and market a series of innovative new products was clear to Wilson: Create and establish an image and reputation for his company as an employer, as an investment, and as a company to trust and do business with again and again. In his drive to reinvent his company's external image to match the revolutionary changes he was making internally, Wilson was ready to change every aspect of the company, even its name.

[9]Dessauer, page 54.

Names matter. Great names like Kodak, Harvard, and Yale matter greatly. Xerox is a great name. Haloid was not. Haloid was just a conventional industrial name. In the early years, it had been a good name: brief, distinctive, and identified with the company's product. But, 30 or 40 years later, that direct identification with haloidal salts was becoming both misleading and constricting.[10] It had no connection with the burgeoning technology that was the future for Wilson's company. And electrophotography—the name Carlson had coined—was a tongue twister. Hard to pronounce, hard to remember, and not even easy to recognize, electrophotography had no particular meaning for most people. Wilson needed a new and better name.

How Haloid became Xerox illustrates the way Wilson—as an entrepreneur with unusual intellectual interests and high aspirations for his company—led and managed his company's development. Only the restraints of familiarity and inertia would support continuing to use the name Haloid. That's easy to see in retrospect, but what is not clear was exactly when—and on what specific, incremental day—it became obvious that *now* was the time to change.

Human beings avoid change because the costs of change are largely concentrated in the here and now, while the benefits extend way out into the future—and the current costs are always much clearer and more visible than the future benefits. Moreover, it is much easier for an individual to make a change than it is for a group to agree on a change. And the larger the group, the more difficult it is to agree on whether, when, or how to change, and even what to change to.

Wilson was ambitious for his company to be special, so he was unusually open to considering name alternatives to Haloid. He was looking for a name that was different, original, and that would com-

[10]Haloid's limitations were not unique. Other corporate names that became outdated include Radio Corporation of America (now RCA), National Cash Register (now NCR); and Radio Shack.

mand attention. Chance always favors the prepared mind. With Wilson's long-standing fondness for the classics and his comfort in an intellectual realm, he was well-prepared when chance came his way.

Xerography became the name for Carlson's process during a delay in formalizing contractual rearrangements with Battelle, a delay of only a few months during the summer of 1948. Jack Hartnett was in Columbus with Wilson for a May conference on the marketing possibilities for electrophotography. Hartnett spoke of *dry printing* as a better description to use for marketing purposes, but while descriptive, dry printing sounded flat, even dull. Something better, something distinctive was needed, but what might it be? Robert Stich, head of Battelle's public relations, had raised that same question with an acquaintance, Professor Robert Jones of Ohio State's Greek and Latin department,[11] and Jones suggested combining two Greek works—*xeros* for *dry* and *graphien* for *writing*—into a new word: xerography.[12]

Wilson liked the classical tone immediately. But would people say the word with the first letter x pronounced as a z? After some give and take on pronunciation, the new word, xerography, began to gain acceptance, and that initial acceptance grew stronger and stronger. (Twenty years later, Chester Carlson still saw no advantage in the term xerography compared to electrophotography and still felt his original name was more technically accurate and "fit better with technical parlance.") Late in May, "xerography" appeared in correspondence between Haloid and Battelle. By July, the term was being used in their contracts.

To encourage widespread use of the term, Hartnett advised against copyrighting the term xerography. It was better to put no limits on the

---

[11]Jones was a member of the faculty from 1940 to 1968 and taught courses in Greek mythology. He once observed laconically that no one ever even suggested he might be paid for his contributing the name *xerography*.

[12]AB Dick's term *mimeograph* was composed similarly from *mime* for *repeat* and *graphos* for *writing*.

descriptive term for a whole new technology and let xerography be generic. Instead, a trademark should be registered for a brand or trade name. Hartnett suggested Xerex as the trademark name, but Wilson rejected that as too close to Zerex, a well-known antifreeze. Instead, Wilson suggested if xerography would be the new generic name for the process, then the trade name could be Xerox. If people would pronounce the name as *Zerox*, it would be clear and distinctive. And it looked and sounded like the trade name they all knew and admired: Kodak. Xerox was an entirely new name with five letters that started and ended with the same letter, an unusual, hard consonant. As a trade name, all agreed on Xerox.

Battelle suggested that the Optical Society of America's annual meeting in Detroit on October 22, 1948—exactly ten years after the date of the original 10–22–38 copy in Astoria—would be a perfect date for a public demonstration of xeroprinting.[13] A xeroprinting machine capable of printing four-inch wide paper at 1,200 feet per minute was designed and built. (How very tight budgets were at Haloid in those days is indicated by the way the total cost of the $25,000 demonstration was allocated. Haloid paid one-third and Battelle paid two-thirds, evenly split between its public relations budget and the Battelle Development Corporation.) The Optical Society agreed to feature the demonstration. But to protect against unseemly commercialization or, even worse, being scooped, the Society stipulated that there must be no publicity about the new process before their meeting. Wilson agreed.

A little later, Wilson learned that America's leading print medium, *LIFE* magazine, was ready to do a major story on xerography. An article in *LIFE* would be a spectacular publicity coup. But *LIFE* would come out one day *before* the Optical Society's meeting, so Wilson stood by his commitment to the Optical Society: There would be no story in *LIFE*.

[13]Dessauer, page 45.

At the conclusion of the Detroit demonstration, Wilson gave an upbeat talk that ended with this observation: "All of us working with this process confidently believe that through it, those two old workhorses, light and electricity, working together again as a team—now as xerography, capturing images through a new method at once simple, economical, flexible, and completely physical—will render mankind another highly beneficial service." The Detroit announcement was a real success—though not so spectacular as would have been a feature article in *LIFE*.

In addition to publicity from the demonstration, Haloid received tentative applications for licenses from 90 different companies. Follow-up appointments were made with GE, AB Dick, RCA, Burroughs, and others. To promote the widespread use and development of xerography, as agreed upon with Battelle, Wilson launched negotiations to arrange licensing agreements with a dozen corporations.[14]

Meanwhile, Wilson continued working on the transformation of his company. One important aspect of change was in improving labor relations. During the late 1940s, as other companies incurred major difficulties in labor relations, Wilson conscientiously kept emotion out of negotiations on economic and other pragmatic issues, and labor relations at Haloid progressed increasingly smoothly. Wilson consistently and specifically committed Haloid to good labor relations through collective bargaining in the 1947 Annual Report: "Again we stress the importance that we attach to the maintenance of good industrial relations. During 1947, we are happy to say that they continued friendly and cooperative. We, as a Company, were faced with a severe problem during the mid-year sales decline and our workers and their representatives cooperated wholeheartedly with us. On the other hand, despite the difficulties of that period we made adjustments in our workers' favor which we felt were fair and justified."

[14]Goss Printing Co. tried to bypass the Battelle-Haloid patents, but the validity of Haloid's patent position was successfully reaffirmed.

As was typical for most companies in the 1940s, Haloid had no pension or retirement plan. Wilson didn't think that was right or wise, so he sought expert advice.[15] He had three objectives in mind: All categories of workers should be included; payment into the fund should be variable, with more in good years and less in poor years; and retirement should be set at 65 to open up opportunities for younger workers.

Addressing Haloid employees in the 1948 annual report, Wilson stated: "We believe sincerely in the principle of collective bargaining and practice it with good will. We try to pay salaries and wages at least equal to those for comparable work in our communities. At the same time, for your security, we try to see to it that the Company's position is kept financially strong. Over a period, and as we can afford it, we shall try to put into effect further measures which will relieve you in part of the fears that beset so many these days; fear of poverty in old age or in slack times.

"We want you to be proud of Haloid. We want your job to excite you, to make you feel that you're a person of dignity, a part of a valuable creative effort. With it all we want you to enjoy it here, and to take pride in your work. We try to conduct ourselves so that you will feel confidence in us and in our determination that all your problems are considered fully and fairly always. On the other hand, we want you to treat our problems just as fully and squarely as we deal with yours and thus to create the kind of organization morale that will be the envy of others. If we all seek that kind of unity of purpose, we cannot help but be happier people and Haloid will be a model of the kind of business that our country needs."

As was always the case for Haloid, money was a persistent concern and a particular focus for Wilson, a speed-reader with a photographic mind, particularly for numbers, as he often demonstrated so effectively. His unusual facility with figures and his evident personal integrity were repetitively significant for Haloid

[15]From Ivins, Phillips & Barker of Washington, DC.

bankers and for the company. In 1946, to raise much needed capital to repay bank loans, Wilson arranged with First Boston to handle a private placement issue of $1 million of 4% preferred stock with four insurance companies.

First Boston's Charles Glavin recalled the meeting with the institutional investors at which Wilson was expected to answer questions. "I was dumbfounded when Joe arrived without a single note or document. Usually, at such meetings, company officials come armed with a hundred booklets and papers. Joe brought nothing except a pleasant smile. He talked easily, informally, for the better part of an hour. It was not a speech; it was a bit of conversation. While he answered questions, I sat fascinated and amazed. He had every figure in his head, every fact at the tip of his tongue. By the time the meeting ended and the men shook his hand, the million dollars was as good as delivered."[16]

Wilson wasn't the only one concerned with needs for cash. Chester Carlson, who had been tested so often in childhood, would be tested again in 1949, long before any products were produced through xerography. His five-year option to pay Battelle's accumulated costs of research—which then totaled $17,000—was about to expire. Carlson still had no money, but he was more convinced than ever of his patented process's potential, and he was determined to get the funds. Pleading with every person he knew—particularly his relatives and those of his new wife Dorris—he raised $15,000 and borrowed the balance to reach the necessary $17,000. Over the next several years, this additional 15% of licensing income would return nearly $7 million, 400 times the cost.[17] Still, Carlson was strained for cash and worried about the pace of progress in xerography.

[16]Dessauer, page 151.
[17]In 1947, Carlson modified his agreement with Battelle as an exclusive license because that made his royalties taxable as capital gains rather than as ordinary income.

Late in 1949, Carlson—already stooped at 43 by the pain of his inherited spinal arthritis—stopped off in Rochester on his way from Columbus to New York City. He wanted to check on progress. Carlson unloaded a string of complaints to Wilson and Dessauer about how little progress Battelle had made toward commercial applications. Battelle's annual development expenditures had averaged only $3,500 over the first five years—a sum that was small both absolutely and relative to its total annual budget of $1 million, and very small relative to the large sums needed to develop xerography commercially. As usual, Wilson, who liked Carlson and respected his brilliance, listened thoughtfully.

On the spot, he offered to retain him as a consultant at $1,000 per month. Carlson agreed—his personal finances were even worse than others realized—and moved into a small rented house near Rochester. Carlson was still poor and brought his lunch in a bag. When John Dessauer invited him to a restaurant, he declined, explaining, "I just can't afford to reciprocate, thank you. Some other day."

Explaining that the avalanche of enquiries about xerography prevented meeting as often as he would have liked, Wilson asked Carlson by memo to "follow a procedure which we have found extremely useful in our own organization. Will you set forth at the beginning of each month the objectives both patent-wise and equipment development-wise which you hope to accomplish and then give me a brief written report at the end of each month as to the progress made in each direction? I am anxious that we be fully informed and in full concurrence that the objectives you are setting for yourself are the same as our desires." In the months that followed, Carlson filed written reports that were typically a page or more on accomplishments, plus one-quarter page on plans. And while Carlson would say almost apologetically, "I want to stay out of the way," he continued to press his contacts at Haloid to file more patent applications.

The decade of the 1940s ended with some guarded optimism. Carlson advised his co-investors that "Haloid Copier is nearing the manufacturing stage. Small scale output is looked for about the end of the year. Baring unforeseen difficulties, production should increase from month-to-month in 1950."

With progress at the company, Joe Wilson was ready to make another kind of investment: a family home, one that would be particularly important for Peggy Wilson. The Greek Revival house at 1550 Clover Street had caught Peggy's eye when they were a young married couple, so one day, she asked Joe to drive by and quietly announced, "That will be *our* home one day." After more than a decade of dreaming, the house came on the market in 1948, and Joe bought it for Peggy as a Valentine's Day present. The home on Clover Street had 16 rooms and 100 years of history, first as the Clover Street Seminary and later as the St. Mark's School for Boys. There were enough bedrooms so all of the Wilson children had their own rooms. As Peggy happily said, "We loved it."

Joe Wilson was unusually adept at and conscientious about keeping work and family separated. He was particularly careful not to bring home, as his father had often done, the tensions and struggles he encountered at work. During the week, breakfast and dinner brought the whole family together. Before breakfast and after dinner, he made the rounds of the children's bedrooms with his cheery wake-up calls in the morning and, at the end of the day, a gentle "nite-nite" to each child after recounting the amazing adventures of Queen Christina, her knights, and her gracious ladies-in-waiting. He was also the "go-to-parent" for comforting back rubs, and he enjoyed giving his children morning rides to school as another time for sharing daily experiences. Every Sunday afternoon, weather permitting, Joe Wilson put on his cook's apron and organized a cookout, usually of hot dogs and hamburgers. At the office, Wilson had standing instructions: "If one of the kids calls to speak to me, please put the call through right away so they'll *know* their calls are always at *least* as important to me as their calls will be to them." As Kathy Wilson recalls with a warm smile, "Not only was he our *father*, he was very definitely *our* father. We all knew we were very important to

Dad and he was there for us in the most direct and engaging way. The house on Clover Street was enlarged to make it just right for the whole family. And that's the same reason Dad made sure the summer cottage at Bristol was built with a big, warm, friendly gathering place designed around the fire so everyone could sit together and talk, play games, and sing songs." (In 1958, a winter home would be purchased in Delray, Florida, with a pool, family room, and terrace serving as gathering places.) "Those houses were carefully *designed* to encourage family fun, and we had a *ball!*"

In late 1948, early in the long search for corporate partners, a lucky break quickly developed into a chance to demonstrate the new technology, this time on television! Wilson believed that Haloid had the proverbial better mousetrap, but what was needed now was a way to tell the world so it could start beating a path to Haloid's door. A TV demonstration would reproduce for a wide audience the show stopper performed for the relatively small group gathered at the Optical Society meeting in Detroit. But the one chance for a TV demonstration came on *very* short notice: Tonight!

The WABC-TV studio was in New York City. So was the xerographic equipment. But there was no toner in Manhattan: All of Haloid's toner was in Rochester. And there was too little time to drive from Rochester to Manhattan. To solve the problem, a plane was chartered to fly toner to New York City. But on that particular day, a heavy fog closed New York's two major airports, LaGuardia and Idlewild (now JFK International Airport). So after over an hour of circling, the plane from Rochester was diverted to Newark, New Jersey. The time it would take a taxi—in heavy, early evening, rush-hour traffic—to make the trip from Newark airport to the Midtown Manhattan TV studio would use up all or almost all of the time still available before airtime. The taxi could still make it, unless it ran into too much traffic. At 7:50 PM, just ten minutes before airtime, the taxi with the toner still had not arrived. If the taxi didn't make it in time, the chance to demonstrate the new technology on TV—the perfect time and way to showcase xerography—would pass by.

Luckily, at 7:55 PM, the taxi with the toner did arrive and the televised demonstration went on as scheduled. Getting toner to the studio just in time was not the only lucky break that evening. Another was in the audience. Among the millions of viewers was IBM's CEO, Thomas J. Watson Jr.

Watson was impressed. The next day, he called Wilson to suggest they get together to discuss a joint program and instructed his associates to investigate ways in which IBM might use xerography. After some urgent study, the best prospects appeared to be in producing the millions of computer-printed address labels used every day to mail magazines and newspapers. But then after several months of negotiating, IBM aborted discussions. Other techniques would be used instead. IBM had no further interest in licensing the Haloid patents.[18]

[18]In 1984, when Steve Jobs introduced the Macintosh at a shareholder meeting, he cited IBM's lack of interest in xerography as characteristic of the inability to recognize the important potential of a new technology.

10

THE UNIVERSITY

I n early 1949, Wilson called a friend to share the exciting news that he was being made a trustee at the University of Rochester. At the age of 40, Joe Wilson would be one of the youngest trustees ever to serve the university. Most other trustees were older than his father. Joe Wilson's leadership of the university would be the largest of his many service commitments and would parallel his commitment to Xerox.

"Congratulations, Joe! You must be pleased!"

"Yes, very. You know how much the University means to me." And then Wilson added, "And this is five years ahead of my own schedule!" Wilson surprised his friend with the deliberate discipline of his personal life strategy and his commitment to planning, which was already becoming familiar to those who knew him well.

Over the next two decades, Wilson would be acknowledged as the principal trustee of the university he led through an impressive era of bold expansion and upgrade that transformed the University of Rochester from regional to national in stature—a transformation that others agreed could only be achieved with Joe Wilson's strategic vision and organized persistence in implementation.

As Wilson demonstrated his leadership, both organizationally and financially, his official responsibilities at the university increased rapidly. After just one year's service, he was named to the executive committee and made chair of the trustee steering committee. In 1954, Wilson was named the first chairman of the corporate relations committee, which was newly created at Wilson's initiative. Its assignment: to develop stronger relationships between the university and the Rochester-area business community by developing strong programs of mutual interest. In August 1956, he was elected chairman of the university's executive committee. In 1958, Wilson moved successfully for a major expansion in the authority of the executive committee. In an informal meeting with the Chairman of the Board of Trustees, Wilson presented an eight-page analysis of the university board's structure, identifying specific areas needing improvement, and a list of 50 local and national candidates for the 40-member board.

Wilson was convinced that having a strong, nearby university would be essential if Haloid were going to recruit successfully the large number of talented people it would need to become the kind of company he intended. And, as an alumnus, he understandably wanted to see his university move ahead. (Wilson also wanted educational variety, so he encouraged Kent Damon, Xerox's Treasurer, to work for Rochester Institute of Technology.) In 1959, Wilson and his father gave the university $1 million with a remarkable stipulation: It was all to be spent within just three years. In accepting the terms of the Wilson gift, the university committed itself to raise the permanent funding needed to sustain the new higher level of expenditures. Typically, having carefully thought out a long-term goal, Wilson developed an effective strategy to achieve that goal and then acted boldly to make it happen. Time and again, this was Wilson's way: goal, strategy, organization, action—all in concert, because each part had been carefully thought through and all parts were interconnected.

Major change was not uniformly accepted or endorsed by the trustees of the university. The Rochester establishment was traditionally very conservative, and some older trustees strongly resisted any change. Two senior trustees resigned in protest in the 1950s, when President Cornelius deKiewiet—encouraged by Wilson and other younger trustees—combined the men's and women's campuses. (The women's college was started in 1910 by Susan B. Anthony, a leading suffragette and Rochestarian.) Wilson and deKiewiet pressed on, and in 1958, expanded the doctoral program and launched three new colleges—in business, engineering, and education.

When the Chairman of the Board of Trustees resigned in 1959, it was clear to his colleagues that Joe Wilson should be the next chairman. In addition to his work at Haloid, they had observed Wilson's effectiveness on the board of managers of the Memorial Art Gallery, which is operated by the university, and on the board of managers for the university's Alumni Association (for which he was awarded a university alumni citation for leadership). In September 1959, Wilson was nominated to be Chairman of the Board of Trustees of the University of Rochester.[1] He was only 50.

Before the vote was taken, Wilson asked for an opportunity to speak. Noting that the authority of a chairman is nebulous until proven and that he must work to win it, he said: "We are embarking upon a difficult though inspiring program of development. I intend personally to devote every resource that I can muster to achieve greater excellence for this institution, and we must feel free to ask the same kind of contribution from every one of you." Noting that they were at a watershed in the university's history and that he was committed to a bold program to make it an institution of greater excellence, Wilson concluded: "I must ask anyone who is not truly prepared to work very hard to please vote No."

Wilson's election was unanimous.

A few days later, he went to New York City to introduce the revolutionary 914 copier.

Allen Wallis, who served as President during Wilson's time as Chairman, later looking back at the university's transformation

---

[1] Always looking for ways to increase person-to-person connectedness, Wilson initiated trustee luncheons and later trustee-faculty dinners.

during the Wilson years, observed: "In a literal sense, he did not bring it about himself at all. To a large extent, he led others to do it, but above all he *inspired* others to do it. He elevated everybody's sights—trustees, administrators, and faculty alike—to the highest pinnacles, not just the attainable mounds. Wilson emphasized that the University did not need to undertake everything. Indeed, it should plan cautiously what it would undertake. But in what it did undertake, it should never think in terms of 'second best,' or 'as good as can be expected,' but always in terms of absolute quality and the highest standards of excellence existing anywhere."

"Joe Wilson had a brilliant mind, but much more importantly, he analyzed and considered all aspects of every question," says Robert Sproull, who served as President after Wallis. "And he did so in a very thoughtful way." Wilson was intensely interested in education and was determined that the university should be great. And for the students, he sought *education*, not just training—though he recognized that the Eastman School of Music and the medical school were both necessarily training institutions. His vision was for a research-oriented university with an undergraduate college based on *education*. As he told students: "Your first job out of school depends on your training, but all the other jobs in your life depend on your education."

A t the university, Wilson applied the managerial techniques he had learned and developed at the corporation, particularly the value of making explicit both strategic goals and the plans for their execution. (He also brought onto the Board of Trustees colleagues from the corporation, including Sol Linowitz.) Wilson and his fellow trustees had a well-defined set of goals for the university and were confident that they had effective plans to realize those goals. So before accepting the presidency, Wallis was asked to visit Rochester for several days to discuss those goals and plans carefully with Wilson and other trustees.

Wilson adhered to the view that trustees do not manage, but do make sure a university is well managed. In his work for the university, Wilson recognized that he was a *corporate* executive and he understood the differences between business and academic institutions and the leadership they would each need. He was personally comfortable with that differentiation and was also just as comfortable performing his appropriate role whether leading or being led. Wilson and Wallis soon developed a close cooperative-consultative relationship, and in addition to their numerous one-on-one sessions, they jointly established an executive committee that met each month. Equally important as the frequency of these meetings was their open character. In addition, Presidents Allen Wallis and Robert Sproull each met with Wilson at his home half a dozen times a year—often with one or more other trustees—to get guidance, particularly on people issues. "Whenever we needed him, he was always there," says Sproull. "Conscientious and hard working, he never passed up a phone call or a letter." Wilson worked effectively to integrate the separate schools into the university as a whole.

To keep the executive committee strong, Wilson persuaded Marion Folsom, who served with distinction in Eisenhower's cabinet, to chair that increasingly effective group. After agreeing on several strong candidates for key positions, Wilson named Linowitz as his successor on the vital nominating committee. A strong executive committee, composed of the capable people Wilson and Wallis recruited, worked effectively to implement Wilson's vision, even when Wilson himself was sometimes too busy to attend.

A proposal to establish a public university for New York State with numerous regional campus locations around the state that would be comparable to the University of California's statewide system gained increasing prominence in the 1960s with Governor Nelson Rockefeller's strong endorsement. This eventually led to the establishment of the State University of New York (SUNY) with 14 campuses. In several instances, the State University absorbed private institutions, and several Rochester area leaders saw an opportunity to merge the University of Rochester into the new statewide system.

While Wilson strongly advocated endorsing the initiative to have a state university campus in Rochester, he disagreed with those who advocated automatically surrendering the University of Rochester's charter and campus to the new university. He wanted the university's president to be authorized to explore what might be involved if it were to become the main upstate campus of the new university. President deKiewiet was later told that the struggling University of Buffalo would be taken over and developed into a major facility. So the University of Rochester and its 8,000 students would continue as an independent institution and would need to develop its own future along the lines of Joe Wilson's vision.

Expansion programs endorsed by Wilson caused the University of Rochester's operating expenses to more than double from $14 million in 1952 to $32 million in 1961. With both a bold expansion of the university's academic programs and a drive to increase quality, the University of Rochester was becoming a great university with several major schools now equal in national standing to the medical school and the Eastman School of Music. As a result, the program was rapidly becoming as expensive as it was inspiring, and a major capital campaign would be needed. But first a new president had to be recruited when deKiewiet left the presidency in 1961.

Wilson led the search for the new president even though he knew that such searches always require extensive time commitments. With strong faculty participation in the nationwide search, an initial list of 200 possibilities was reduced to 20 serious candidates. Trustee-faculty teams interviewed each candidate and eventually selected Allen Wallis, then Dean of the University of Chicago's graduate school of business. Wilson had intended to step down as Chairman once the new President was installed, but Wallis said: "If I do accept this job, it will be with the expectation that you will remain as Chairman." Despite his personal plans, Wilson promised to continue serving for five more years in order to convince Wallis to come to the university.

In the 1963 university development campaign, the Wilson family, again at Joe's initiative, established the Katherine Upton Wilson Scholarships for the children of Xerox employees. And the company funded the Haloid-Xerox Professorship in International Economics.[2] Wilson was explicit about the importance of investing in the university to make Rochester the vibrant intellectual community that would attract the scientists, technologists, and managers Xerox would need to fulfill his strategic vision. "The quality of life here [in Rochester] is greatly affected by the quality of the University."

In addition to raising new money through a capital campaign, the trustees naturally looked to the endowment to produce more and more spendable income each year. Even though endowment income increased as the University of Rochester's endowment achieved one of the best investment records in America, the percentage of operating budget covered by endowment income actually declined because total spending was rising so rapidly to support the university's strategic transformation.

During the 1950s, the endowment's market value increased from $68 million to $170 million. Then, with growth stocks dominating the portfolio, it surged to over $400 million by the mid-1960s, in part because Wilson had steered the university into making a $196,000 investment in Haloid stock that grew an extraordinary 600 times to be worth $120 million. But growth stocks pay little or no dividends. So while the university's commitment to a larger, stronger academic program was in harmony with the splendid increases in market value being achieved by the endowment, the cash income available for current spending was not keeping pace. This was building strong pressure to increase the flow of spending money the endowment provided to the university.[3]

The funds available for spending on current programs at most universities were traditionally and conservatively limited to cash

[2]*Fortune*, January 1967, page 168.
[3]The income constraint was further exacerbated by the reality that endowment funds were segregated into support for different schools (and often designated for quite specific purposes), so they were not available to the central administration.

income,[4] so most institutions naturally invested primarily to maximize such income. With war and the Depression not very far behind, the perceived prudence of such a conservative approach seemed to make good sense, particularly to the senior trustees of the nation's foundations, colleges, and universities. And academic administrators—recognizing that the typical endowment was doing all that could be done to maximize current income from the endowment by investing in bonds and high-yield stocks[5]—were grateful for the funds made available and certainly didn't complain that future growth, however unintentionally, might be retarded.

The endowment of the University of Rochester was very different. It was not only one of the ten largest in the United States, it had gotten there through radically different investments. The university's primary investment objective was not income and stability, but growth. The University of Rochester, it was argued, had been around for a century[6] and would be around for centuries to come, so the primary mission of the endowment was to support the university's future ascent to long-term greatness. To those in charge of investing, the endowment was fulfilling its mission quite splendidly by maximizing long-term growth. If current cash income seemed small, relative to the size of the endowment, they pointed out that dividends had been rising rapidly, thanks to the splendid growth of the companies in the portfolio.

Given the university's rapidly expanding academic program commitments under Wilson's bold leadership, the challenge to the

[4]Endowment investment policies and practices grew out of the personal trust business, which was dominated by the separation of interests between the current income beneficiary and the remaining interests in capital. Trustees were expected to avoid favoring either party. An easy way to avoid any questions was to seek relatively large dividend-paying stocks and to "balance" the portfolio 50–50 in stocks and bonds. Without careful consideration, the same Procrustean asset mix was often applied to endowments.

[5]These practices of owning a high percentage of bonds and concentrating equity investments in high-yield stocks were roundly criticized in the *Barker Report to the Ford Foundation*.

[6]Founded in 1860 on land that had been Azariah Boody's cow pasture.

university's endowment managers—who were distributing current income that was less than 3% of the endowment's market value, only a small fraction of the 15% total return being earned—was blunt: If they were saving and investing the 12% difference every year, what were they saving it for? Moreover, the longer the endowment grew at its superior rate of gain, the stronger the case became for spending more *now*.

J oe Wilson was committed to growth. His own direct experiences at Xerox, his indirect experience observing IBM, Eastman Kodak, and other companies creating their own futures, and the splendid success of the endowment's sustained commitment to growth stocks all confirmed his belief in investing for long-term growth at the university.[7] Not only did he have the understandable aspirations of a proud alumnus and devoted trustee, Wilson also knew that having a leading university would be important to his company's success in recruiting and retaining the talented scientists and executives needed to continue Xerox's rapid growth trajectory far out into the future.

To achieve his strategy of advancing the University of Rochester into the front ranks of American universities, Wilson needed money—a lot more money. The issue boiled down to choices of growth: growth of the endowment or growth of the University of Rochester. Wilson's challenge was to protect the endowment's policy of investing for long-term growth by engineering the consent of the finance committee to release more funds each year from the endowment to support the university's expanding operation. To do this, Wilson and deKiewiet initially tried to combine the finance and executive committees into one, but older trustees blocked this idea. Wilson then arranged to have the two groups meet together to

---

[7]Joe Wilson was well-acquainted with Hulbert Tripp, the university Treasurer and an avid growth stock investor. Wilson had inspired Tripp to invest early in Haloid, and Tripp acquired a sizable investment for the university's endowment and, then mortgaging his own home, made a very large investment for himself. In both cases, the results were spectacularly favorable.

discuss development programs, and then meet separately to decide on the specific steps of implementation in their respective areas of responsibility.[8] This change brought the conservative "investment" trustees into serious, open discussions with the "program" trustees who were working on strengthening the academic offerings.

With greater shared understanding, the walls of separation were soon coming down, but defining the appropriate balancing point for a long-term spending policy was still needed. There was no agreed-upon calculation of just how much spending from the endowment would really be appropriate and prudent. "We knew we needed a new discipline if we were going to move away from the archaic spending limit of cash dividends-plus-interest," says Robert Sproull. "So with Monte Carlo computer simulations of the future, we worked out a Spending Rule: 5% of a 5-year moving average of market value." With continuing market appreciation, this worked out to current spending of a little less than 4% of the current endowment market value. While increasing spendable funds by one-third, the policy still looked sensibly conservative and prudent. Back-testing showed that this formulation would always produce more income each year than the year before.[9] To provide the unassailable documentation Wilson needed, finance professors Michael Jensen and Bill Meckling ana-lyzed expenditures, ran numerous Monte Carlo simulations of prob-able future scenarios and produced a 100-page report.

At Wilson's request, Professor Jensen and then-Provost Sproull organized a series of Saturday seminars for trustees—meeting with just two or three trustees at a time—to take them through the logic and the Monte Carlo simulations. But showing senior trustees the math was one thing. Getting their agreement to a major change in institutional policy was a very different matter. "You've made a great case and I can see you're all for it, but I just feel so uncomfortable"

---

[8]He also arranged that at the age of 70, trustees would become honorary.
[9]In the early 1970s, when the stock market fell substantially, cash distributions to the university's annual budget actually had three successive "down" years.

was the way more than one trustee expressed his feelings. But, according to Sproull, "When Joe spoke in favor of the change, with his wonderful mind and great personality—and his soft-spoken, but forceful presentation—they *all* voted with Joe." The investment committee and the full board of trustees agreed to move to the new Spending Rule and thereby substantially increase the funds released from the endowment to the university budget.

"Joe Wilson was the key," said Sproull. "He understood exactly what we wanted to do and why. We needed his help to get it across" because Wilson had immense respect among the Rochester establishment. "As other trustees saw it, Joe stood head and shoulders above the others in intelligence and integrity. This, far more than persuasive argument, was what enabled Wilson to get done what he wanted to achieve. If he wanted something done or a decision made, others just naturally came aboard. It was really quite personal. He could communicate well and directly with people as people, whether they were on the factory bench or in the executive suite."

Wilson would face other challenges at the university. During the 1960s, student unrest and protests disrupted many U.S. colleges and universities. At the University of Rochester, concern centered on its management of the Center for Naval Analysis. After lengthy discussion, which Wilson consistently encouraged, he concluded one leadership meeting with a characteristic statement: "If it is the right thing to do, and it seems to be, then we will have to do it and see it through."[10] By the phrase "see it through," Wilson made it clear that whatever student protest might develop, the decision of the Trustees would be sustained, and that assuring this result was the direct responsibility of the Trustees, both individually and collectively.

Wilson's tenacity to purpose and self-discipline were made abundantly clear in his private counsel to President Wallis: "Some of us have put our blood, sweat, tears and fortunes into building this University for the past 20 years or more. All those efforts and hopes

[10]Letter to Blake McKelvey, June 16, 1981. The CNA contract was signed in 1967.

are jeopardized by the present situation. Yet it would be better to stand on principle, even if that destroys what we have worked for, than to let the institution be changed in ways that make it no longer worthy of our efforts and our hopes." With this solid backing, President Wallis took a strong public stand that led to class attendance actually going up during a called-for two-day student strike. This was followed by the students abolishing the student government organization because it was so out of touch with students' views that it had voted 24 to 1 for an action very few students would support.

Wilson's persistence was nicely balanced by his capacity—unusual in most successful people who are used to making final decisions—to give thoughtful advice *and* comfortably accept a president's decision to go a different way. This fit with Wilson's consistent ability to defer to the decision of the individual whose responsibility it was for that decision, whether in the company, the family, the city or the university.

In 1966, Wilson once again took the lead for a major fundraising drive, whose goal was to raise $38 million in private funding with $50 million more from government grants and loans. Wilson organized the capital campaign with characteristic care. First, he assembled a list of 90 companies in and near Rochester, listing their annual profits next to their past contributions to the university. Then Wilson, Folsom and other trustees visited each company where they announced Kodak's gift of $6 million and Xerox's comparable gift, which Wilson asked Kent Damon to record as "nearly $6 million" to avoid upstaging Kodak. Wilson was indefatigable in his personal leadership throughout the campaign, once again, leading from the front, arranging that his parents' proviso bequest come from his inheritance, not his brother Dick's.

When the campaign appeared to be losing momentum, at least partly due to the sharp 1966 drop in the stock market, Wilson announced a stunning personal gift of $15 million, the year's largest personal gift to *any* university in the United States. (Joe and Peggy

Wilson had already provided $5 million in their wills, but Wilson decided to make a major increase and announce it at the most effective time.) Wilson stipulated that his additional gift be used to establish professorships "because we want the university to maintain the remarkable momentum it has, and because we feel very keenly that the new buildings will achieve their full purpose only as the very best teaching takes place within them."[11]

In 1972, the Wilson Scholars program was launched, allowing 30 students in each entering class to work one-on-one with professors in each student's area of special interest. The program would enable the university to attract "exceptionally bright young people who can be expected in the future to make important contributions to society in the tradition of one of the University's greatest benefactors."[12]

Wilson's gifts to the university totaled $23 million in market value. As President Wallis said, "More important than his gifts, it was his character, counsel, guidance, and spirit that made the University worthy of the support that he and many others have given it." Dr. deKiewiet, speaking from an earlier association, added, "The Joe Wilson who was both alumnus and trustee, is not to be measured in ticker tape, or bricks and mortar. He was a considerable intellectual influence in both university and community. He was like a coiled spring, charged with fervor rather than mere power. His fervor had a moral content . . . that came from the loyalties which he professed."

"If this university lasts for one thousand years, three men will have made the greatest contributions," said Robert Sproull. "Rush Rhees who served as President for 30 years and showed George Eastman the way to philanthropy in his later years;[13] George Eastman who went 50–50 with John D. Rockefeller to build the medical school and then built the Eastman School of Music (as well as the Eastman Quadrangle

[11]*Rochester Democrat and Chronicle*, June 1, 1967. In 1968, Katherine N. Wilson died at 85 and left $5.5 million to the University.
[12]Chancellor W. Allen Wallis, *Campus Times*, April 10, 1972.
[13]While he never attended, he was committed to education and left all of his residual estate to the University of Rochester.

at MIT). And the third great benefactor—whose non-financial gifts were far more important than his financial gifts—was and is Joe Wilson."[14]

As important as the university and the daunting task of its transformation were to Wilson, the challenges and the essential role he performed at the company were always greater.

[14]After Wilson's' death, an annual Wilson Day was initiated at the university. The inaugural program consisted of concerts, poetry readings, and lectures by Nobel laureates and Pulitzer Prize winners. Sproull described a meeting he had at the university with Joe Wilson's widow: "I had a meeting scheduled here with Peggy Wilson. Rather than walking, I'd taken my car to another meeting so I could be back on time. As I came into the parking lot, I saw Peggy driving her black Mercedes. There was only one open space to park—the one reserved for the President—and she could so easily and sensibly have slipped in there, but she drove three or four blocks away to park and walked back to my office—where she presented a check for almost $5 million."

11

WORST OF TIMES, BEST OF TIMES

For Joe Wilson and his company, the 1950s were both the best of times and the worst of times. The worst of times as seen from the late 1940s, and the best of times as seen from the early 1960s. By the early 1960s, Wilson and his company would know they had created a spectacular product, and would be earning extraordinary profits, but in the late 1940s, Wilson and his company were struggling with such daunting problems and risk of failure that their major challenge was clear: Escape total defeat. If Haloid had stayed with the business it had in the 1940s, it would surely have been snuffed out in the following decade. (In 1950, to save money, Haloid people ate in the cafeteria—the Eastman Kodak cafeteria, a custom that held over from the days when Haloid was a customer of Kodak.)

The 1950s were, in many ways, the decade of Joe Wilson's greatest achievements. While the payoff—surely greater than Wilson or anyone else had ever expected—came mostly in the 1960s, the great struggles, major investments, and crucial decisions were made in the 1950s. During that decade, xerographic sales shot up from less than $100,000 to more than $24 million and opened the way to the extraordinarily successful 914 copier and the zoom-zoom sixties.

Wilson understood that to capitalize on the great promise he saw in xerography, he had to transform Haloid on every major dimension because xerography was too big for Haloid *and* Haloid was too small for xerography. That's why Wilson had agreed with Battelle on the importance of engaging several other companies in researching the many possible applications of xerography other than office copiers, where Haloid maintained exclusive rights. Wilson appreciated at an intuitive level how powerful the technology of xerography could be. So in 1950, he hired Frank Steinhilper to create a patent department that would establish a remarkably secure protective perimeter. Wilson was determined to do all he could to take his company as far as possible into whatever business xerography might become—and to make Haloid a success by making xerography a success.

Wilson's managerial style combined consensus and strong leadership. In an era when subordinates were generally expected to communicate with their seniors in writing while seniors communicated orally—"write up, talk down"—Wilson clearly preferred writing for *all* communications. He distributed pads of notepaper on which was printed: "Don't say it, write it." Consensus was developed across a rather broad group of people and was typically facilitated by memoranda that met his own mandate to "put it in writing." Drafts of memos would be sent to as many as 20 associates with a request for comments, with a follow up warning note to truants. (Peter McColough, a future CEO, often turned his memo of comments in *after* the warning to truants, saying he had hoped to discuss the subject face-to-face, but since other tasks had kept him too busy, here were his written views.) Wilson always chose which, if any, suggestions to use in the final document, took care in formulating his stands, and was collected and deliberate in developing conclusions, which were often presented with the phrase, "It is our profound conviction that . . ."

In his continuous concentration on advancing Haloid, Wilson's fertile mind generated innumerable ideas, which would soon appear in the many short memos he sent out each day. "You know, he was a great guy for memoranda," said Hartnett. "It would drive me nuts, but I had to bear with it because that was his manner of work. He would have a dictating machine and—zing—you'd get a three-line memo. You might get 15 of those in just one day! And many of them required a lot of digging to get the right answers."

Wilson's office procedure was controlled and orderly, and Wilson was habitually thoroughly prepared for meetings. Tickler files were kept on a wide range of matters that would need future follow up. Well before meetings, his secretary would bring in the appropriate file so he could review all past communications and carefully prepare for the upcoming meeting. Telephone calls that came in during meetings or during the long blocks of time he scheduled for thinking things out or writing important memoranda were deferred, so the return calls were bunched up during specific time periods.

Management meetings were well organized, "buttoned up," and decision-focused. Wilson permitted a reasonable amount of free flow during discussions, but if anyone rambled too far off track, he would firmly bring the discussion back to the topic at hand. And while almost never raising his voice, Wilson could speak quite sharply if he felt time was being wasted or preparation was inadequate. Recalled McColough, "Joe's patience would get pretty thin if people were being difficult—and very bright people can be very difficult—or worse, staying too long on one thought or point." There were no company secrets. Both good and bad news was shared very openly. As Wilson said, "We'll share all we know with you so you can share all you can do with us." Wilson's systemic thoroughness was balanced by an unusual ability to make major decisions quickly when speed mattered.

A s the magnitude of xerography's potential grew steadily larger and clearer, the scope of change that would be needed in finance, marketing, manufacturing, and every aspect of management grew increasingly clear to Wilson. He recognized that if he were going to transform Haloid into the dynamic company he was already envisioning, Haloid would need a very different group of managers now that the war was over. As he said, the company needed

executives "who would want to make Haloid grow *and* could personally grow with a fast-moving company." As Haloid's business
grew, Wilson understood that its management must grow at least as
rapidly, but that most individuals could not change fast enough to
keep up. New people would be needed and past leaders would have
to be replaced. As Wilson put it, "Haloid must be manned by people
who are creative, who are imaginative, who are not in a rut, not
bound by tradition [and want to be] part of an organization that's
not afraid to take on a new kind of challenge, not afraid to drop off
any product when the facts show that it should be dropped."

The decade of the fifties started with the 1950 introduction of
the first commercial product based on xerography: the Model A
copier. After all the risks taken and the investment and efforts
expended, this introduction of a new product using the new technology seemed such a triumphant confirmation of all the past years'
struggles that Joe Wilson graciously arranged to have his father
make the first public announcement.

In 1949, Mr. JR, as Chairman of the Board, proudly announced
that "the first commercial adaptation of xerography—the Xerox
Copier Machine, Model A—will be made in 1950." After that bold
announcement, everyone at Haloid scrambled to complete the
design and build the Model A machines. While hopes and expectations at Haloid had been high, the finished product was so difficult
to work with that it required a skilled operator to perform the 12
separate steps and took several minutes to make a single copy. And
as an office copier, it all too often produced poor results. The Model
A was not going to be the success everyone had been counting on.

The Model A was a flop—a complete flop.

With very good reason, the mood at Haloid was glum. Fortunately, Lew Walkrup was visiting from Battelle, and he quickly identified one of the problems: the location of the lights. With some
adjustments, the Model A was soon producing reasonably good
copies, but the machines were still crude, ungainly in appearance,
and too slow. Cumbersome as it was, the Model A did make use of

xerography, so the Haloid team wanted to test their pride and joy by lending machines to major potential users. Six machines were built by hand and placed on trial with users. The test results were consistently negative.

The machines failed on every dimension. Costly to build, the machines were very hard to use: They had too many steps, they were too complicated, and they were too dependent on everything going just right. Copy quality was unreliable and all too often disappointing. The process was too complex and took much too long. And there were *no* suggestions from test users on how to improve the dismal Model A.[1] No wonder the mood at Haloid was so glum.

A few days later, Walkrup called from Battelle. Taking the call, Wilson was surprised to hear Walkrup sound very upbeat. "Say, do you fellows know what you've got here?"

"Lew, what are you talking about?"

"Joe, our researchers are almost certain that the Model A would be *perfect* for making paper masters for offset printing. They want to try making paper masters, particularly for Addressograph-Multigraph's offset equipment."

"That could prove interesting!"

"Interesting? Joe, it could be a *bonanza!* A-M has nearly 80,000 installations!"

Another round of tests was quickly organized in cooperation with large companies that were high-volume users of offset masters,

---

[1] Some of the Model A's problems produced amusing stories. For example, Eugene Feurst was demonstrating xerography and the Model A to the Board of Directors. The powdered toner took 10 seconds to fuse at a temperature of 375°. With all of that heat, the paper put into the fuser caught on fire. Quickly, Feurst threw it to the ground and stamped out the fire. What looked like—and was—a disaster was no problem for Feurst. He reached down for a spare copy he'd made well before the demonstration and had put on the floor just in case. Picking it up he triumphantly passed that spare around to all of the directors so they could see firsthand the wonders of xerography. At another demonstration in the late 1950s, a prototype of the 914 produced a copy but burned it to ashes. After a long silence, someone said, "Maybe we could sell it to the CIA."

and after a few weeks of testing, the results came back: Users were now enthusiastic. Ford Motor Company reported that "Multilith masters prepared by the xerographic process instead of by conventional methods save time, money and critical materials. From drafting board to the first run-off copy from the Multilith master is a matter of minutes, at an approximate total cost of $.37, including materials, labor, and overhead. *This compares with a cost of $3.12 for the first run-off copy from the zinc plates which might otherwise be required.* Test runs up to twenty thousand copies have been made from the xerographic master and the last copy is as good as the first."[2]

The paper plate master business soon proved crucial for Joe Wilson. It saved his company. (As previously explained, Haloid's traditional photographic paper business—including Haloid Record—was in serious terminal decline, and Wilson had already had to cut the dividends.) Haloid's very survival from 1950 to 1959 would depend on making paper plate masters for offset printers on a modified Model A, renamed the Lithmaster.[3] This product was critical to Haloid in two ways. First, it was a good product. Revenues from Lithmaster machines and supplies exceeded $2 million by 1953 and the available market was large and easily identifiable. Second and at least as important, Haloid had a successful product that proved xerography *could* work. This ray of hope was the essential encouragement that the company's staff and directors needed to continue following Wilson's lead and sustain the commitment to xerography. As so often happens with inventions, xerography was still a solution looking for a problem, but at least with Joe Wilson, that search would be systematic and determined.

In 1951, xerography received another boost when Battelle and the Army Signal Corps announced the development of a camera that would take electronic pictures using any light source and with no risk of fogging from atomic blasts. Taking just two minutes for

---

[2]Dessauer, page 66.
[3]Lithmaster machines were built by Rochester's Todd Equipment Company.

pictures to develop, it was soon dubbed Two-Minute Minnie. It was a breakthrough for Wilson and would lead to Haloid's next commercial success: the Copyflo.

I n 1953—at only 43—Joe Wilson had a heart attack while climbing the stairs at the Albany railroad station: It put him out of work for several months. (Typical of his disciplined ways, Wilson used this time to read the entire Great Book series of classics published by the University of Chicago.) Wilson's doctor advised, "Joe, if you don't stop—really stop—working so very hard you *will* kill yourself." But Wilson couldn't stop working for long, so after he began working again, his doctor told Wilson that he must leave the office and go home each day at eleven in the morning. But after a few months, Wilson decided to add another two hours onto his time in the office and changed his daily schedule: He stayed at the office until 4:30 PM, but reserved 90 minutes during the middle of the day for quiet time alone, lying down in his office on a sofa bought for that purpose, listening to the classical music he loved on the radio and taking a nap or quietly thinking through one or more significant business issues. Leaving at 4:30 PM, he would be home in less than 15 minutes, so he always had ample time before and during dinner at 6:00 PM for serious conversations with his children about their activities and, particularly, the books they were reading in school—which he often read, too.

Wilson was determined to mask the seriousness of his heart attack and the serious risk of a recurrence. He kept both secret, filing his medical claim quite deliberately "lost" in a mass of complex filings to prevent a leak to the press—but was always mindful of the personal health risk facing him. As Linowitz observed many years later, "Joe was short on energy for many years. He would literally force himself to get up and go even when he was pooped as hell."

Unusually capable of sustained self-discipline, Wilson was determined to avoid gaining weight and quite literally ate to live, never complaining about his regimen. A carefully restricted diet at lunchtime became part of his settled routine: one sandwich (usually peanut butter and jelly), a bowl of soup—Campbell's tomato was his particular favorite—a piece of fruit, and Hydrox cookies. (He knew the difference and would not accept Oreos.) When an important visitor was coming for a luncheon, Wilson knew the routine would have to be changed appropriately for such special occasions—so the soup and sandwich were served on china and silverware he brought from home. At home, Joe and Peggy Wilson avoided alcohol during the week, deciding that such abstinence would be necessary for Joe to do his job really well. Wilson also gave up smoking and the chocolate he loved.

While Wilson was keeping his health problems under wraps, none of the successes to come in the sixties were yet visible. And although Haloid may have looked okay from a distance to outsiders, the reasons for Wilson's deep concerns about the future were increasingly evident to insiders. Revenue and profits from military contracts for the war in Korea were temporarily masking reality: Haloid's basic business, as Wilson had anticipated when he told Dessauer to look hard for new technologies, was in serious trouble. Competition was hurting sales. Profits, of course, were hurt even worse, and forced layoffs were increasing. As Haloid's old business faded, the hoped-for payoff from the new xerography business kept getting deferred.

Time and again, potentially promising developments in xerography proved disappointing. Xerographic possibilities that failed included a product that was based on oscillography to record stress of materials in torpedoes and guided missiles, another product that was expected to record seismography in oil-well logging, and yet another that was intended to gather test data at atomic installations.[4]

[4]"A History of Haloid", by William O'Toole, in *Rochester Commerce*, October 1956.

These disappointments made the success of Copyflo all the more important.

Copyflo printers, introduced in 1953, produced enlarged paper copies in readable size from continuous rolls of microfilm, eventually at the rate of 20 to 30 feet of copy a minute.[5] Wilson cited an example of the potential savings: "A B52 bomber requires some 175,000 different drawings of various assemblies. They often need as many as 100 copies of one drawing. Untold hours of the precious time of engineers are spent making copies. We believe our device will free them for more fruitful activities." Copyflo was a huge machine—as large as a printing press—and each unit cost a daunting $130,000, so demand for these machines was understandably small. Still, after spending $4.3 million to develop xerography—with a cumulative *loss* of $428,000 to show for his efforts—Wilson could now see the first small xerographic profit. In 1953, it was $51,000. Increasing profits would necessarily be a function of increasing sales and Wilson could be quite resourceful in selling and, fortunately, was quick on his feet. During one Copyflo demonstration, when someone forgot to attach the output onto the take-up roller and paper was spewing all over the floor, Wilson calmly called to an assistant, "Grab the end and run it out so everyone in the audience can see the wonderful copy quality up close!" Wilson's save-the-show initiative worked so well that it was made a standard part of all future Copyflo demonstrations.

From a manufacturing perspective, a Copyflo machine was little more than a custom-built prototype with a metal cover. If there had been much more demand, it would not really have mattered: Haloid could not have produced more than the few machines it was then producing. Realistically, Haloid was just an assembler and had no competence as a volume manufacturer of precision equipment. Clearly, neither Copyflo as a product nor Haloid as a company could compete in the very big market for small, low-cost machines: office copiers.

[5]*New York Times*, October 26, 1958. Section III, page 2.

Meanwhile, Lithmaster installations increased rapidly to more than 1,200 in 1954. Haloid's Lithmaster equipment was leased at $720 per year and annual sales of supplies averaged $900 per installation. With nearly 80,000 Addressograph-Multigraph multilith installations as an almost captive market, the future looked quite promising. Xerography was producing a good and growing business base that would, in time, enable Wilson's Haloid to introduce the 914—and become Xerox.

Wilson continued to focus on research and the development of xerography, and kept encouraging Dessauer to increase the budget he proposed for research on xerography. Knowing how tight finances were, Haloid's controller, Harold Kuhns, would anxiously shake his head, saying over and over again, "Gee! Gee!" as he saw the costs mounting higher and higher. There were no assurances of adequate revenues, but Wilson kept pressing on. "The whole bent was toward research," recalled Hartnett. "Here was a process, but not a product. So the crowning effort had to be in research. We all knew that. And, of course, it meant sacrifices all along the line. I had no capital expense budget for the sales division of the business for years. No one could buy a chair for an office—or a typewriter. I had no money. None. No appropriations, at all. It all went into research. It had to."

Wilson was deeply interested in the technology and research that would get all the money. Fortunately, the technology was all so new that anyone who was very bright and really interested could catch up to the technological frontiers: They were not very far ahead. Wilson had such an open, quick, and retentive mind and such a logical and inquisitive approach to problem-solving that he developed a particularly strong competence with the new technology. Over their many years together, John Dessauer said he would spell out the various alternatives for Wilson—and then Wilson would choose the way to go: "Joe really made *all* the decisions. He asked for advice and asked for ideas. He never claimed that all the ideas were his, but the one who used them, the one who had his neck out if the plan should fail was Joe Wilson—and none other. He was a top-notch delegator and did not interfere with things decided upon except to ask for progress reports. Even in the licensing negotiations with RCA, Battelle and Rank-Xerox, it was he and only he who made the decisions."

Joe Wilson was no technologist, but he took the time to understand the technology *and* to develop a real understanding and rapport with each of his company's technologists. He sensed the potential of the crude device that did not work. He then organized and guided the several different capabilities and disciplines—financial, marketing, production, and technological—that all had to come together and stay working together for many, many years to make that revolution succeed. As Linowitz observed: "Joe was remarkably capable of doing the job he did—as he did it. He didn't have the technology, but he was able to inspire people who did and bring them together and keep them together for many, many years of quite limited, ever-discouraging, results. He surrounded himself with people who were young so they did not have the experience with old ways or the training in the old ways that would cause them to say: 'No, this won't work!' "

Wilson recognized early on that he had to change Haloid away from the experienced "old hands" who were reluctant to change, and that he needed to empower young people who were keen to learn and try new ways. This also meant, of course, that these same young executives had little experience in management or in leadership and would need to learn these high-order skills on the job. To compensate for the inexperience of his managers, Wilson frequently used outside experts and consultants on a wide range of issues. Wilson's appreciation of the technological possibilities and his considerable understanding of individuals and of his overall organizations, compared to what would be needed for success in overcoming the great challenges ahead, were two sides of the triangle on which he would build his company. The third side was finance, another of Wilson's strengths.

Dessauer went on to describe the challenge Wilson faced: "Money was the main problem. The company was fortunate in being modestly in the black, but not far enough. The members of our team were all gambling on the project. I even mortgaged my house to invest in our company—all I had left was my life insurance. My neck was way out." Pausing, Dessauer glanced at the ceiling and then went on, "Hardly anybody was very optimistic in the early years." Wilson's strategic situation was easily described: "We were spending money we didn't have for a product nobody wanted."[6]

From 1953 to 1961, Wilson never looked back. He accelerated spending on xerography to a total of $87.6 million: cash flow from operations contributed $43 million; R&D charge-offs, $7 million; and debt and new stock issues, $37 million.[7] Large investments went into plant and equipment, including machines put out on lease, and a full $23 million was spent on R&D and patents.

While Wilson's disciplined focus was on developing commercially successful products using xerography, these products were the stepping-stone means to his real end. "Joe wanted to grow a great company," recalled Peter McColough. "A company we could all be truly proud of in the field of information communication and human understanding. Joe had a strong feeling about the opportunities ahead. He had great faith in the value and importance of developing better systems to disseminate information—if Haloid could survive the unknown period of time it would take to get from here to there.

"Joe was always afraid—all of us were always afraid—of a new technology coming along that was better than xerography. It would have been arrogant or naïve to assume that xerography would always sustain its technological leadership." Noting that he was

[6]New Yorker, John Brooks.
[7]"There Isn't Any Profit Squeeze at Xerox," Fortune, 1962.

young enough to have another chance if things didn't work out, McColough added: "Joe was old enough so that if xerography didn't work in five years or so, he would be too old to start all over again." Maybe so, but in the early 1950s, Joe Wilson was still a young man—a man in a hurry to move Haloid out of its increasingly evident danger and into the future by opening up opportunities through xerography.

Wilson always paid attention to Chet Carlson's views on the importance of patents. Carlson was often helpful, observing with a chuckle, "Remember, I'm really a patent attorney. Inventing was something I did after hours—in my kitchen." With Carlson's urging, Wilson organized a commission to study the situation at both Haloid and Battelle. Sixty-two potentially patentable devices were identified, but none had a patent application yet filed. (Carlson once said an inventor would be doing quite well if 10% of his patents resulted in a commercial product, but felt strongly that it was penny-wise and pound-foolish to save the cost of patent applications while risking the irreparable loss of patent protections that could be vital to a small company's future.[8]) Describing himself as intuitive, Carlson was also a prodder and a pusher who was most effective in one-on-one discussions. While usually right in his judgment, he could often be emotional so Carlson was advised to put his important recommendations in writing so Wilson would be sure to take them seriously.[9]

Wilson wanted to advance the development of xerography in any direction that offered real promise, while Carlson wanted to focus all efforts on one great product: copiers. In November 1953, Carlson complained that Haloid was "dropping the ball" by not developing an effective copier—and not even appearing in the annual National Business Show where 3M announced the first *dry*

[8]Linowitz, page 93.
[9]Others described Carlson as more artist than scientist, because scientists discover things that are already there, like Plank's Constant or black holes, while artists create new things, like Beethoven's *Fifth* or Picasso's *Guernica*.

copier, Thermofax. Pointing out that neither Thermofax nor Verifax were archival—because their copies faded over time—and that their copies cost nearly 20¢ a piece, Wilson replied to Carlson: "When you say we missed the boat completely, I, of course, believe the opposite. I believe that if we had taken the wrong boat two years ago, we would be infinitely worse off now.

"Now we know what the real copying competition is. Let's assume it's Thermofax and Verifax. They have shot their wad and while they will make improvements steadily, they probably won't make a fundamental change. Now we know what we have to do. Either we can beat these processes inherently or we cannot. If we can, we'll develop processes to much tighter specifications than we would have two years ago and thus save ourselves hundreds of thousands of dollars. If we cannot, we also will have saved hundreds of thousands of dollars and we will devote ourselves to profitable lines of application rather than to dead ducks." (One of Wilson's best decisions was a "not" decision—*not* to commit to the diffusion transfer process because it had no patent protection. American Photocopy did commit to diffusion transfer, and so did six other manufacturers. Their intense and growing competition drove down prices and profits and eventually, they *all* failed.)

In 1955, the Copyflo II Continuous Printer was introduced. These machines sold for from $72,000 to $177,000, with monthly rentals of $800 to $1,500. With Copyflo and other xerographic product introductions, Haloid's sales had quadrupled to $32 million, and Wilson's strategy was clearly gaining momentum. In October, Wilson went to Chicago for a showing of Copyrama, a carefully staged product extravaganza designed to showcase advances in Copyflo equipment that involved a truck filled with Copyflo II and other copying machines going from city to city across America. Wilson gave an introductory speech surveying the contributions made by Carlson, Battelle, and Haloid: predicting that many new and valuable tools for business and government would come from Haloid's laboratories in the next few years. He concluded with an inspirational message: "Thus, we have come, we think, to the threshold of a major thrust forward with an exhilarated, dedicated organization imbued with a philosophy of pioneering, growth, willingness to accept risks, finding new ways of designing, producing, selling and financing—and a philosophy which fully requires that the joy of such a business career comes solely from the fact that we are part of a free society."

For Wilson, the importance of having superior, innovative products developed through R&D had been clearly demonstrated with Haloid Record in the 1930s. Seeing how vital this new product had been to Haloid's ability to weather the Depression, Wilson would again and again return to the profound meaning of that lesson: A company should create its own demand with a "new product consciousness" and an appetite for innovation. The same lesson was taught twice again by the Lithmaster and the Copyflo—and both were essential to financing Wilson's bold strategy through the 1950s.

Transforming Haloid in less than two decades from a weak, small photo products supplier into Xerox, a worldwide giant and technological leader, depended on Joe Wilson's creating a vision and consistently communicating that vision to engage the interest and commitment of Haloid's people, particularly the growing numbers of scientists, technicians, engineers, managers, and sales representatives needed to fulfill the promising, but still very uncertain, potential of xerography. That's why Wilson focused first on research and why his commitment to basic research and product development was persistently outsized. Research expenditures increased eightfold from $250,000 in 1947 to $2 million in 1958. As Wilson explained: "We put the utmost emphasis upon research and development and intend to continue to do so." As usual, Wilson put his actions into inspiring context: "We believe with Oliver Wendell Holmes that: 'The mind of man is the only instrument that, when stretched, does not return to its original dimension.' At Haloid, we stretch *our* minds through research. The most vigorous research program in Haloid history is under way with increased personnel, facilities, and expenditures. The program has been called an unusual example of the way a small company can develop."

In addition to the challenges that any small company in a mid-sized city might expect in attracting large numbers of new workers, Haloid faced the special challenges of Rochester's being a deeply conservative, establishment city that was skeptical of outsiders and people who were "different." In 1950, Realtors would show homes to African-American families in only two wards: the third and seventh. And ten years later, the social situation was not very different. "Don't bother looking in Pittsford" was sensible advice to a Jewish couple moving into Rochester, one of whom was to take a key position in producing the 914.

By the mid-1950s, Wilson recognized that a growing internal problem, the decline of the old Haloid photographic products business, was accelerating and pushing more and more workers out of their semiskilled jobs. Having been deeply affected by the Depression and the harm caused to families and communities by the loss of jobs, Wilson wanted to know, "What can we do to take the sting out of these people losing their jobs? Maybe there's a way to help ourselves too: We're going to need many more skilled metal workers in our xerography business."

With Wilson's stimulus, Haloid reached an agreement with Rochester Institute of Technology to teach Haloid workers with at least ten years' service how to read blueprints; how to use machine tools; and some basic mathematics so they could switch from the paper coating division to machine manufacturing. Lasting 15 weeks, the program was carefully named a "retraining program," rather than a training program. During the program and after assignment to jobs in the machine shop, participating employees were paid at their full prior rates until their production in their new jobs brought them up to an even higher pay level. "Of course, I do not mean to say that everyone has to be ambitious for promotion," said Wilson. "There are some who are content, and justifiably so, to remain as they are.

These words are addressed only to the others, the ones who want to go ahead."[10] Citing Haloid's burgeoning need for more technically trained workers, Wilson was pleased to report the near doubling in participation in the program from 47 to 88 workers between 1953 and 1956. While this retraining program helped individual workers, Wilson knew that time was truly running out for the old Haloid business, adding urgency to his drive to find and develop more new products and markets for the xerographic side of Haloid.[11]

Despite all his personal modesty, Wilson *was* the indispensable man—and he knew it. When Wilson made the go-for-broke commitment of his family's company—the business his parents, his brother, and his wife and children all depended on financially—to xerography, he knew there was no other person who could provide the leadership necessary to achieve the success he envisioned when making his decision. And as much as Wilson talked continuously about his vision—and celebrated results achieved by his colleagues— no one else would ever have the same full and tenacious grasp of where they were going and why, as well as how to get there. And Wilson knew he must continually balance and reconcile conflicting interests and pressures to lead and build Haloid.

"Joe never stopped growing," says John Glavin, who would per- form a vital role in marketing. "All his life, he was a fascinated stu- dent who read a *lot*." After reading *The Phenomenon of Men*, which was written by a Jesuit, Wilson told Glavin, "This is as close as I can come to what I really believe: The struggle to find the truth; get- ting ever better." While never religious, even serious churchgoers

---

[10]*Haloid-O-Scope*, February 1967, Volume No. 4, No. 2.
[11]One of Haloid's major lenders, Massachusetts Mutual, was already identifying the commercial production and sale of xerographic equipment and supplies as having promise: "These products represent only 4% of sales and have yet to contribute to the company's profit. Xerography is a brand new development in the field of reproducing documents and does not involve chemical solutions. This division of Haloid is regarded within the trade as having very important possibilities."

like Glavin believed that, "In his own spiritual way, Joe was very devout."

Wilson continued to read very widely, was always deeply interested in ideas and ideals, and both found and gave inspiration to others through his frequent citations of great thinkers. Often, after having family dinner at six, he and Peggy would retire to their bedroom where he would read for several hours. A speed-reader with a photographic mind, particularly for numbers, Wilson read several books each week. For relaxation, some were Westerns and mysteries. Other books on his list were works of history, philosophy, or biography. Wilson also read corporate reports and the many memoranda that came in response to his admonition: "Don't say it; put it in writing!"

At home, it was necessary to find a workable solution, too. Joe and Peggy Wilson worked out a program of extraordinary concentration. She would concentrate on raising their children while he concentrated on building Haloid. "Everything Joe had—of time, talent and treasure—went into developing Xerox," said Glavin. "Nobody else was ever so dedicated."

While primarily concerned with the development of people at the company, Wilson faced sometimes awkward relations with his father. For example, in the early 1950s, Mr. JR came by limousine to the office daily, but only for a very few hours. In his office, he shaved with an electric razor at 11:00 AM each morning. A little later, he would corral several people—most often secretaries—and take them off for lunch at the Howard Johnson's restaurant at Eight Corners that JR had acquired for his son Richard to operate. Once there, he'd order drinks, insisting that *everyone* join in—often for two rounds. Word got out that those who went to lunch with Mr. JR couldn't be counted on for much work in the afternoon. This routine clearly conflicted with Joe Wilson's careful discipline, but he decided to endure it. And as Mr. JR's health declined, Joe made a regular practice of going to his parent's home for a long visit each Sunday.

In the late 1950s, Mr. JR's health had deteriorated so much that he had not visited Haloid for over a year. Then, still a director, he came to a Board of Ddirectors meeting and asked a question.[12] It was not a very good question, but Joe Wilson asked Harold Kuhns to provide an answer. Kuhns was giving a somewhat simplified answer when Mr. JR cut in and, turning his head toward his son, reached high up in the air and slammed his right hand down hard on the table, his eyes full of fire: "God *damn* you, Joe! When I ask a question around here, I expect a good straight answer!"

[12]The Board of Directors was never important at Haloid. Wilson had seen how very difficult a Board could be during the fight with Mosher and had never seen a Board make significant contributions. The weakness of the Board was assured by Wilson's use of it as a holding pen for executives who had passed their peak performance.

12

JOE WILSON

Wilson concentrated on vision and strategy—and recruiting exceptional people. "When I first interviewed at Haloid," recalled McColough, "Joe asked me, after a day of meetings and demonstrations of Copyflo, what I thought. I told him candidly that I wasn't very impressed with the equipment they were producing—and that other companies seemed to be making better, cheaper copies. He responded gravely and earnestly: 'In 20 years, we'll make better copies than they will—both faster *and* cheaper.' That's why Joe was a true innovator. Having good ideas, as consultants and advisors so often do, is only 2%. Getting it done through people is 98% of leadership."

Central to Wilson's leadership was his unusual ability to engage with others and overcome his personal shyness, which he could and would hide, but could not escape. Time and again, he had to get himself "up" for meetings, particularly with strangers. Yet Wilson was a listener with a remarkable ability and a deep commitment to listening and understanding. In his office, Wilson worked at a large mahogany desk, sitting in a big high-backed, leather-bound swivel chair. When visitors came in, he would rise and move to join them at a cluster of comfortable leather-cushioned chairs. Typically leaning slightly forward and toward his guests, it was clear he wanted to be certain he heard every word. His eyes engaged with others' and, as colleagues often said, "Joe's smile could charm the birds out of the trees." Speaking with confidence in a calm, steady voice, he unconsciously signaled both his seriousness and his sincerity with a habitual physical gesture of opening his hands with palms up. By the probing questions he asked and the direct, candid answers he gave to questions, each person he met with knew they were getting Wilson's undivided attention and felt the subjects they discussed together were the most important conversations in the whole world.

Still, given his shyness, Wilson's outward manner was often reserved and quiet. As Peter McColough put it, "In a room of VIPs, Joe would appear the *least* important. Joe had such depth of self-confidence that he was comfortable with others leading or being in authority—as at the University of Rochester—and delegated substantial authority to others at Haloid."

Wilson had two primary interests: concepts and individuals. Each individual person was important to him and many experienced the directness of his contact. "Joe Wilson had great respect for people of all ages and of all stations in life," said John Glavin. "He listened so intently. And he never forgot you and who you were. I remember him sitting on a small child's chair in our home, asking my wife, Aline, one question after another—and always *listening*." As Aline Glavin added, "When Joe Wilson listened to you, you *knew* you were the only person on earth with the most important ideas. This made him very charming."

"Joe could easily and naturally go from a king to a pauper," said public relations expert David Curtin, "changing gears to relate well to each person as an individual."

At home, Wilson truly believed in reasoning and talking things out, even with children. When his daughter was caught smoking, instead of a traditional parental disapproval and prohibition, Wilson's reaction was measured and respectful: "You'll decide, of course, but smoking is *not* a smart choice. The Surgeon General's report has just come out and it's packed with solid information on the harm that comes from smoking."

On another occasion an expected confrontation became an exercise in reasoning and self-determination. "Dad, it doesn't make sense to me to be studying liberal arts anymore. So I want to stop going to college and do something much more practical." His daughter was a sophomore in college and, knowing her father's strong commitment to education, she had been afraid to raise the subject—particularly when, following years of strictly ordered Catholic schooling, she'd been "rambunctious" at college. "Go upstairs," said her father, "and write out the pro and con reasons, as you see them, for this decision." After nearly an hour upstairs, she returned and handed over her list of reasons. Wilson read them carefully. "You know how I feel about education, so there's no need to discuss that. Your argument and thoughts are well developed, and so I will support you in your decision." (She went to Kathryn Gibbs Secretarial School, and then years later graduated cum laude from the University of Rochester with a bachelor of arts degree.)

"Joe Wilson learned that I was an assistant scoutmaster," recalled Bob Gundlach, a prolific inventor-scientist, "and he knew my troop, a racially mixed troop sponsored by the Baden Street Settlement House in Rochester's inner city, would be missing out on summer camp because it was without any parents or a scout leader to accompany them. Joe wanted to know if I'd take the troop for two weeks of summer camp. Explaining that I'd only been employed for six months and so had only *one* week of vacation coming—which I'd planned to take with my new wife—I said I couldn't do it. Joe quickly explained that I'd get my vacation as planned *and* Haloid would be pleased if I would also take the kids to camp—on company time. That sort of approach helps explain the dedication of employees to do all they could to make our company thrive. The value of real teamwork is beyond calculation. Joe was way ahead of his time."

13

IBM, RCA, AND GE

While he was far too optimistic in his estimate of how long it would take to create a major business based on xerography, Wilson was very realistic in recognizing that this was much too large a challenge for Haloid to attempt on its own. Haloid was small, its profits were very small, and all of Haloid's capital was needed just to sustain the old Haloid business. Little Haloid could not possibly finance the research and development—and then the production and the marketing—of major new products that would need to be sold to hundreds, even thousands, of new customers. Military contracts could help fund Haloid's R&D, but Wilson would also have to find major corporations to help finance the large, capital-intensive conversion into the worldwide business he hoped to build from his new technology.

Financing was just one of the several areas where Wilson knew he needed help. The R&D unit that Dessauer headed was much too small and inexperienced to take responsibility for a major technology development program: How could Haloid afford a major new product development effort that might run for many years, replete with uncertainties and potential detours and delays? Haloid was really only an assembler of equipment, not a major manufacturer, and Haloid was building Copyflo machines one at a time: How could it convert itself into a mass-production manufacturer of complex, precision equipment? Haloid's sales force was both small and outdated: How could it be converted into a modern, nationwide sales and service organization? Outside its niche of small, industrial markets for reprographics and photographic paper, little Haloid was virtually unknown. How could it hope to create a national and then an international market for important new products *and* a strong brand name and recognition? Finally, how could Haloid's small-company management group, with its limited experience, be transformed into the management team that could successfully lead a large, fast-growing, global enterprise that would successfully capitalize on a series of innovative new products?

Haloid was about to provoke some of the world's leaders in industrial technology and marketing with what they would see as a major direct challenge. Realistically, how could Haloid hope to survive, let alone prevail, in the coming competitive battles for new technologies and new markets, battles that would go on and on, decade after decade?

Wilson recognized how very great these challenges were, and he was realistic about how limited in experience and resources Haloid really was. However rational and realistic Wilson always was, one of the most important reasons for his successful transformation of Haloid into Xerox was that he was very wrong on his estimate of how long it would take to achieve commercial success with xerography. He thought it would take only a few years. It took much longer—several *times* longer. If Wilson had known how long it would actually take, he would never have undertaken the venture that led on to triumph.

Recognizing that Haloid lacked the resources and capabilities that would be needed, Wilson, again and again, sought relationships with much larger organizations to get help for Haloid and xerography from larger outfits' research capabilities and financial resources. Part of the help Wilson needed could come from the government.

As Wilson later said, "The federal government showed vision and courage by giving us important financial support to achieve objectives of value to them, and from this sponsored research and development, important values have come to the government, as well as to the public generally." Military contracts were crucial to the development of xerography, but military contracts would not be nearly enough.

To develop the major products that would truly capitalize on xerography in commercial applications—clearly Haloid's great opportunity—Wilson needed to partner with the nation's giant industrial corporations. Of course, these very same corporations could become Haloid's most formidable and dangerous competitors. Wilson knew he would have to take the risk of getting larger companies interested in the new technology.

In working with large industrial organizations, Wilson never tried to monetize the near-term benefits of Haloid's leadership position by charging high licensing fees. Instead, he shrewdly took a broader, longer-term view, making it easier for others to join in working on developing the technology. He also sought the nonexclusive right to enjoy the research results produced by every Haloid licensee, understanding that "We will have any number of auxiliary research organizations working together—and we will share the results."[1]

In the early 1950s, initial developments were encouraging. Even before it had started producing any computers, IBM was looking for output devices for its tabulating machines that were faster than a typewriter's top speed of 200 lines per minute. Because Haloid's technology imaged and printed an entire page at once rather than producing a series of single characters, it could produce output ten *times* as fast, at 2,000 lines per minute. This seemed quite promising, so IBM again engaged in negotiations with Haloid. In 1951, it received a license to use xerography in its punch card accounting

[1]Dessauer, page 80.

machines.[2] Although small and only incremental, this was progress. At the same time, negotiations with RCA that took place in both Rochester and Princeton were developing constructively. In 1951, RCA signed a contract for a limited license to use Haloid's technology in facsimile recording. In addition, research was accelerated by a series of urgent military contracts during the Korean War.

Wilson was committing more and more of Haloid's limited resources to his dream that Haloid would find *the* big breakthrough, hopefully in office copiers, that would give it a major new product success. His nightmare was that some other company, a much larger company, would make it to market sooner.

That nightmare came in 1953. After years of working with Haloid—apparently cooperatively and according to a series of contractual agreements—RCA, one of America's giants in technological innovation, stunned Haloid with a surprise announcement: It had successfully developed an office copier called Electrofax. Based on xerography, RCA said its copier used a *different* xerographic process and that Carlson's patents did not apply. RCA claimed that its process was unique: Specially coated paper, not a selenium drum, was the photoreceptor. RCA conceded that a mere methods patent *might* be claimed by Haloid. Although it was sure that such a claim would not stand up in court, RCA was willing to pay a very modest fee for an explicitly unrestricted license to use all of Haloid's methods patents. Of course, this meant that RCA would pass them along to any other company that might be interested in RCA's new technology.

No wonder Wilson was very upset. As Wilson saw it, RCA had unilaterally changed a crucial and carefully constructed agreement with Haloid. As Wilson wrote to Linowitz: "Haloid's determination in the face of adversity is an obvious one, one that does not spell 'vulnerability,' but one which accounts for the fact that we are going to be tenacious and stubborn about our interests because we have

[2]Linowitz, page 78.

hazarded so much to get where we are."[3] Wilson went on to specify that Haloid's objective in entering into the xerographic field had always been "to become a larger, much more prosperous company and to develop broadly a new and revolutionary process." To achieve its long-term objectives, Haloid had adopted some basic policies:

> To keep for itself exclusively certain fields in which it had know-how. For example, office copying, microfilm enlarging, and the like. To license apparatus in fields where it did not have know-how but to retain for itself the manufacture and sale of supplies because of the highly sensitive nature of them and their effect on the process, and to provide profits for itself from their sale to many fields. To use exclusive licensing where strategically appropriate in order to secure a substantial financial help or development help which would be impossible through the use of non-exclusive licensing.[4]

Wilson recognized how tough and combative an adversary RCA could be: RCA was strong in both finance and technology, and RCA was big, with a reputation for being rough on competition. Wilson noted that Haloid had spent $900,000 developing xerography over the prior five years, 20% of its profits. For RCA, a similar proportion of *its* profits would have been $62 *million*.

RCA's Electrofax copier used specially coated paper and made only one copy at a time. While that single copy limit was an important constraint on RCA's product, Electrofax was still a serious threat. The key question was whether the Carlson patents would apply. On this question, RCA and Haloid sparred seriously in various ways over several months, usually through their respective lawyers. Hoping Haloid would not have to launch a long and expensive lawsuit order to protect its position, Wilson instructed Linowitz to send each of

[3]Linowitz, page 88.
[4]Memorandum to John Dessauer, April 16, 1953.

RCA's Electrofax licensees a shrewdly constructed "look carefully" letter, advising them to be very careful of violating patents and exposing themselves to costly lawsuits.

Meanwhile, Wilson characteristically looked for constructive ways to work cooperatively with RCA, as he always did with any interested major corporation. Although RCA was combative, Wilson kept looking for ways to avoid confrontation and to find points of agreement. Despite many difficulties, a satisfactory arrangement was eventually worked out (Haloid even became a supplier to RCA of the zinc-oxide paper used by Electrofax copiers). Later, RCA licensed its technology to several other manufacturers. Eventually, the superiority of Haloid's reusable selenium drum and its plain paper copying would prevail in the marketplace, and the once-threatening storm would pass.

But it could easily have been very different. As the years went by, Wilson came to believe that the crucial factor was General Sarnoff's preoccupation, as RCA's CEO, with developing color television. If developing copiers had been Sarnoff's strategic priority, Electrofax might have been developed faster, effectively changing the competitive dynamics that Wilson called "5 × 5." If the 914 copier had been introduced five years *earlier*, the market would not really have been ready for copiers and some of the necessary materials would not have been available; five years *later* would have been too late, because other copiers would have been so widely accepted that the 914 could not have achieved the necessary volume and would never have received the essential bank financing.

Winning that first battle with RCA was modest comfort for Wilson, because he knew the development of Electrofax suggested the coming of a broader competitive war. With many large companies actively searching for new ways to produce copies, the risks were proliferating that somewhere, somehow, some competitor—or maybe several competitors—would discover a technological breakthrough and produce a copier that would sweep the market. Wilson understood that, even though he could not identify the specific competitor that was most threatening, Haloid was in a desperate, do-or-die race to develop a successful copier and get it to market in time.

D evelopments with IBM were entirely different from the frustrations with RCA—and very encouraging. In September 1953, Joe Wilson and Tom Watson enjoyed a long and mutually encouraging meeting in Watson's office. As Wilson reported by memo to his father (with copies to nine colleagues), Watson said he "understood perfectly" that a recent development in xerography achieved by RCA could not be made available to IBM until after Haloid had completed the final stages of negotiations with RCA to make this possible. Watson expressed his pleasure that more progress was coming and emphasized to Wilson that "his policy of seeing to it that licensees are required to make their developments available to others working in xerography should be a cornerstone of policy and that he hoped we would never deviate one jot from it."[5]

Wilson concluded with a summation that illustrates an essential dimension of his leadership—the thoughtful enthusiasm he so consistently articulated to keep his team inspired and determined: "I was more than happy with the whole discussion. It revealed a depth and penetration of xerography consciousness in their thinking and in their planning which, despite the assurances of their Engineering Department, I really had not dared believe was possible. My impression is that our relations with this highly important potential user of xerography could hardly be improved upon at the moment and that we have an almost infinite amount to gain by working with them just as closely as we know how. They are going to solve a great many machine development problems for us and will make xerography as well known a word as 'typewriter' in office management circles or I miss my guess—assuming that we perform."

Another partnership licensing opportunity that loomed large in

[5]Letter from Joe Wilson, September 14, 1953.

Wilson's hopes and thinking during the 1950s was with General Electric for the development of a xerographic process that would produce better, easier-to-read X-ray images. *LIFE* magazine found the process dramatic enough to warrant a full-page xeroradiographic picture of a hand.[6] Haloid restricted the GE license to xeroradiography and secured an agreement that any patents that grew out of GE's work would automatically be licensed back to Haloid, and through Haloid to its other licensees for possible use in fields other than X-ray reproduction. This fit the pattern of progress Wilson was seeking to harness through the research and development capabilities of large corporations.

For several years, Wilson hoped that GE would develop an innovative product that could spawn a large new market for xeroradiography, potentially generating large royalties for Haloid on a breakthrough product alternative to X-rays. It appeared particularly promising in detecting breast cancer as well as in military and industrial applications. However, GE scientists were unable to find a xerographic process that did not require a much higher intensity of X-rays than was generated in a newly improved photographic film system developed by DuPont. As a result, the dangers of increasing the power of X-ray machines overwhelmed the benefits of the more easily read final print, so this GE venture was aborted.

GE was also interested in computer printout, and at one point announced what it called ferromagnetography. Dessauer and Clark visited GE labs and were shown a rotating wheel drum that looked promising. They thought GE and Haloid should move to get a patent on the process, but the system could not be manufactured at a practical price, so it too was dropped.

While IBM, RCA, and GE scientists were looking for ways to capitalize on specific aspects of xerographic technology, another approach—which any of these giants could easily have taken—was

---

[6]Battelle had done the first work on this system, discovering in 1949 that selenium-coated plates were even more sensitive to X-rays than to visible light.

somehow never tried: simply acquiring all of Haloid. IBM's CEO Thomas J. Watson Jr. later confided: "The biggest mistake I ever made was not buying Haloid!"[7] Chance, and the long-term significance of initiatives taken or not taken when chance presents opportunities—particularly in such dynamic environments as war or free markets—was particularly important in the case of Joe Wilson's company.

In early 1954, IBM reopened discussions with Wilson and Haloid. Now IBM sought an exclusive license to manufacture or, if Haloid were the manufacturer, to distribute an automatic, xerographic office copier. (Dessauer, according to Linowitz, saw IBM's design as much too close to Haloid's to be anything but a copy and thought that IBM was pirating specific ideas Haloid had been discussing in confidence with IBM.) At this time, Haloid was doing quite well in the supplies business, selling to users of the Copyflo and Model A machines. It was anticipating doing much more business by selling supplies to RCA's customers. Wilson once suggested that Haloid's best strategy for the still undeveloped copier business might well be to let IBM take over the manufacturing and marketing—both areas of great capability for IBM—while Haloid concentrated on selling supplies to the large number of customers that Big Blue was sure to create.

For Haloid, the attraction of getting International Business Machines to take over the heavy lifting was clear: IBM had deep capital resources, outstanding manufacturing capabilities, a great sales

---

[7] Rumors of a combination with IBM came up again as the 914 was taking off. In his book, Linowitz explained what may have prevented an acquisition: "Our aggressive promotion of licenses also served my second purpose, because it involved us with the major competitors of the great corporations that might otherwise have looked at this little company with the interesting patents as a tempting acquisition. Because we were so tied in through licenses with GE and Western Electric and Stromberg-Carlson, an RCA or an IBM could not possibly buy us up without creating an antitrust issue that the Federal Trade Commission and the Justice Department could not ignore. I described this patent and licensing program as the creation of a 'protective picket fence' around Haloid and later Xerox; and inside that fence we were indeed able to cultivate our own garden."

force, commanding stature in the marketplace, and superb management. Moreover, it was the much-admired global leader in business equipment. To be both fair and realistic, Haloid was only an assembler, not the high-volume precision manufacturer that IBM was known to be—and IBM had already mastered the numerous challenges of organizing a national sales and service organization capable of dealing with sophisticated customers and complex equipment. If IBM could create the business by selling copiers nationwide, and even worldwide, Haloid could work with this strong base, and concentrate on selling supplies where it had a proven capability—year after year—to all those customers IBM would create. While Haloid would be limited to supplies, that "limited" business would be a very large opportunity for a company as small as Haloid. This was clearly a win-win strategy for both companies. Or so it seemed, particularly to IBM.

For IBM, James Birkenstock led the negotiations. In his warm, friendly, avuncular way, always expressing deep appreciation for Wilson's leadership and for all that Haloid had so far accomplished, Birkenstock would typically begin by saying, "I must tell you as a friend" that such an arrangement would work best for Haloid. Wilson almost agreed.

In what would, in retrospect, be seen as a nearly disastrous strategic blunder, Haloid offered IBM a license, in August 1954, to manufacture and market a xerographic copying machine. In the proposal, Haloid would receive a large royalty and would be free to build and sell its own copier so long as it was not too close to IBM's design. This would have been a great mistake. Haloid would have been limited to sales of supplies to IBM's customers, and as Wilson later came to appreciate, IBM would surely have encouraged other companies to produce supplies, too. So selling xerographic supplies would have soon become just a highly competitive, low-margin business: Achieving leadership in supplies would have been at best a Pyrrhic victory.

Months later, having decided to build its own xerographic office copier, IBM responded. Fortunately it insisted that it was only interested in an *exclusive* arrangement and needed a guarantee that Haloid would never go into the copier business itself. This, too, was a major strategic blunder. Because IBM demanded too much, Joe Wilson had to refuse. He was not willing to go that far even after Birkenstock cautioned Haloid executives about the enormous costs and risks that would so clearly dominate the business future for everyone in the industry. Discussions with IBM were broken off again in late 1954.

IBM made overtures to Haloid again in early 1955, and by April, the proposition was again explicit: IBM wanted an exclusive license to build and sell an automated desktop copier. IBM's insistence on an exclusive license was clearly significant. In order to deal intelligently with IBM's proposal, Wilson decided he needed to understand more fully xerography's potential in an automated office copier, so he set up a small-copier committee with Chet Carlson as chair.[8] The committee worked for six months, generated lots of ideas, and in its final report concluded that the xerographic copier looked very promising and should definitely *not* be turned over to IBM. With this report in hand, Wilson again refused to give IBM an exclusive license. So discussions again came to an end for the time being.[9] The committee agreed, preliminarily, that such a machine would have to be as large as a four-drawer filing cabinet and weigh 1,000 pounds. To make success possible, Haloid needed to succeed with a new technology and a series of enabling inventions and developments. In addition, Haloid would also face enormous marketing problems because the whole concept for Haloid's copier was dramatically different from any other copier on the market: Competitors made their profits on *supplies* and sold their machines at a low cost, while Haloid planned to make its profits on *machines* that would cost nearly 10 times as much as the machines being placed by competitors. And in addition,

---

[8]Others on the committee were Harold Clark, Clyde Mayo, George Mott, Bob Vyverberg, and two new men—Donald Shepardson and Fred Schwertz—who wrote the report.
[9]In 1972, in a Federal Trade Commission consent decree, Xerox agreed to provide open licenses, expecting this would leave competitors approximately two years behind it *and* that this would give Xerox a productive challenge to keep advancing in order to stay ahead of the competition.

over the next few years, Haloid's copier program seemed remarkably capable of attracting every sort of technical problem. As Wilson later said, "This was *not* an easy time."

Wilson then asked the Study Project 914–813 committee, chaired by Harold Clark, to re-examine the company's strategic situation. That committee concluded that Haloid should go into office copiers on its own, but Wilson was still reluctant to take the go-it-alone gamble. The stakes were so very high; the margin for error so very small. This would be a classic all-or-nothing, bet-the-company situation. Wilson was playing to win, but in free markets as in war, taking unnecessary risks is dangerous and good entrepreneurs strive to avoid them. As an effective entrepreneur, Wilson was much more a risk minimizer than a risk taker.

Wilson's entrepreneurial grand strategy was clearly designed to create a major corporation that would grow to dominate its industry, just as IBM had done in business equipment and General Motors had done in automobiles. Therefore, it was the beginning of a memorable experience when his secretary announced: "Mr. Wilson, you have a call from a Mr. Alfred Sloan." The caller was the brilliant, logical executive who had transformed a sprawling mixture of different automotive parts manufacturers, assemblers, and financial companies into the world's largest and most respected manufacturing corporation: General Motors.

As usual, Sloan spoke directly: "Mr. Wilson, reports of your work remind me very much of our situation when we were striving to rationalize the automotive industry's new technologies. This required new ways of conceptualizing and managing our business. And now, it seems to me, you are engaged in the same extraordinary challenges. You certainly have my best wishes for your success, and my admiration and respect for all you are doing, sir." Wilson, like Sloan before him, needed innovations in marketing, manufacturing, management, and service. And to make those innovations possible, like Sloan, Wilson needed creative financing, another hurdle that Sloan had tackled at GM with car loans from GMAC.

14

GATHERING STRENGTH
IN FINANCE

J oe Wilson had unusual capacity to inspire others to envision a very different, much better future for his company, and great ability to inspire others to join with him in the adventure of pursuing his goal. But he also had a realistic understanding of what he would need to get where he wanted to go, particularly the people and financial resources that were needed. Wilson's balanced combination of vision and resources with action and decision gave his company strength in both ends and means. Wilson's financial priority, as with every effective entrepreneur, was clearly on cash flow. Not sales, not profits, but *cash*. For the first few years of the decade, Haloid's sales averaged less than $14 million and profits less than $500,000, but cashflow was steadily building up.

Wilson had studied corporate finance at Harvard Business School, was good at it and enjoyed it, and had a special facility with numbers. (He had once considered becoming a finance professor or going to Wall Street.) Even more important for his company, Wilson understood the importance of demonstrating consistently prudent financial discipline, having clearly articulated business plans designed to capitalize on opportunity, *and* having a record of consistently matching those plans with effective action, so lenders would be confident that they would always get back the money they lent to Haloid. Wilson also knew that he and all other Haloid investors would want, as much as possible, to avoid dilution of their equity.

Something of a stickler for accuracy—his own accuracy and the accuracy of others—an attitude all bankers like to see, Wilson had an impressive ability to retain figures in his head and to use them in presentations.[1] Another favorable factor was the discipline with which Haloid managed its financial affairs. Wilson insisted on very tight cost disciplines, and it showed: Haloid's offices were obviously shabby, assembly lines were set up in lofts, and engineers worked out of cramped spaces in buildings with colorful names derived from Wilson's focus on cost-saving: the House, the Fur Shop, the Toy Shop, and so forth.

Wilson concentrated on achieving success where success really mattered: research, manufacturing, sales, and service. Combined with his profound personal modesty and those indelible lessons from the Depression—"patch it up; fix it up; make it do; do without"— Wilson resisted spending money on anything else, particularly executive offices[2] which were notoriously shabby. Without such concentration on his strategic imperatives, Wilson could not have enjoyed the success he achieved—and might not have succeeded at all.

To finance his massive commitment to developing xerography and transforming Haloid, Wilson pursued a many-dimensional strategy to obtain the necessary capital and organizational resources:

[1]Wilson was charmingly, but not *always* consistent: Ever the English major, Wilson was annoyed by poor usage, such as *almost perfect* when there were no degrees of perfection or *monies* when money was a collective in the singular—or when files were misplaced. Still, long after the 914's introduction, he was still asking his secretary, "Please make a carbon."

[2]However, in early 1961 at the urging of John Davis, Wilson approved a survey of suitable office space in downtown Rochester. By spring, two floors were leased in the tower being built as part of Midtown Plaza—the first covered downtown shopping mall in the United States. At least part of his motivation was to give a boost to the renewal of downtown Rochester.

- Contracts with the U.S. government to develop new ways to utilize xerography, particularly when military developments might then be converted into future civilian products. During the 1940s and 1950s, military contracts were the major source of financing for the R&D required to convert xerography from Carlson's shoebox into important commercial products. They were also vital to Haloid's profitability. (In 1951, 35% of Haloid's $13 million in sales was to the U.S. military, for example.) Moreover, as a U.S. citizen, Wilson linked these government contracts with his patriotism and lifelong interest in national service.

- Cooperative agreements and cross-licensing with major U.S. industrial research and technology corporations like GE, IBM, RCA, and Bell & Howell were an effective and low-cost way of engaging these major companies' financial and R&D resources in the pursuit of xerography's potentials.

- Joint ventures in international markets with local companies to gain access to their manufacturing facilities and distribution capabilities around the world.

- Developing the credibility necessary for raising substantial capital funds in both the debt and equity markets, long before the development of the open capital markets that small growth companies now take for granted.

- Using subcontractors for most of the manufacturing so Haloid would not need to make major investments in plant and equipment.

- Not spend on unnecessary costs such as nice offices or even "proper" production facilities.

Finally, Wilson and everyone else in management worked very long hours. They were, after all, as Wilson often said, "on a soul-sized mission."

The cash saved or raised through these combined strategies enabled Wilson to invest boldly in developing xerography. Over the years from 1947 to 1953, Haloid earned $2.3 million, but all of this and more had to be reinvested *defensively* to protect what was left of Haloid's traditional and rapidly declining business against its increasingly strong competition. Even as the old Haloid business required reinvestment of virtually all its earnings, Wilson poured *twice* as much as the company earned each year into developing xerography, and most of the millions invested in developing xerography had to be raised from outside sources through increased debt and new stock issues. This difficult job devolved to Joe Wilson and his Treasurer Kent Damon.[3]

Financing for Haloid was initially modest in scale and done on the basis of personal relationships with bankers, relationships that Wilson and Damon developed with patience and persistence. Because Haloid and Wilson were known to the Rochester banks, and the bankers were known to Wilson and Haloid, the local banks provided most of the needed money. If more credit were needed, the Rochester banks had good relationships with their correspondent banks in New York City, particularly Morgan Guaranty and First National City Bank. As Wilson carefully explained to him, Damon's principal responsibility was to develop and manage Haloid's relationships with the commercial banks and insurance companies that Haloid relied on for money—lots of money for such a small company to borrow—

[3]Responsible for overseeing accounting, Damon also worked on taxes and the annual report. After graduating from Amherst and then Harvard Business School in 1947, Kent Damon served four years in the U.S. Navy and went home to Fort Dodge, Iowa, where he spent three years working for Tobin Packing Company. Feeling stymied in his career, he hoped to transfer to Tobin's headquarters in Rochester. He had met many Tobin people from Rochester and hearing them talk with pride about their hometown, even though he'd never been to the city, Damon thought it would be a fine place to live and raise a family. When he was told that a transfer couldn't be done for some time, Damon decided to look for work in Rochester and wrote to every company in the city with sales above a certain threshold. Damon's list included Haloid, where Harold Kuhns was a close friend of the treasurer of Tobin. Kuhns read the letter, got a favorable evaluation from his friend at Tobin, and hired Damon.

particularly since it was going to pour all that borrowed money into developing xerography, a new and unproven technology.

Wilson and Damon concentrated on finding banks that were already comfortable lending to IBM and other office equipment manufacturers that leased their equipment to end-users. Such lenders would know from their own experience that business equipment leases were superb collateral for loans. With Wilson articulating Haloid's strategy and demonstrating his financial mastery, Damon arranged the necessary loans from a deliberately diverse group of banks and insurance companies. In arranging Haloid's financing, Wilson's primary concern was avoiding over-leveraging the balance sheet with so much debt that restrictive covenants might be imposed on the company. To avoid this, Haloid used a nuanced blend of private debt placements, convertible bonds, and preferred stock.

Capital was raised on the promise of xerography, validated by Joe Wilson's evident mastery of all aspects of Haloid's financials, his overall strategy, and his confidence-inspiring manner of presentation, plus Damon's carefully documented five-year projections. (Tall, thoughtful, and deliberate, Damon, like Wilson had an appropriate abundance of what political leaders call "gravitas" and bankers call "character." Character—and meeting financial projections on a regular basis—are what give lenders the confidence to lend even more.) As Damon put it, "They got to know us and recognized we were conservative in our projections. We lived up to them. We exceeded them." Damon was good with numbers; Wilson was even better *and* knew their context and meaning. "I was very impressed," said Damon. "Joe was such a bright man. He got right through to the guts of the matter very quickly. He was always way ahead of you in his thinking." Even better, as would be seen again and again, Wilson was unusually quick to see the merit of other peoples' ideas, acted decisively to put them into practice, and celebrated their originators. As McColough remembered, "He never identified personally with an opinion—and was delighted by the superior ideas of others."

As the financial specialist on Wilson's team, it was important that Damon always took the role of *helper* in his work with the company's operating executives. "Instead of reacting to every proposal as though, like Harold Kuhns, he was the only one left to defend the last cash in the treasury," says Horace Becker, "he always wanted to understand the whole picture. . . . Kent would sit right down with you and ask: 'Help me understand why we have to spend this money. Explain to me what we need to do and why that's important.' And after you gave him a good explanation and he really understood and was convinced, he'd say, 'Well, I guess we've just got to find the money.' By contrast, Kuhns was a bookkeeper and was always beating up on me on costs. So I had to fight back—harder—with Kuhns. But Kent was a man you could confide in and you could work with."

As much as Haloid needed money—which might have tempted executives at other companies to use aggressive accounting policies to maximize reported earnings—Wilson always insisted that Haloid follow unusually conservative accounting policies. While using accelerated depreciation for *tax* purposes, as did many other companies, Xerox's accounting was very unusual: Wilson's company used the same double declining balances accelerated depreciation for internal bookkeeping purposes *and* in reporting operating earnings to investors. (Most companies used accelerated depreciation for tax reporting, but straight-line depreciation for reporting to investors because this raised the level of earnings.) But conservative accounting and a disciplined focus on generating free cash flow did not impede Wilson from taking bold actions that advanced his company toward his long-term vision.

In 1953, Wilson went looking for 40 acres of land near Lake Ontario because he wanted direct access to a large amount of fresh water for a new manufacturing plant. A lawyer named Barrett, who had an option on a large parcel in Webster, asked: "Would you like 1,000 acres of farmland—*plus* a corridor of land so you could pipe water from the lake?" On the spot, Wilson went from seeking 40 acres to buying 1,000 acres. (A major manufacturing complex of over 40 buildings now covers 58 of those acres.) To buy the land in Webster and build modern, efficient buildings required arranging a substantial long-term loan. Focused as he was on conserving cash, Wilson had a nice balancing ability that enabled him to seize an unusual opportunity and to decisively reach his longer-term objectives and visions. In early 1954, Wilson and Damon borrowed $3 million in 20-year notes at 3.6% interest from Massachusetts Mutual Life Insurance saying, "We are certain that we shall find it beneficial and money-saving to consolidate our operations on a single site. At present, we are scattered all around Rochester, and our inadequate space hampers us from using modern and efficient methods of operation. Besides, it makes no provision for future growth."

By the end of the 1950s, the capital that Haloid would require to build and lease thousands of copiers would be enormous. However, Wilson was not intimidated. He also was not deterred by the potential nightmare that any one of a dozen corporate giants— all with keen interest in getting into office copiers—would somehow achieve a technological breakthrough in three or four years that would make xerographic machines obsolete. This would leave Haloid horribly overexposed. Instead, Wilson found the challenge stimulating and was attracted by the imperative to continue developing improvements. He focused on making sure that Haloid would always be selling the very best product.

One of Wilson's astute moves to increase cash flow was so original that many people did not immediately recognize how shrewd it really was. At first, it looked like a mistake. But it was no mistake. It was a low-cost way to raise significant and much-needed equity capital. Effective January 1, 1956, Haloid purchased, with common stock valued at $3.8 million, the worldwide patents on xerography from Battelle. (Haloid agreed to pay $3.5 million in shares of common stock—25,000 shares in January, 1956, and 10,000 shares at the end of each of the next three years. For the period from 1959 to 1965, Haloid also agreed to pay 3% of its domestic xerographic sales up to $20 million annually and 1% in excess of that figure, plus 25% of domestic xerographic royalties with 50% of these payments in Haloid stock valued at $60 a share, up to a maximum of 5,000 shares a year, all totaling $3.8 million.)[4]

The great advantage of this arrangement to cash-needy Haloid was that the stock payments replaced what would otherwise have been large cash payments of royalties, and eliminated the need for additional outside equity financing. Of course, Wilson knew when he bought them that the patents would expire in just 3½ years. The rapid expiration of the patents actually gave a strong boost to Haloid's cash flow, the real money that could be used in the business, because Haloid could amortize the cost of those patents in just 3½ years, adding over $1 million per year—an amount equal to Haloid's total profits—to pretax cash flow. And because this particular asset, unlike plant and equipment, would never need to be replaced, it was all *free* cash flow at just the time when Haloid really needed the money. The combination of amortization and profits gave Wilson the money needed to develop the 914.[5]

Initial interest among institutional investors in owning Haloid stock developed tangentially and through informal networks. Bank trust departments first learned of "something going on" at Haloid from their commercial loan officers. Others learned of Haloid through their investment analysts. (Haloid, following a common practice at the time, used a particular stock brokerage firm, Adams & Peck, to communicate to institutional investors the "authorized" figures for such big variables as machine placements and copies per

[4]In 1955, Wilson and Linowitz had gone to Columbus, hoping to offer 25,000 shares of Haloid plus $500,000 per year for three years and a continuing royalty of 3% of sales until 1965. (The $500,000 was equal to the 8% royalty then in effect.) Clyde Williams of Battelle suggested 10,000 shares a year instead of cash. A decade later, each 10,000 share block was worth $5 million.

[5]Linowitz proposed a clever three-way strategy that would have had the University of Rochester buy the patents and lease them to Haloid at a lower rate than Battelle was charging, but Wilson rejected this scheme to capitalize on the University of Rochester's tax-exempt status as "gimmicky."

machine. Morgan Guaranty Trust Company held the largest block of Haloid stock of any institutional investor. Peter Vermilye, a senior investor, recounted the story: "A brilliant Dutch analyst on our staff made the original recommendation, so I arranged a meeting with Joe Wilson. The first time we met, he told me 'Our earnings will triple in three years!' That was the sort of statement an investor would obviously remember. Even more memorable, he was right! Earnings *did* triple. When we met again a few years later, he again said to me, 'Our earnings will triple over the *next* three years!' Again, he was right: Earnings *did* triple!"

A few articles appeared in the business press, such as when *Fortune* included the company in a short list of "delicious" growth stocks. A GE scientist, who had left General Electric for Battelle, talked about Haloid with the manager of GE's Elfun Trust, a mutual fund for the officers of GE that invested in small technology companies. After some study, the portfolio manager bought 10,000 shares saying, "Except for the 5 percent limit on a mutual fund's ownership, I would have doubled my initial investment." All too soon, Elfun Trust was a *seller* of Haloid—but only because the share price was going up so rapidly that it made that one holding too "out sized." Similarly, for portfolio diversification, the University of Rochester, an early investor, had to sell stock to stay below the endowment's policy limit on the market value size of any one holding.

Wilson was expanding his company's sources of credit *and* building institutional interest in owning Haloid common stock. He knew he would need both. And he would need to transform his company's whole organization.

15

BUILDING THE
ORGANIZATION

Joe Wilson understood what venture capitalists all understand:
Cash is essential, but the success of venture investing depends
on building a successful organization. Wilson knew he needed
able, motivated people just as much as he needed money.
"Wilson attracted quite a large number of unusually capable young
people who responded positively to the values he espoused and
lived," says Erik Pell, a senior scientist. "He was straight and honest
and a gambler with vision." By the mid-1950s, Wilson's hiring in
sales, research, and production was transforming Haloid.

When he became president, Wilson had known that Haloid was
a disadvantaged company. In any direct competition with established industry giants, Haloid would never be able to fulfill Wilson's
aspirations. So Wilson made sure that Haloid was more imaginative
in its approach and more focused. For example, Wilson knew his
company needed more and better managers *and* more and better scientists and engineers. But in recruiting top engineers and scientists,
Wilson knew Haloid would be in direct competition with universities, as well as IBM and Bell Labs and other well-known, high-status
organizations with enormous research budgets. To compete successfully for the best people—the ones everyone else wanted—Haloid
focused on convincing engineering professors at selected colleges to

identify their best young engineers. The early years of an engineer's employment—and the feedback professors received from their recent graduates—were important in determining how professors felt about recommending Haloid. To get faculty support in recruiting during good times, Wilson knew Haloid would need to show that it would also hire steadily in lean times, so this is what Wilson very deliberately did.

Wilson also encouraged Haloid researchers to attend scientific conferences to meet other researchers, partly to encourage interest in the new technology, but mainly to identify talented people who might come to Rochester. Erik Pell, who had worked for 10 years at GE's Schenectady facilities, provided the following explanation for why he left: "It was a rather standard large corporation and I couldn't warm up to it. We were there for only one reason: to make a profit. Everybody wants to work for a company that is more than a corporate profit-maker."

As he talked with job candidates—and with institutional investors—Wilson was just as willing to discuss Haloid's problems and limitations as the promising potentials he saw ahead, typically putting his company's prospects into the context of a broad vision of the benefits to humankind of improvements in communication and education. Many candidates reacted in what became a quite typical fashion: "I interviewed with Wilson and on the train back to Pittsburgh came to a clear conclusion: 'If that remarkable man ever offers me a job, I will go there!' "[1] He was soon offered a job and promptly headed back to Rochester.

When he gave managers significant new assignments, Wilson made a practice of having a long, personal discussion with each one to instill a full understanding of the responsibilities the manager would be taking on and how they would affect the company and other people involved. In these discussions, they would evaluate together the costs and risks as well as the major goals of the

[1]Fred Schwertz.

assignment, and then Wilson would follow up with a memorandum, detailing the agreed-upon plan of action. The executive put in charge was not interfered with thereafter, but Wilson expected regular progress reports and would applaud good performance or criticize poor results. If the project itself ever turned out to be ill-advised, Wilson would reach out and personally take full responsibility. John Dessauer called them "contracts in cement" and considered them one of Wilson's greatest managerial strengths. "He took the time to come to you, to draw you out and get the facts. He knew how to motivate us."

With the company growing more rapidly than most individuals could grow, many of the old Haloid managers couldn't keep up or fit in with the future Wilson was developing. They'd done all they were capable of doing in bringing Haloid up to $8 million in sales. Wilson would now be taking his company to 250 times that size, and the work would soon be beyond them. For many of the employees of the old Haloid Company, all they could see was that top management was risking their company on a very expensive, very risky project in which they had no part. According to Linowitz, "One of Joe's greatest accomplishments was that he managed to keep all these people productive and mostly cheerful, through the long years of discouragement. Those were the years when key people in Haloid remained with the company simply because they saw the stars in Joe Wilson's eyes."

In addition to recruiting outstanding young talent, Wilson knew that to achieve the organizational transformation he intended, he would have to move older men aside. Instead of letting eclipsed people go, Joe Wilson—who couldn't bear to fire anyone—moved men like Jack Hartnett and Harold Kuhns off to the side where they were comfortable in new job responsibilities. After that, Jack Hartnett had a heart attack, Wilson moved him up to Chairman of the Board, an honorary title and an increasingly notorious parking place, and made Hartnett's friend and colleague, Homer Hurst, sales manager.

But, always reluctant to demote or dismiss an executive, he assured Hartnett that he would continue to be responsible as an "overseer."

Wilson was sensitive to others' feelings and concerns, and they knew it. But he was always clear and strong as a leader. And they knew that too. Time and again when someone was not working out, Wilson's first thought was, "It may well be that the fault is ours for putting him in the wrong kind of job. If we've somehow mismatched his skills and our needs, we'll have to try him at something else." Wilson anguished over having to fire anyone, particularly someone who had been with the company for several years. He would insist the company work with the individual to find another position, saying: "We do these things because so many of our people have moved to Rochester at our urging. It's unfair to release them when they've made such a sacrifice for us." Even serious malingerers in the factory would not be terminated without going through arbitration. After hearing all the evidence, even the arbitrator's eyes would sometimes roll in wonder that the company had been so restrained.

Nor was Wilson comfortable demoting people. Over the years, McColough would learn that when Wilson would say something like, "As part of your buildup of corporate experience, Peter, it's time for you to have the Controller report to you . . . so let's start that next week," it often had a double meaning. While it was surely part of Wilson's steady expansion of McColough's experience, it could also mean, as McColough would soon discover, that the executive also needed to be reassigned to a less demanding job.

Wilson felt that if he ever had something disagreeable to say to anyone—like changing the size of his sales territory—the longer ahead of the actual event he could tell the person, the better. That way, the individual would have time to adjust to the coming reality and prepare his or her family, so they would see the change in a positive light and view the employee as personally wanting it or even, perhaps, initiating or bringing it about. Wilson would bring the employee to Rochester and schedule a full day of meetings, often including his father and other senior executives to show that the change was being taken very seriously and that the meeting was truly important, not only to the individual as a person, but to the company. In addition, Wilson would explain that the salesman would be held "whole" in earnings until the future growth in earnings from the new smaller territory caught up to the current level of earnings.

Still, Wilson could and would put long-term executives on the shelf with an office in an area that soon became known as no man's land. There they could stay as long as they liked, but if they ever complained or said they were feeling unproductive or the equivalent, they would soon be gone. Dave Raub's sudden departure provides an example. Raub—who had been put on the shelf—had accumulated $2 million, primarily through Xerox stock options. So Wilson knew he was well off. One day, Raub was in conversation with Wilson when he said very off-handedly, "Joe, I've been thinking. Maybe it's getting to be time for me to be thinking of possibly retiring some day." Raub got no particular reaction and certainly no resistance—that day. But the very next day, he got a final paycheck with a warm note from Wilson: "Dave, we're all so happy for you that you've chosen to retire at an early age so you can do all the things you've always wanted to do. Joe."[2]

---

[2]While he set the pattern of consistent discipline at work, Peggy set the boundaries at home. Joe couldn't. He wanted the kids to be happy and, if he sent them to their rooms or said, "No TV," he would soon relent and often add something extra. In effect, of course, he was rewarding the kids for misbehavior. And Wilson had difficulty setting appropriate money boundaries for his children. He was proud of providing well for his family, but did not teach the children how to handle money particularly wisely. A teenage daughter would charge lunch almost every day at the Country Club of Rochester and regularly treat two or three friends. Asking one of the kids to run down to the store to buy a paper, he would give $20 and not ask for change. Regarding the family fortune that his achievements created, Wilson told his father, "Don't leave money to me. I'll be OK on my own. Leave it to the kids." And he arranged with his parents that their promised bequest to the University of Rochester would come from his share of their estate, not his brother's.

On setting up trusts for the children, Wilson waited two years before taking action, so it would look "right" for the company. Originally, he had arranged for

Wilson's search for fairness was central to his company's labor relations practices. He had an unconventional view of workers that was particularly unusual in the confrontational labor-management climate of the 1940s and 1950s. He treated workers as associates rather than as employees, always referred to them as personnel, and had a real desire to relate directly with each individual person. He did this by walking through the plant at Christmastime, thanking each individual by name or nickname, recalling specific experiences and details about their wives and children, and knowing their number of years with the company. His meaning was clear: We're all on the same team; we're in this together.[3]

These one-on-ones were important to the workers and very important to Joe Wilson. As the company grew, Wilson still wanted to shake hands with each person so he could have enough time for a meaningful conversation and thank them individually. By 1955, the process was taking so long that the starting time had been pushed all the way back to Thanksgiving.

Given the pressures of rapid growth, tight finances, *and* the uncertainties of a new technology, tension was a constant problem as highly committed executives and workers grappled in darkness for the uncertain future. "We were all on edge," says McColough. "After

---

each child to receive 25 percent of the principal at 30 and 25 percent at 35, but he reduced those ages to 25 and 30 to give them more responsibility, the other 50 percent remaining in trust and making annual distributions. (Ironically, Wilson's thoughtful, two-year delay later resulted in an IRS suit for $19 million in estate taxes on Wilson's $43.5 million estate. Because the delayed date on which they were finalized was so close to his date of death, the IRS claimed that the trusts for the Wilson children had been established "in contemplation of death" and as a means to avoid estate taxes. After a trial, the U.S. Tax Court cut the IRS claim back to just $2.2 million.)

[3]At the annual July company picnic, T-shirts with "My Daddy works at Haloid" printed on them were given out to all the workers' children. One adult shirt was made and presented to Wilson, who wore it proudly because his father, JR Wilson, was still employed.

all, we were betting our lives and mortgaging our homes to bet on our company. We all had the right attitude and *believed* we had the right stuff."

Most executives and most workers were new to the company and to each other. All were experiencing rapid change in their work. Many worked very long hours. All were aware of both the excitement of working to create a major revolution and the anxieties of knowing they had taken on a major challenge without knowing exactly how to overcome it. With time compressing everything, it was not clear they would ever make it. Under the pressure of urgency, tensions rose and frequently flared into anger.

To reduce tensions, Wilson turned, characteristically, to a consultant. He engaged Dr. Paul Brower, an industrial psychologist he had met with two years earlier in Cleveland. Dr. Brower encouraged executives to assess their own abilities, jobs, and aspirations. He advised individual members of Wilson's management team on how to deal with particular problems and how to recognize why their individual managerial styles might conflict with the individual styles of their peers. He also demonstrated specific ways they could help reduce the tensions both were experiencing. Wilson worked hard to expand the areas of cooperation: close, cooperative relationships between proud and talented individuals were essential to the transformation of Haloid.

To find people with the flexibility to change and the creative energy to innovate and drive change, Wilson very deliberately sought young people with lots of energy who embraced change as a way to pry open opportunities. Large numbers of enthusiastic new people were added in a steady flow as Wilson and Dessauer increased the research organization from 15 employees in 1947 to 170 in 1959. Most new hires were under the age of 40; a very substantial number were under the age of 30. (By 1960, nearly 70% of Haloid's people were under 40.) In addition, several intellectual "rainmakers" like Nobel laureate John Bardeen, co-inventor of the transistor, were retained as consultants.

"Joe Wilson was a person people trusted—trusted very deeply—and were glad to follow," said McColough. "He took a very long-range view of business and industry—and a long-range view of where to take the company. As an organization builder, Joe Wilson put the imprint of his values on the whole organization. His *personal* integrity and moral tone became established *corporate* values."

Wilson was a consistent leader on matters of integrity. For example, in 1956, Itek, a high technology company with strong military contracts, introduced a machine that was, surprisingly, faster *and* easier to use than a machine just developed by Haloid. Wilson intercepted Haloid's new product on the loading dock, ready for initial shipment: "Sorry guys. The project is dead. We are not going to ship something we know is second best."

When a senior executive once took a bribe, he was fired immediately. To reassure others without citing the specific misbehavior, a memo was issued that day saying that the reason for termination was "not trivial."

Wilson was also usually self-disciplined. Even with all the stress and frustration of constant innovation and frequent disappointment, he maintained his composure almost all the time. "*If* he was ever angry, those steely blue eyes would look right through you—*if* he ever got mad," recalled Gloria Chapman.[4]

Characteristic of great leaders is the assured consistency with which their personal compass and commitment to high values not only guide their own actions, but also serve as assured, reliable standards which everyone in their organization can confidently use to

---

[4]The angriest Gloria Chapman ever saw him was when he rushed into the office one morning to dictate a strongly worded letter to an employee, pointing out that the "way to the boss's heart was *not* to have one's wife challenge the boss's wife to a game of chicken—and then drive out of the company parking lot without saying a word!"

One of the few times Wilson lost his self-control in public was at a Friday dinner hosted by the union. Abe Chatman, thinking he was respecting Wilson's religious practices, arranged to serve Wilson fish while all the others had roast beef. Wilson's "I'm *not* Catholic," outburst was swift, and a plate of roast beef was quickly provided.

guide their own actions and decisions. Joe Wilson's personal integrity inspired a widespread confident commitment to integrity in policies, practices, and beliefs that gave individuals confidence that doing the really right thing was always right—and expected—at Joe Wilson's company.

Over and over, Wilson played the decisive role of persuading capable individuals to give up promising careers elsewhere and join Haloid. The success of this crucial recruiting depended on two salient factors, both provided by Joe Wilson. First, Wilson had what recruiters call good taste—a special gift for identifying talent—and an equal gift for attracting talented people to Haloid. The more obvious factor was Wilson's quite remarkable ability to articulate and project the opportunities unfolding through xerography with a warmth, candor, and sense of excitement that many found inspiring. This was particularly important to the young and ambitious people he focused on, knowing he needed young people with energy who were focused on the future.

Wilson urged each of his senior colleagues to search for strong young people, and assigned Jack Hartnett to recruit a new sales manager. When Hartnett asked, "Can we really afford a topflight man?" Wilson replied: "We can't afford to be without one."[5] So Hartnett retained a search firm, Ward Howell Associates, and soon had more than 50 candidates to review. He interviewed several and came down to three finalists, but couldn't decide which to select. He turned to Wilson for help: "Joe, I'm in a dilemma. I've whittled the candidates down to three finalists, but they're all so good that I don't know which to pick." After reading Hartnett's summaries of the three men, Wilson was puzzled: "So what's your problem?" Hartnett explained they presented an embarrassment of riches and asked Wilson's reaction. "I already *have* reacted. They *all* look like the kind of people we want. Let's hire all three. When xerography starts rolling we're going to need good men—and lots of them. If we don't grab them while

[5]Dessauer, page 86.

we can, we may lose the best of those available. These three sound perfect; all young fellows who've made their mark by the age of thirty-one. Let's hire all three!"

Wilson offered to interview the three finalists. John W. Rutledge, a graduate of Northwestern University and Harvard Business School, had served as a Navy Lieutenant in World War II and was sales manager of Lehigh Coal and Navigation, a conglomerate whose British owners had just abandoned its promisingly aggressive asset redeployment strategy and were going to stay with the old lines of business. Seeing no major opportunity for his career after that abrupt change in strategy, Rutledge resigned. So did a Canadian lawyer and Harvard MBA who had served as a British Naval Airman during the war: Charles Peter McColough, a Vice President and Director at Lehigh. The third was Donald Clark, a Phi Beta Kappa graduate of Wesleyan and an MBA who had graduated with distinction from Harvard. He had served as a lieutenant in the Army Air Corps and then spent six years at GE as a market analyst.[6] These strong credentials were why Wilson wanted to hire all three.

But it wasn't that easy. McColough only visited Haloid because he happened to be in Rochester for another meeting with a different company, and didn't want to embarrass the recruiter who was a personal friend. The recruiter had urged McColough to consider Haloid and might have cooled on recommending him for other openings if he didn't at least stop in to see Haloid. McColough was looking, but he was *not* looking to move to Rochester in remote Upstate New York.

McColough's initial visit to Haloid started badly: The first interview with the head of sales, Jack Hartnett, was in a shabby office with obviously old furniture and just an orange crate for a bookcase with a black metal lunch box sitting on top. "Only later," McColough said, "did I learn that the company, by necessity, had very strict controls on any expenditures, so all available funds could go into the development of xerography: hence the makeshift bookcase and worn out furniture.

[6]Dessauer, page 87.

Also, Hartnett, was just recuperating from an illness and on his doctor's orders took quiet lunch hours in his office: hence the lunch pail."

Morever, during the morning, McColough had seen a demonstration of xerography, including the clunky Model A, and was impressed—negatively. "The copier I saw on that first visit made copies that were OK as copies, but the process was much too complicated and required far too many skills and way too many steps for most companies to even consider using it in their offices."

After lunch at Mr. JR's Howard Johnson's, Hartnett took McColough to see Joe Wilson, who was at home nursing a cold and expecting only a very brief visit. "I was not impressed by the technology and said as much to Joe." Wilson acknowledged the very real problems and agreed that the plate master business had limited potential, but he enthusiastically took the very long view. "Our machine *is* primitive, but the day will come when we too can make 9,000 copies—in one hour!" Wilson assured McColough that in time, xerography would be faster and better quality than offset. "He really could see the whole future just that clearly," said McColough, whose planned short visit lasted a full three hours. After that, he was hooked.

Inspiring articulation of his strategic vision, thoughtful personal attention to each individual as an individual, and discipline—particularly self-discipline—were three of the essential characteristics of Wilson's approach to leadership. A fourth characteristic was Wilson's obvious and sustained personal commitment. This encouraged others to follow his lead in bringing the technology from its crude beginnings into commercial realization, making it the most profitable new office product of the 20th century.

Wilson was continuously determined to avoid one kind of problem that had little to do with technology but could interfere with the strategic transformation he was determined to achieve: disruptive labor relations. He had been very upset with Haloid's adversarial labor relations in the thirties and was familiar with the three

traditional levels of labor relations: hostile, arm's length, and progressive. Having moved Haloid away from hostile, he now wanted
to move up to progressive. He turned to Bill Asher, the Assistant
Personnel Manager, and said: "Bill, labor relations in our country is a
pretty sad affair. We need dependable labor relations so work stoppages will not constrict our future growth. Your job is to make labor
relations at Haloid work, and work well, so we can rely on not having labor problems as we build up Haloid *and* so we can set a beacon
for other American companies to follow."

Wilson always felt that Kodak's "no-union" policy was morally
wrong, and he made a practice of consistently working cooperatively
with the Amalgamated to achieve the "progressive" level of labor
relations. Quarterly meetings were held to discuss specific ways to
adjust working relationships, to share information in absolute confidence on how the company was doing, and to exchange views on
ways to increase cooperation. The mutual interdependence and
cooperation eventually achieved was clearly shown when Haloid
wanted to change certain work rules and union leader Abe Chatman,
said: "We understand what you want to change and why. We *will*
agree with you, but only after you've given us two to three years to
get it set up the right way with our members."

The Amalgamated had matured as a labor union in the 1920s,
and its leadership knew how to work *with* employers. They would
discuss issues and the objective basis for recommended changes, and
then they would reason together on decisions. Similarly, Wilson
understood the great importance of never threatening the security
of the union as an organization, and made several decisions to assure
its leadership that the union's security was also important to Haloid.
While executives at other companies might instinctively fight on
principal if a labor union wanted a union shop, Wilson was fine with
a closed shop and explained his logic as such: "We will never do anything to threaten the union's sense of security because if ever we did,
they would defend themselves—at *our* expense."

However, when a different union—the United Auto Workers—

tried to organize technical workers in Boston, Asher was sent to block and prevent that initiative. Eventually, after a prolonged struggle, he was successful. However, he certainly appreciated Wilson's call near the end of the intense negotiations: "Bill, if you go down on this effort, much as we all hope you'll prevail, you should know how I really feel: It won't be the end of the day, Bill."

Developing progressive labor relations would depend on Wilson's taking a direct interest in working with the Amalgamated, particularly during contract negotiations and on his being resourceful and adaptable to circumstances. For example, in 1948 and 1949, Haloid's earnings had been so low and uncertain that nothing was paid into the profit-sharing plan, so the Amalgamated decided to insist on switching to a defined benefit pension plan, and that change was agreed upon. Then, when Xerox stock took off—taking management's profit-sharing plan way up in value—the Amalgamated leaders were understandably distressed, so Wilson asked Asher to develop a retirement plan that would fairly blend a profit-sharing plan with the defined benefit plan.

In the 1940s, 1950s, and early 1960s, Wilson negotiated all labor agreements himself. (In the later years, he would turn the detailed negotiations over to Asher.) In contract negotiations, Wilson consistently insisted that the Amalgamated make a rational, factual, and logical case for each of its proposals. In the early 1950s, he consistently rejected one particular logic—using Eastman Kodak as a standard for comparison. Wilson simply did not consider Haloid in the same league with Kodak. But this changed as Haloid's position improved and by the mid-fifties, Wilson was ready to accept pay parity with Kodak as fair.

In 1955, Wilson agreed to a 5% pay increase and wrote the following to the Amalgamated's Abe Chatman:

It was a great pleasure for us to be able to respond to your points that the prosperity of Haloid warranted this improvement in our people's living standards. As we have said many times to you and your associates, it is our firm policy to maintain favorable conditions for our people when it is economically possible for us to do so. We are also happy to be able in this way to emphasize the fine relationship which, in our opinion, exists between the Union and Haloid. We are determined that this association shall be even more closely knit together as the years pass. I think the best proof of our intent here is that we are making this change now on a purely voluntary basis. Under these circumstances, our contract need not be modified in any other way if this is in accord with your understanding.

In return for this action on our part, we ask only that you and members of the Union cooperate with us fully in our determined effort to continue to make Haloid profitable. We pointed out to you in our discussions that the only reason which justifies our taking this action at this time is because the affairs of the Company are good. All of us would be blind if we did not also point out that several aggressive competitors are vigorously trying to take business from us. We can only remain profitable if every Haloid person will accept his responsibility to make a contribution toward more profit. We must be able to move ahead with new products, new processes, and new methods; and we are entering into this arrangement now because of your assurances that this need is fully recognized by you, your associates, and members of the Union.

In the entire field of Industrial Relations, it is our intention to do our very best to develop programs which are broadly useful to our people, to see that they are administered equitably, and yet to keep clearly in mind that the greatest benefit for everyone is to advance the interest and prosperity of the Company itself. Certainly it has been brought to all of us during the last five years of Haloid's increasing prosperity, that in no other comparable period of our history have we been able to do as much for our people as we have recently. There is only one reason for this. Haloid has been successful and, therefore, has benefits to share. This lesson, I hope, has been learned by all of us. I sincerely hope you keep it in mind as we ask you to undertake difficult but exciting tasks next year.

During Wilson's years, his company suffered only one labor strike. In that year, the company had actually been too effective in the negotiations and the union negotiators had settled for too low a wage increase. The workers voted against it and went out on strike. As a union leader, Abe Chatman was in a jam. As labor relations manager Bill Asher later recalled: "Chatman said, 'If you so much as *dare to increase your offer*, we'll never speak to you again!' " To sustain its credibility, the union would have to demonstrate that it had fought hard for an additional increase and won it.

On the other hand, Wilson was worried about having clerical and technical workers organized, so he worked out a reciprocal pledge with the union in the late 1950s: The union would not try to organize clerical and technical workers, and Haloid would not resist the union organizing all units doing work comparable to the work done by members of the bargaining unit. Wilson assured the union leaders: "We will not interfere with your right to organize workers in our other locations if they are doing work comparable to the bargaining unit here in Rochester. We will always inform the Amalgamated if we acquire or open an operation, and we will not interfere with the union's right to organize those units."

Wilson was particularly effective in negotiations, whether negotiating contract terms with the Amalgamated, patents with Battelle, or agreements with major companies. Unfailingly polite and unflappable, his friendly smile signaled a keen interest in the person-to-person understanding so often vital to successfully resolving important negotiations. Wilson was quick to focus on areas of mutual interest and possible cooperation, and would follow up with warm letters of appreciation that emphasized any areas in which actual progress had been made. As negotiations approached a conclusion, particularly in labor negotiations, Wilson typically sent a long letter enumerating the specific terms being agreed upon, with the benefits to each party clearly identified.

Fairness was so important to Wilson that he didn't simply wait like a judge for others to bring issues of fairness to him: He went looking for them. Again and again, he found them. In 1951, Joe Wilson asked Asher: "Bill, have you noticed that women only work in two areas of our company: They're either clerical or factory workers. We have no women who are executives or even in line to become executives. I think that's disgraceful. What do you think?" In a few weeks, Haloid hired a woman MBA who later went on to become a corporate officer. (Years later, another woman MBA, Anne Mulcahey, would become CEO of Xerox Corporation.)

Maintaining morale among managers as well as workers was a continuing and major challenge during the long years of tight cost controls and Spartan offices and manufacturing facilities; uncertainty and doubts about the chances of success expressed by Old Haloid hands; lots of new people joining, often in important new positions; and the constant pressure of striving to innovate in hundreds of different areas of manufacturing, design, and marketing.

Tension was a constant at Haloid. Committed young executives, engineers, and production workers, most of them new to the company and new to each other—and all experiencing rapid changes in their own jobs—were working very long hours. All were aware of the excitement of working to create a major technological revolution and very aware of the anxieties of knowing they had taken on a major challenge without knowing exactly how to overcome it. With little knowledge of the problems facing other work groups, each individual unit naturally saw its own priorities as *the* priorities and seldom showed much appreciation for other units' problems, triumphs, or failures. Understandably, in these stressful circumstances, tempers flared and things were said that increased the friction and seriously threatened to impede overall progress.

Wilson organized a series of personality and leadership tests, took them himself, and asked all the senior executives to do the same. Wilson's ratings were by far the highest. Next came Jack Rutledge, a Mensa with an IQ of 160. After that there was a significant space before the others' scores.

R utledge was smart, tough, and effective. He understood the issues and had great capacity for hard work and the ambition to become CEO.[7] "Jack had an idea a minute—and two or three a day were really good ones," recalled David Curtin. "Very creative."

Rutledge built the Haloid sales force into one of America's most effective sales organizations. This required fighting on two fronts. First, he had to clean out the many people who couldn't do the new kind of work, but were still on the payroll. This was particularly hard because Wilson couldn't bear to fire anyone, leaving Rutledge alone with a task he hated doing. However, in a few years, Rutledge replaced virtually all the old salespeople and *every* branch manager. Yet, in keeping with Wilson's policies, these men were not terminated. They were transferred to other positions, making the work even harder for Rutledge.

At the same time, Rutledge had to find and hire the many new people the company really needed. As Curtin remembered, "It's hard enough to hire lots of good men, but it's really hard when they can see that the guys you've got are second rate and really worry about maybe joining a group of losers. But Jack did it." Rutledge's sales organization increased very rapidly—in one year by more than 40%—

---

[7]In addition, he was very aware of turf, territory, and power. In 1957, Dave Curtin was on the West Coast, which was Rutledge territory. Curtin was greeted with considerable suspicion. However, over a few weeks of sales visits, Rutledge and Curtin got to know and like each other. It helped that they had both been at Okinawa—one in the Navy and one as a marine.

while the service organization doubled in size. Impressed by all he was achieving, a reporter from *Fortune* asked Jack Rutledge: "What do you do in your spare time?" His blunt reply: "I sleep."

Rutledge was brilliant and decisive. If he could have built close relationships with other executives, he might have been a natural for CEO. But he turned increasingly to liquor to get respite from the continuous emotional strains of being known as "the hatchet man" and the stress of being on the road all the time, traveling all over America as he fired and hired—and hired some more—salesmen. Drinking with others and then drinking alone, Rutledge soon became a heavy drinker. "We're *all* alcoholics in our family!" explained Rutledge's brother and he knew what he was talking about. In time, lunch for Rutledge would regularly include two martinis—and sometimes three. The pills Rutledge took for high blood pressure mixed badly with the alcohol. And this combination mixed very badly with his anxieties about public speaking.

Once when told that he would be introducing Joe Wilson at a large gathering in San Francisco. Rutledge was seized with fear and shuddered, "Oh no!" But there was no way out. He was told that he must. So Rutledge rose, nervously fingering the microphone, and wishing he were safely back in Rochester, forced himself to go ahead, completely blowing it by saying in his rich, deep voice, "We're delighted to be here with all you Angelenos." The crowd of proud San Franciscans hissed. Luckily, Joe Wilson converted the dreadful moment into something of a joke and broke the tension, but the event added to the barriers already accumulating to block Rutledge's career and seriously limit Wilson's eventual choice of a successor.

"Joe really was terribly straight-laced *almost* all the time," recalled Dave Curtin. "The exception—once each year at the two-to-three-day planning conference, usually held at Niagara Falls—was a traditional game of craps, a complete break from the rigors of work because playing with dice was impossible to intellectualize. Craps began as a safety valve, and then with time, became a 'cult' game within the company." Recalled Curtin, "The only thing that got Joe

The Xeroprinter being demonstrated by John H. Dessauer, Haloid's research head, Chester Carlson, and Haloid President Joseph C. Wilson (circa 1948). (*Photo credit:* Photograph provided for use by Xerox Historical Archives. The original owner of the photograph is unknown.)

Joe Wilson at the 914 manufacturing assembly line, Orchard Street, Rochester, New York (circa 1960). (*Photo credit:* Provided courtesy of Xerox Corporation.)

The 1952 Haloid Annual Picnic. L–R: John M. Hayashi, Joe Wilson, and an unidentified person. (*Photo credit:* Photograph provided for use by Xerox Historical Archives. The original owner of the photograph is unknown.)

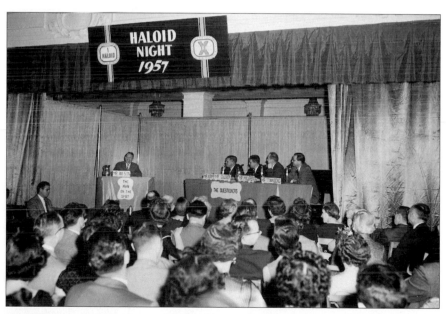

Joe Wilson, "Man on the Spot," during a "Haloid Meets Its Owners" question-and-answer program that was part of the annual open house activities for Haloid employees and their families at Haloid Night, March 2, 1957. The questioners were Braman Adams (Adams & Peck, New York City), Allan Gulliver (Merrill Lynch, Pierce, Fenner & Beane, New York City), Hanry Maijgren (Assistant Treasurer, The University of Rochester, Rochester, New York), and Edward Townsend (Vice President, The First Boston Corporation, New York City). (*Photo credit:* Provided courtesy of Xerox Corporation.)

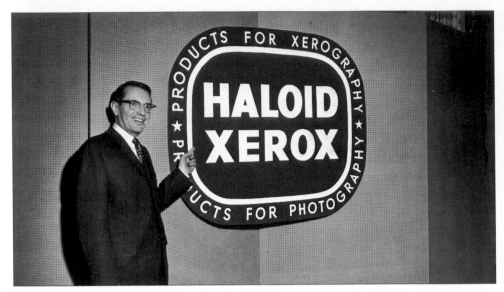

Joe Wilson with a sample of the proposed trademark that was displayed to employees during Haloid Xerox Night, February 15, 1958. On April 15, 1958, Haloid shareholders voted and the name of the company became Haloid Xerox Inc. (*Photo credit:* Provided courtesy of Xerox Corporation.)

Joe Wilson and Sol M. Linowitz, 56th Annual Meeting, May 1, 1962, held at the Distribution Center, Xerox Webster Plant Site, Webster, New York. (*Photo credit:* Louis Ouzer.)

L–R: C. Peter McColough, Sol M. Linowitz, John H. Dessauer, Joseph C. Wilson (date unknown). (*Photo credit*: Robert Isear.)

Board of Director's Meeting 1962 (?). Joe Wilson speaking with Herman M. Cohn. (*Photo credit*: Henry Grossman.)

Joe Wilson at the introduction of the Xerox Magnafax Telecopier, also known as the Telecopier I. This joint venture between Xerox and The Magnavox Company resulted in the first non-xerographic desktop fax machine capable of sending and receiving documents over any distance using a regular telephone. Television coverage was set up at both the Los Angeles and New York Hiltons for this coast-to-coast demonstration of the product in April of 1966. (*Photo credit*: Provided courtesy of Xerox Corporation.)

In the Academic Procession to Commencement Exercises, Harvard University, June 15, 1967, are (front to rear, left to right): Professor Randall Thompson, faculty escort, and Leonard Bernstein, honorary degree recipient; Dean George P. Baker, faculty escort, and Joseph C. Wilson, honorary degree recipient. (*Photo credit*: Photograph provided for use by Xerox Historical Archives. The original owner of the photograph is unknown.)

Mrs. Dorris Carlson (left) and Mrs. Marie Curran Wilson (Peggy) (right) next to a replica of Mr. Carlson's first xerographic apparatus. Picture was taken at Firsts in Xerography: Technology, Archeology and Art, an RIT/Xerox exhibit held at the City Center of Rochester Institute of Technology, October–November 1981. (*Photo credit:* Photograph provided for use by Xerox Historical Archives. The original owner of the photograph is unknown.)

Joseph C. Wilson, Mr. Wilson's grandfather and former mayor of Rochester, New York. (*Photo credit:* Photograph provided for use by Xerox Historical Archives. The original owner of the photograph is unknown.)

truly excited was the game of craps!" Names were coined and took on insider significance. Curtin was Big Zeus while Wilson was El Supremo.

Once when Wilson had had much too much to drink during a relaxing evening of shooting craps after a planning conference, he was heading for the bathroom. He tried to pass a "boxed" column that had mirrors on all four sides, but bumped pretty hard into the column, looked up and, mistaking his own image in the mirror for another person, apologized politely, "Oh, I'm terribly sorry," before walking on.

Wilson rarely also caused tension. As an October planning conference was winding down over cocktails, Dave Curtin and Don Clark launched into a soft-shoe dance and patter song written especially for that occasion, called "No Poon at All." Each verse won more and more laugher. When it finished, Wilson cheerfully called for a repeat. But during the encore, Damon and McColough began playing with sugar cubes as though they were dice, an obvious signal that they wanted to start up the now traditional game of craps. Wilson was miffed by their distraction and began to lecture them about cooperation and fairness. Then, recognizing the increasing flush on McColough's face, Wilson changed course and challenged him to a game of craps. Fortunately, Wilson lost.

16

GOING INTERNATIONAL

Technologies show little respect for national borders. The better the technologies, the faster they disperse around the world, which is why Wilson had to move quickly to internationalize Haloid's business to keep ahead of rapidly globalizing demand and to preempt potential competition. Otherwise, indigenous companies in the major national markets would inevitably find ways to produce copiers to meet local demand in their respective home markets. And, if given the chance to establish a home-market base, they would surely launch competitive initiatives into other countries, even into North America, Xerox's home territory (which is exactly what several Japanese companies would do in years later).

Wilson understood that if it were only exporting from America, Haloid would, in nation after nation, encounter serious problems such as complex trade restrictions and regulations, plus all the obvious difficulties of building a large international sales and servicing organization. Haloid needed to become established overseas, particularly in Europe, and the only feasible way to do this was to combine with strong partners who could sell, service, and manufacture xerographic equipment and reduce the demands on Haloid for management and capital. In 1953, agreement was reached with Adressograph-Multigraph that it would sell xerographic products outside North America. However, as natural as this linkage appeared at that early time—because plate makers were a natural add-on to A.M.'s product line—results were disappointing and the venture was abandoned.

As he considered other ways of expanding internationally, Wilson had a three-phase strategic challenge:

- First, establish a strong "first-mover" advantage and market position, particularly in nations with major domestic market potential such as Japan, England, Germany, France, and Brazil.
- Second, establish substantial market share in all the major markets to prevent any local competitors from gaining enough of a beachhead to be able to attack Haloid's product line and pricing structure.
- Third, be sure Haloid itself developed the most advanced products in order to preclude potential competitors from developing a new or improved technology that might somehow leapfrog xerography.

With such major strategic challenges before him, Wilson recognized that Haloid's resources were far too small to expand sufficiently rapidly into a series of major overseas markets on its own. Haloid did not have, and could not get, all the money that would be needed to finance overseas manufacturing facilities, nor could it afford the heavy cost of building a major sales and service organization in each national market. Challenged as it was in America to expand sufficiently in managerial capability in order to stay on top of its accelerating business, Wilson knew that Haloid could not even think of taking on the considerable management challenges of operating effectively in a series of major international markets. Haloid would need help—a lot of help—in international marketing, manufacturing, and finance.

Linowitz cautiously wondered why Haloid should take all the risk and go to all the trouble of developing its own channels of distribution, so he proposed inviting IBM and RCA to bid for the international rights to distribute xerographic products, particularly Copyflo and the nascent office copier. As Linowitz saw reality, Europe was large and complex, comprising many nations with different currencies, taxes, import constraints, business customs, distribution systems, and marketing practices. And after Europe, would come Asia, the Middle East, South America, and Africa. Such international giants as IBM and RCA had already mastered the necessary complexities of building and managing international marketing and manufacturing organizations in their existing businesses and were already well-established with strong finances. Besides, nobody at Haloid had any experience in international business, and Wilson had never been abroad.

Wilson understood the risks, but after his typically careful consideration of Linowitz's cautious proposal, he quietly and firmly rejected it. This was no time to give away international opportunity and certainly no time to bring giant competitors such as IBM and RCA into Haloid's fledgling business.

Wilson recognized, of course, that he and Haloid had no experience in Europe, so, in a familiar pattern of seeking the advice of experts, he turned to a specialist consultant, Fenton Turek, an expert on marketing in Europe. Turek's report outlined a comprehensive ten-step program, but Wilson wanted to move much faster and felt that Turek's report contained disappointingly little he did not already know, so he simply decided to skip most of the time-consuming, deliberate steps in Turek's handsomely printed report. Wilson would go to Europe himself so he could explore directly the possibilities of either establishing wholly owned subsidiaries or joint venturing with local business-equipment companies in the United Kingdom, Germany, and the Netherlands.

By coincidence, the Rank Organization's local representative in America knew of London's interest in acquisition opportunities, and had written a very favorable memo on Haloid to his superiors. When Tom Law, the amiable managing director of a subsidiary,

Rank Precision Industries, was in Chicago, Bell & Howell CEO Charles Percy suggested he visit Haloid.[1] Law recalled the favorable memo and decided on his way back to London to stop off in Rochester to meet Joe Wilson. Law and Wilson charmed each other as both recognized the other's unusual capabilities. As he left Rochester, Law extended an invitation to demonstrate xerography to Rank's senior executives: "I believe our Board chairman, John Davis would be interested. Of course, I cannot promise anything but a warm welcome. But if that attracts you, please do come to England."[2]

It wasn't much, but it was enough for Wilson to accept and boldly promise that two months later, xerography would be demonstrated in London. Those two months were kept very busy: Wilson sent an assistant to New York City to research the names, addresses, and officers of two to three possible partners in each European country; scheduled a 30-day trip for May 1955; organized a team of engineers and technicians to assure a successful demonstration; and hoping serious business discussions might develop, asked Linowitz to go with him. He got letters of introduction from Tom Gates of the Morgan Bank and Tom Watson of IBM and wrote letters to both Tom Law and John Davis projecting how much he and his team were looking forward to their visit. An advance man was sent to London to scout out the right location for several days of demonstrations—he chose the Hotel Picadilly ballroom—and a large supply of spare parts were gathered up and shipped to London, along with the transformers needed to adapt to England's 50-cycle 220-volt electrical system.

Leaving North America in the spring of 1955—each for the very first time, the Wilsons and Linowitzes steamed out of New York harbor aboard the *SS United States*, heading for England and then on to the Continent. Their intention was to partner with one company in

---

[1]Pell, page 80.
[2]Dessauer, page 102.
[3]One possibility was a major company in Aschaffenburg, Germany, run by John Dessauer's brother.

Britain and another on the European mainland,[3] but three dozen company visits would make it discouragingly clear that a not-yet developed, expensive machine based on a new technology and requiring several million dollars of up-front investment was not a compelling business proposition. It wasn't even interesting—at least not to most corporations.

But one company *was* interested: Tom Law's employer, Britain's Rank Organization. Rank had the organization and the ability to commit ample funding for manufacturing, sales, and service—not just for England, but for all of Europe—so the Picadilly Hotel demonstration would be crucial.

Best known in North America for its J. Arthur Rank films and best known in England for its chain of movie theaters, Rank was moving away from films and the movie theaters that had been lucrative cash cows during and immediately following the war when even mediocre films gave Britons at least some entertainment. (In 1947, the British Government, concerned about a balance of payments crisis, had imposed very heavy duties on foreign films, which had been supplying 70% of British screen time. The import duties created a void that British film-makers filled with cheap, shabby films. In response to wide public protest, the import duties were eliminated in the early 1950s and the stop-gap, British-made films were suddenly valueless.)

As movie audiences shrank and ticket sales plummeted, the fixed operating costs of theaters pushed Rank into increasingly serious losses.[4] By the mid-fifties, Rank was determined to get out of the movie business as quickly as possible and into growth businesses. John Davis took charge of the massive strategic transformation and went looking for new technology-based businesses to acquire with the cash created by liquidating Rank's old film and theater business. He was intrigued by Tom Law's report on Haloid.

At the Picadilly Hotel demonstration, a sensible precaution

[4]These losses accumulated to £8 million over just three years.

nearly resulted in a Copyflo disaster. A final test was run. Instead of producing a copy, it produced a fire—still a frequent problem—and acrid smoke quickly filled the room. In less than an hour, Davis and Law were scheduled to arrive. Windows were thrown open to clear the smoke and burnt parts were feverishly replaced. Five minutes before Davis and Law were to walk in, the smoke was gone, the equipment repaired, and Wilson and his team were set to go—but just barely.

Davis and Law entered, smiling from under their bowler hats, exchanged greetings, inspected the demonstration machines, and then watched the demonstration. Davis and Law limited their appraisal to one repeated word. "Quite. Quite." The meaning was unclear and would stay unclear after they left, again saying "Quite!" Were they really interested?

Fortunately, Davis was very interested, and the next day, he invited Wilson and Linowitz to confer in his office. As Linowitz recalled, "Joe was concerned that we might scare them off by appearing to want much more than they were ready to contribute. And with good reason. Ours was a baby not yet born because we only had the one process and it was not very developed."[5]

Negotiations between Haloid and Rank continued over several months and several trans-Atlantic trips that culminated in an historic meeting held in Davis's enormous Edwardian office in London.[6] Wilson wanted Rank to make a major capital investment of $1.5 million. Wilson also wanted a major share in European profits. Davis wanted Rank to have full rights to all 129 xerographic patents. Davis also wanted the marketing rights everywhere outside of North America. Since Rank was rich in cash, Davis was ready to put up all the money needed—$2.5 million—for half the profits. Wilson countered that if and when profits rose to a higher level than

[5]Linowitz, page 72.
[6]An alternative, proposed by Bernard Mason with backing by Sir Harold Webb, to put up half the capital to establish Haloid-Xerox Ltd., failed to materialize.

projected, the patents contributed by Haloid would have proven more important than the capital contributed by Rank. Davis suggested a two-thirds share to Haloid above £600,000; Wilson countered with a threshold at £500,000. After several hours of discussion, Davis sighed in frustration: "Oh, for heaven's sake, let's toss a coin and have done with it!" Wilson shrugged, "Why not?"

Davis took a shilling from his pants pocket and tossed it into the air: "Call!"

"Heads."

The shilling landed, rolled and fell—tails.

"Gentlemen," announced Davis solemnly, "England wins."

Davis won the coin toss for Rank, but the business grew so rapidly that Haloid was the real winner. The joint-venture company was informally agreed upon on December 19, 1956, and two months later, John Davis decided to visit Rochester, accompanied by his financial adviser Ronald G. Leach. "We took a train," Leach later explained, "because we had never been through New York State. We wanted to see the countryside from a train window. It was beautiful. But we were hardly prepared for the kind of reception that waited us in Rochester."

After a six-hour train ride from New York City, they were met at the platform in Rochester by Joe Wilson and Sol Linowitz and a TV camera crew. Linowitz insisted the visitors repeat getting off the train because their first "arrival" had not been correctly recorded. (Always attentive to publicity and appearances, Linowitz had arranged the coverage for the evening news on the Rochester TV station that carried his weekly interview program.)

Davis was a guest at the Wilson's home where, when not in serious meetings, Davis and Leach teamed up to play croquet against Linowitz and Wilson. At a dollar a game, the British side won enough for Davis to make cheerful reference to improving the balance of payments between their two countries. More importantly, John Davis got to know Joe Wilson. "I still hadn't the foggiest idea of whether Haloid's machine would really work well, but what I did

know was that this man, Joe Wilson, was a person of utter integrity—
simple, direct, truthful. One could do business with him with complete confidence in his word. Ronald Leach shared that feeling. I
have sometimes felt that my admiration for Joe had more to do with
the creation of Rank-Xerox than my confidence in his product."

Croquet was not the only game being played. "Occasionally,"
recalled Davis, "when I spoke of going out to see the factory in
which the machines were being manufactured, Joe quickly suggested another game of croquet. If it wasn't that, there was invariably someone he wanted me to meet. After a few days, when we still
hadn't seen the plant, I awoke to a revealing truth and said to Joe,
'You don't *have* a factory, do you?' He grinned broadly and answered,
'So, you've found me out!'"

Davis was not long concerned. As he soon learned, Haloid's
plant was still producing photographic products and the rather simple xerographic device was just an assembly of parts made by subcontractors, so Haloid didn't really need a manufacturing plant.

Wilson's engaging personality was key to attracting Davis, and
Wilson's modesty was important to his not being put off by Davis—
who saw himself as a Very Great Man—and saw Wilson as a small
town guy who was suddenly thrust onto the world stage. For all his
grand boldness in demeanor, John Davis—later Sir John—did not
appreciate what xerography could become. He badly underestimated the potential, and as Haloid progressed, his initial underesti-
mation became more and more serious. Thinking he'd dabble by
putting in just a few pounds, Davis had unwittingly given the store
away in the joint venture negotiations. Wilson later decided that
the agreements would have to be renegotiated for the long-term
success of the joint venture, not because the terms were too good
for Davis's company, but because they were too good for Wilson's
company.

Rank-Xerox was officially formed on May 1, 1957, with $3.3 mil-
lion capitalization, and Wilson and Linowitz were soon back in
London for the first meeting of the board of directors. (They went

by ship because Peggy Wilson was uncomfortable flying.) The sense of adventure and wonder that Joe Wilson felt as the international expansion of Rank-Xerox unfolded was evident in his reports to his company:

> A bright sun was slanting down on *The United States*, as she paused last April 23rd to pick up the pilot a few miles from Southampton. With that pause began for Sol Linowitz and me, as well as our wives, the most exciting and stimulating time of our lives.
>
> On the pilot boat were two emissaries of The Rank Organization, our partners in the exploitation of xerography overseas. They had flowers for the ladies and a magic wand to whisk us through customs and onto the boat train. We arrived a little later at the Dorchester Hotel in London where more flowers and hospitality of the most pleasant kind were awaiting us in our rooms. The next day, Sol and I began a round of inspections and meetings which caused our enthusiasm for this partnership to climb steadily.

Obviously impressed, Wilson reported: "In some ways, the climax came on Friday when over three hundred people from all branches of British industry and government attended a luncheon at Grosvenor House, one of the large London hotels. The function was given by Rank-Xerox and it was done impeccably. My job was to convince these people that xerography has some kind of future."

Wilson was comparably excited in his reports on his following visit to Germany's Hanover Fair, the most important West European business fair: "Throughout these visits, it was exciting for Sol and me to read the story of xerography written in German, French, and Italian; to hear people bursting with interest in it; and to realize that throughout Western Europe now, thanks to the extraordinarily good promotion of The Rank Organization, this word—xerography— already means something."

Despite Wilson's considerable enthusiasm, the marriage with Rank had not been made in heaven and did not always run smoothly. Rank-Xerox was losing money due to lack of demand both for flat plate machines and for Copyflo. Davis and Law, were understandably impressed—unfavorably—by the lack of acceptance of Copyflo in the U.K. and on the Continent, and therefore were quite unsure of the market potential for an office copier. At the same time, Wilson had reason to be concerned about progress at Rank-Xerox. Rank had two different divisions in separate locations with different managements and separate accounting, so they often argued over the allocation of costs of design changes in the machines. Some difficulties were more embarrassing than expensive. When Rank-Xerox began marketing the 914 copier, they discovered, after the first dozen units had been shipped, that the doorways to British offices were smaller than the doorways to U.S. offices and the machine would have to be recalled and downsized—not enough to force redesign of the interior mechanism, but enough to be costly and unnerving for John Davis.

As usual with joint ventures, there were misunderstandings on both sides. In London, John Davis was concerned about Haloid's concentration on the large and costly 914 when the apparent demand in Europe was for small, cheap, desktop copiers, and a European marketing survey had produced very discouraging estimates of demand for the 914.[7] But Davis's opinion of the 914 shifted favorably as success after success accumulated in the United States, and he eventually became so optimistic that he asked Wilson to explore with Battelle the possibility of Rank acquiring Battelle's shares. While not expecting any interest at Battelle, Wilson agreed

[7]IBM was known to be considering getting involved in marketing—and maybe manufacturing—the 914 in Europe through its international company, IBM World Trade. Meeting with IBM's James Birkenstock in New York City, Wilson explained that Haloid would market in the U.S. and Canada on its own, but IBM World Trade would have to negotiate with Rank-Xerox on overseas business.

to raise the question during one of his trips to Columbus. No sale. Battelle was quite happy with its shareholding and expected to exercise all of its stock options.

To assure sufficient financial strength for the long term, Wilson proposed a solution for a nagging dispute with the Rank Organization over the proper financing of the development of the joint venture. After Rank had completed its initial investment in Rank-Xerox, Wilson offered two possible solutions, giving Davis the choice between a 50/50 split in financial support and share of profits or a 60/40 split in both support and profits up to an £800,000 investment level. Wilson reasoned that either plan would impel Rank-Xerox to press ahead promptly with the manufacturing and marketing he felt were sorely needed to assure the 914's success in Europe. Davis opted for 50/50.

In the spring of 1958, Wilson and Linowitz went to London for the Rank-Xerox Board meeting and a leisurely day visiting Davis's home in Kent, where they again played croquet. Then in September, Tom Law visited Rochester, and one week later, Wilson and Linowitz returned to London. In October, Linowitz was again in London as part of a series of ten monthly meetings to accelerate progress at Rank-Xerox. In addition, Wilson sought to take direct responsibility for Japan and Latin America, but Davis "all but slammed the door" on these changes. Later, Davis would relent on Latin America in exchange for an increase of two percentage points in Rank's share of Rank-Xerox profits. (The long and intense trips abroad were particularly strenuous for Wilson. He continued to suffer from angina far more than he would acknowledge.)

In their negotiations, Davis would try to exploit Wilson's good nature and his desire always to have amicable relations and avoid interpersonal controversy. Linowitz said he felt he should stay with Davis and Wilson after dinner, because they would go out for a drink and start talking about a major issue, such as the division of profits earned by Rank-Xerox. In such a situation, Wilson would so want to reach a positive compromise that he might overreach: "We *could* increase the sharing point by £100,000." Davis would deliberately say nothing, staring dourly back until, to break the silent tension, Wilson would say, "Well, John, if *that's* not satisfactory, we could go up £200,000."

Wilson was increasingly recognized abroad for the leadership he was already so well-recognized for in the United States. While internally proud of his growing recognition as a business leader, Wilson was careful to share the spotlight with his associates. When Davis invited him to join the Board of Directors of the Rank Organization, he was privately delighted, but said nothing in Rochester, and wrote to Davis urging him to be sure any announcement recognized the important contributions to the development of xerography that had been made by Carlson, Dessauer, and Linowitz.[8]

J oe Wilson's vision and enthusiasm combined with his appreciation of the power of inspiring symbols. He made a striking proposition at the 1958 planning conference, when Haloid had just set a sales record of $25 million. Already thinking of Haloid as an international enterprise, Wilson suddenly announced, "When our sales reach $100 million, our *next* year's planning conference will be held . . . in . . . London!"

Despite genial "Oh, sure" smiles and friendly applause, almost no one took Wilson's promise too seriously. But Wilson *was* serious. And as Wilson spoke, the idea of going to Europe caught Bill Asher's imagination. In 1962, during a discussion of wages, Joe Wilson opined: "I guess a company that's about to break through $100 million in sales can afford to consider a generous wage settlement," and Asher reminded Wilson of his earlier offer to celebrate in Europe. That afternoon, Dave Raub got a request from Joe to think ahead on just how that year's planning conference could be held in Europe. (Ironically, because the salary level cut-off was one notch above his, Asher would not be going to London.)

[8]McKelvey, VIII, page 31.

The trip to London was, of course, a major event: 50 couples would be in London together for three days. Knowing that most of his colleagues had never been to Europe, and that such long distance travel was expensive, Wilson encouraged everyone to consider taking their annual two weeks' vacation as a private extension to the group trip to London. At Wilson's careful direction, extra efforts were made in preparation to assure success. Peggy Wilson and Toni Linowitz hosted a tea for the Xerox wives at the Wilson home. There, they explained what to expect in London: Ladies always wore hats; as many as six or seven wine glasses would be used at a formal dinner; buttons would be found on the bedside telephones in hotel rooms to call for valets, maids, and room service—so the ladies should have some fun and use them. Pictures were taken of each of the wives so they and their husbands could learn everyone's names and connect names with faces. Haloid printed 3" × 8" guidebooks with these pictures of the executives facing their wives with short position descriptions under the men's pictures and home addresses under the women's. Each person was given a travel kit with such items as Dramamine, Aspirin, and Band-Aids.

Wilson was careful as usual about planning ahead. Knowing that this would be the first trip to Europe for nearly the entire group, he sent a memo around to his young "innocents abroad" colleagues, noting that they would be meeting many new people who would naturally be watching them closely, and recommended that since wine would be served at dinner, everyone should be careful to take only one cocktail during the reception before dinner.

Once in London, planning meetings were held each day, with entertainment during the evenings: theater with very good seats as Rank's special guests one night, and on another, the Americans dined in the homes of their British counterparts. Walking the streets of London, stopping in at pubs, riding the underground, and seeing St. Paul's, Buckingham Palace, and London's red double-decker buses were both fun and memorable. Several of the Upstaters saw former Prime Minister Anthony Eden give a street-corner speech in his district, handling Labor and Communist hecklers with skill and aplomb. All this was capped by a formal dinner at the Houses of Parliament.

On the next night, Rank hosted a major black tie banquet in the Dorchester Room of the Dorchester Hotel. Long tables were covered in dark blue, green, and red felt. Candelabras were filled with lighted candles. And centerpieces for the tables were composed of wooden Beefeater dolls that had been specially made at Rank's Pinewood Studios. As each couple entered, the master of ceremonies, in a full, deep voice, boomed out his formal announcement of the couple's names.

Some guests had their own tuxedos, while others wore tuxedos that Rank rented for the occasion. Of course, the rental tuxedos were British in design, so the Americans found them unfamiliarly tight and stiff. Dinner began with a large plate of lobster bisque. Unfortunately, Dave Curtin's black tie had two characteristics: It was quite flared, and it was a clip-on. As he began to eat his bisque, the clip-on tie fell off—and into the tureen of bisque. Curtin recalls with a laugh, "Ladies of the aristocracy on my left and right were quite solicitous. They fetched the tie out of the bisque, cleaned it up quickly, and helped me put it back on."[9]

Bold as Wilson's drive to go international clearly was, back home he was looking for a strategic partner—because he needed help.

[9]Haloid provided the opportunity for many new experiences. Joe Wilson and Dave Curtin were on the first jet liner flight from Los Angeles to New York City, but the flight's take off was delayed for three hours while a fighter jet dashed to Seattle to get a missing part.

17

GOING IT ALONE

By early 1958, Joe Wilson was again looking for a corporate partner. Once again, he focused on IBM. Wilson worried that Haloid just didn't have enough money to do all the things he wanted to do nor all that he believed Haloid should do. He was also concerned that Haloid did not have all the capabilities it needed. Aware of the costs and risks he was facing, Wilson went back into discussions with IBM, hoping to organize a joint venture to which Haloid would contribute its patents and designs and IBM would contribute its great manufacturing and marketing capabilities.

Both IBM and Haloid now knew more. Haloid now recognized that manufacturing and marketing a high-volume copier would seriously overload its financial and organizational resources *and* its production and management capabilities. IBM was now convinced that a xerographic copier was quite feasible, and had even completed the design for a copier that would be positioned between the 914 and the already planned 813 desktop copier.[1]

This time, IBM proposed it would make and market xerographic copiers with the IBM logo. Again Haloid declined. Then IBM's negotiators proposed that Haloid take up the design IBM had developed

[1]Pell, page 97.

for a mid-sized copier. They gratuitously adding several disparaging evaluations of Haloid's manufacturing capabilities, apparently as a negotiating "stick" to go with the "carrot" of cooperation with Big Blue.

The strategic attraction for IBM was clear: IBM dominated the business equipment industry worldwide, and IBM's electric typewriter division—with its ubiquitous salesmen in dark blue suits, white shirts and "rep" ties, calling regularly on thousands of companies—dominated the office equipment industry. IBM's Watson was looking for more products than just typewriters to distribute through his sales organization The costs of having that organization in place were relatively fixed so incremental sales from a new line of copiers would add nicely to corporate profits *and* increase compensation for the salesmen.

IBM's Birkenstock, in his always paternal way, claimed he was trying to help the young Haloid executives. He wanted them to recognize how far over its head Haloid would be getting if it launched a new kind of product competing directly against the industry giants. The worldwide business equipment market was huge, fast-changing and very uncertain. Technological breakthroughs were to be expected, and they could come from virtually anywhere. Price competition could and would be rough. Haloid would be in a perpetual competitive war that the larger corporations could not afford to lose. Haloid would be very wise to go into this treacherous market with a friend—a very good, very big friend. "You have no abilities in manufacturing and very little experience in marketing," counseled Birkenstock. "So here's the best way forward for you: We'll manufacture the machines and take care of all the direct marketing *and* split the revenues with you 50/50 *if* you can just wait until we size the market."

"OK," said Wilson, "We'll listen." Always deliberate and shrewdly cautious, Wilson was looking for ways to minimize the risks taken by Haloid and was well aware of the enormous risks involved in going ahead all alone with a completely new business venture. IBM's electric typewriter division was cautious too, and wanted to do market research before making a major commitment. Because IBM's in-house market research group was too busy in 1959 to take on the assignment,

IBM decided to commission Arthur D. Little, Inc. to study the market potential. To assure the validity of the market research, Haloid agreed to give Arthur D. Little access to the detailed design characteristics planned for both the 914 and 813 copiers. (The 914 was planned as a large console machine while the much smaller 813 would sit on a desktop.) In return, IBM agreed to share with Haloid the results of the Arthur D. Little study.

Arthur D. Little's market demand study took nearly a year to complete. The results were presented in December 1958.[2] Based on interviews with 80 large potential users, the study's conclusions were summarized in a cover letter that recommended IBM "terminate consideration of the 914 as a new market opportunity" and further concluded that the "813 is not a good market risk."

Arthur D. Little's report provided a dismal appraisal of the market for the 914, concluding:

- There was no trend toward centralized copying.
- The 914 was too big and cumbersome for normal office use.
- The 914 would often need its own separate room and such rooms were seldom available.
- Considerable market development expenditure would be required.
- IBM's electric typewriter division was not equipped to sell such a large and cumbersome machine; its salesmen were used to carrying 30-pound typewriters into customers' offices, *not* 650-pound copiers.
- The 914 was far too costly to be competitive with products already on the market.
- Direct copying had little if any recognizable advantage over duplicating, which was clearly faster.

[2]"Investigation of Two Haloid-Xerox Machines as New Product Opportunities in the Office Reproducing Equipment Field," Report to International Business Machines Corporation by Arthur D. Little, Inc., December 1, 1958 [C-61613].

- Offset produced better quality when copy quality mattered.
- Decisively, very little interest in the proposed 914 had been shown in *any* of the interviews.

As for the 813, Arthur D. Little advised that since that machine was two years away from introduction, it must be anticipated that competitors' product improvements would by then almost certainly negate all of the 813's currently expected performance advantages. While an exception *might* be found in the high-volume segment of the market, total projected unit sales volume in that segment would be too limited for the company to achieve good profit margins. Bottom line: a very limited market, with total market demand of only a few thousand machines, so the whole initiative should be aborted—now.

After this report, IBM's experienced executives quickly lost interest. At the big Business Equipment Show at the Waldorf-Astoria in New York City, Tom Watson took Joe Wilson aside to tell him the bad news: IBM was no longer interested. (An IBM marketing survey in Europe, where IBM had been considering getting involved in marketing and possibly manufacturing the 914, had also produced very discouraging conclusions regarding potential demand for the 914.) James Birkenstock strongly advised Haloid executives to forget their office copier dreams.

Haloid's only real hope was that the Arthur D. Little study was wrong.

The impact of Arthur D. Little's assessment was all the more powerful because it was essentially in line with the conclusions of Stewart, Dougall & Associates, a Park Avenue consulting firm Haloid had hired earlier in the year to conduct a similar study: That study concluded the 914's potential was "extremely limited" as no more than a very specialized machine. Then Haloid had commissioned yet another study by Ernst & Ernst, and its conclusions were only slightly more favorable. If the volume estimates coming from these three studies were right, Haloid's massive investments in xerography might *never* be recovered.

Wilson kept shaking his head and saying, "I cannot believe it. *I simply cannot believe it.*"[3]

Joe Wilson's intuition was right. All three studies were wrong—very wrong.

Only 20/20 hindsight would enable anyone to recognize why these studies were so far in error. In 1958, everyone *knew* that "copies" meant either very low volume carbon-paper copies or high volume duplicating. Nobody loved using carbon paper because it was difficult to use, particularly for multiple copies. Duplicating was messy work—and it was exacting: Masters had to be typed error-free, so even small typing mistakes could mean a complete reworking was necessary. That's why people answering Arthur D. Little's questions and Ernst & Ernst's questions were mentally anchored in their own personal experience, which was soon to be completely obsolete. Demand for multiple copies *was* limited, particularly demand for five, ten, or 15 copies, given the way office work was being done at that time with messy, tedious *carbon* copies.

Arthur D. Little had also made a classic mistake in designing its market research. They studied the demand for copies at the point of *origin*, not at the point of *receipt*, which is where the real demand potential might have been recognized. As the Arthur D. Little researchers oriented their study, they were really studying the demand for carbon paper and carbon copies *and* how many customers would be willing to pay more than $10,000 for an unfamiliar machine that could serve as an alternative to *carbon* copies. The answers to those questions were clearly negative.

The market standard copier was Kodak's: It sold for only $350, was a proven product, and came from one of American's most admired companies. As a competitor, Haloid would face the daunting problem of being compared to that standard. The 914, as planned, was huge—so where would users put it? Even worse, the cost of Haloid's large machine seemed very high. Purchasing agents who specialized in buy-

---

[3]Dessauer, page 89.

ing paper, pencils, and staples in $50 or $100 orders *might* spend $350 for a proven copier, but where would they get authorization to pay a price of, say, $10,000 just for a new kind of copier? And who would even consider paying so very much for a new kind of machine from a company no one has heard of? Realistically, nobody would even begin to consider paying nearly thirty *times* as much as the $350 that was widely accepted as the price for a good copier.

The obvious strategic response to purchase price "sticker shock" was, of course, familiar to IBM: leasing.[4] But leasing had two major problems. First, a lease really just spread the purchase price out over, say, five or ten years. Leasing changed the cash flow and protected the customer from the risk of technological obsolescence, but the customer would sooner or later still be paying the full purchase price plus financing costs, and would know at the start that he was making a very "big ticket" decision—for just a copier.

Leasing's second problem was that prospective customers would differ widely on how much they would each use the 914. At a fixed monthly lease rate—set at a level that would be "right" for average-volume users—high-volume users would be getting the bargain of a lot more copies than they would be paying for, so Haloid would be leaving money on the table. And low-volume prospects would never install the machines: For them, the cost–benefit ratio would be much too high. So, Haloid's situation looked pretty hopeless. The obvious decision was to give it up and quit—now.[5] But the *obvious* decision was not the *right* decision.

Fortunately, Haloid asked for and got IBM's permission to interview the Arthur D. Little team that had done the market research,

---

[4]Leasing came to IBM from AT&T where Theodore Vail developed the concept of "renting" equipment to make it easier to become a customer than buying expensive gear.

[5]Howard P. Colhoun, Arthur D. Little's lead researcher in the photocopy industry, had been serving clients such as Polaroid, and Eastman Kodak as well as IBM and had been asked by Polaroid at about the same time to assess the potential demand for their instant cameras. Colhoun had reported to Polaroid that the demand for instant cameras was quite limited for several reasons: Polaroid's early cameras were

and Haloid learned a lot in these interviews. Given the way they had conducted their study and the way they had asked their questions, it was no surprise that they had arrived at their negative conclusions.

"If you accepted the validity of the way Arthur D. Little designed their study, you'd have to accept their conclusion," says John Glavin. But Glavin was sure he could interpret the data very differently, and as he did, he came to a very different conclusion.

As Haloid and Arthur D. Little researchers talked about the study, two important variables—which had *both* been left out of the discussion so far—became increasingly evident. First, Haloid was in an almost desperate situation: For Haloid, xerography was its one best chance of future *survival!* In contrast, all the other copier and

---

rather large and heavy, they produced only black and white prints; the process was neither familiar to nor convenient for users and it could be quite messy. Users were unsure of the results they would get. The Polaroid process was expensive. And Polaroid was as much of an unknown in the consumer photography market as Haloid was in the business equipment market. "As we now know," reflects Colhoun, "despite all those problems, Polaroid later developed a very big business with their cameras. The point is this: innovation is not static. It's *dynamic*—particularly if the technology is fertile and allows continuous progress!" After making his presentation of findings to Polaroid, Colhoun had been asked: "Young man, would you go ahead with this product?" Colhoun replied "That's not the question we were asked to research and answer, but I will answer your question if you will first answer one question for me: How much have you already spent versus how much more do you *expect* to spend?" The answer: 98% of the total had already been spent. Colhoun then continued. "If you have spent 98% and need only 2% more to be ready to go to market, then the answer to your strategic question is clear: Go!" Asked *why* he would go forward in spite of the grim picture produced by his research, Colhoun explained to the group at Polaroid: "I've been doing new product research in technology long enough to know how very hard it is for people, when looking at an unfamiliar and innovative new product, to answer the questions we or any one else can ask about what and how much they will buy. The potential customers simply can't anticipate Polaroid's camera being cheaper, smaller, lighter, easier to operate—or offering color. And they can't anticipate themselves becoming more experienced, skillful and comfortable as *users*. These dynamics can all be working favorably for you as the innovator. So the 98% already spent is *sunk cost* and it really only costs you 2% to complete the development and get to the market. Ask yourselves this question: To launch this product can Polaroid afford the 2%? *That's* your decision."

duplicating companies were being very protective of their *past* business—including Addressograph-Multigraph, which was already using xerography to make the plate masters. All of these other companies were making good or better profits on the many machines that they had installed over many years on long-term leases and for which they were now receiving monthly payments. So they naturally wanted to preserve their established ways of doing business. They saw the innovation of xerography as a threat to their existing businesses and to their companies, *not* as an opportunity.

The second factor was even more important. Wilson had played his cards close to the chest and had not told Arthur D. Little everything. The decisive factor in positioning the 914 was a major innovation in pricing.

Good ideas are, in retrospect, simple. And, in retrospect, the simplest ideas are often the very best ideas. And so it was with pricing at Haloid. Amidst all the complex struggles in developing xerographic technology, in financing a major corporate expansion, and in designing and manufacturing the 914, one simple idea virtually eliminated what would have been the most daunting problem in marketing the 914: sticker shock. The 914 machines would have cost far too much to purchase or lease. IBM was quite used to leasing, but at IBM, leasing was by the *year* so no one ever imagined leasing by the *copy*. Charging by the copy transformed the central question from "Will you pay $20,000?" to "Will you pay 5¢?"—and *that* truly transformed the business.

Joe Wilson's core insight said it all: "The machine is just a means to the end: The end is the *copy*—the visible print on a piece of paper!" Wilson's team transformed his business by understanding a simple but profoundly different way of defining Haloid's purpose and the business it would build. The *copy* is the product, *not* the machine. And the price was 5¢, not $20,000.

18

5¢

"Joe Wilson structured the corporate environment to provide overall guidelines and then devolved to others the responsibility for implementation," according to John Glavin. "He selected very good people and was a great motivator, drawing people out so they would really want to reach out *with* him."

Wilson was never particularly interested in the detailed work of managing implementation. The nitty-gritty often bored him. And he could get annoyed by anyone who really expected him to parse through all of the specific details of how to hire a 500-member sales force or 300 engineers for manufacturing. He expected others to work out the details of execution and believed that if you got the big picture right, the rest would naturally come along. At one year's planning conference, presentations were being made on the sequence of steps that would be followed to implement a major strategic program. After getting luncheon at a buffet table, Bill Asher happened to sit beside Wilson.

"Don't you think this morning's presentation went well, particularly the good homework done to work out the specifics of implementation of our major new initiative?"

Wilson turned, shook his head, and smiled: "I hate to admit it after what you just said, Bill, but I find all this detail pretty boring."

When Wilson appointed Glavin as Marketing Manager for the 914, he made it clear in their one-on-one discussion of the job that led to Wilson's "concrete contract" with Glavin that the challenge was to find the solution to two key problems—find a way around the big "sticker shock" barrier, and find a low-cost way to service the 914s so they would keep making copies.

To learn first-hand about the competition in copiers, Glavin organized a group of volunteers to go out in the area around Rochester. They were to talk to customers to learn which copying machines they were using, how they were using those machines, what they liked and didn't like, and what they were paying for competitor's copiers. They talked to more than one hundred users and learned a lot by asking just a few questions.

"Users didn't really know how many copies they were making *and* they didn't know their copying costs," recalled Glavin, "but they liked being able to make more copies quickly and easily. And they were making many more copies than they had thought they were making—which we learned when they double-checked *after* we asked them.

"More important, secretaries *disliked* the competitors' products. But the companies that were already using Haloid's ten prototype copiers *loved* them because Haloid's copier was neat and clean, made good copies, and was pretty fast."

Even so, there were problems. The prototype machine was big: It weighed more than 600 pounds. "And we needed to increase our reliability because even though we repaired the machines quickly enough, customers wanted our machines to *always* be working."

When the test period was over, the strongest possible data came: The companies testing the prototypes *all* wanted to keep "their" machines.

Glavin's group agreed to repeat their research in the metropolitan area extending from Philadelphia to Baltimore and Washington. At each visit, they asked the users the same few questions, and after each day's interviews, they got together at their hotel to share what they had learned. "We were feeling pretty good—and getting pretty encouraged by what we were learning," recalled Glavin. "Then . . . Bingo! The bell rang one night and it rang *really* loud and clear! One of our guys had called on the Social Security Administration in Baltimore and reported to us that evening: 'Social Security is using all sorts of copiers: Apeco, Thermofax, Electrofax, Verifax, etc. They make copies in *very* large volume, John.' "

"How large a volume?" asked Glavin.

The reality was way beyond any expectation: "They produce copies by the carload."

"Did you say carload?"

"Yes, John. By the carload! The Social Security Administration produces enough copies to fill a whole railroad freight car every few days. They buy by the carload and they produce by the carload—every few days. And they're doing all their work on copiers and duplicators that do a pretty poor job and are messy—and are slow!"

With this stunning information, Glavin knew, and everyone else in his group knew, that the copier business—once their new copier was introduced—was certain to boom and that their company had a wonderful competitive advantage. It had far and away the best copier if the problems of pricing and service could be solved. But Glavin wasn't sure where to find the solution to those two problems. Finding their solution was part of the "concrete contract" he had with Joe Wilson.

Luckily, the solution for machine service found Glavin one evening—in an airplane at 34,000 feet. Glavin had had a long, hard day and knew he'd have more than two hours on the flight he was taking to be in place for the next day's series of visits and calls on prospective customers. As the flight attendant came down the aisle offering drinks, Glavin, who was 6'4", noticed that the stranger sitting next to him was also quite tall. Smiling, he observed: "I guess we both can really appreciate being able to sit up front with the extra leg room."

"You bet! After another long day out on the road selling, it's good having enough room to stretch out—and enjoy a good drink." Turning to the flight attendant, the man continued, "I'll have a double bourbon, please."

As the two men sipped their drinks, Glavin, an engaging, outgoing man, was in the mood for conversation: "Did you say you're in sales?"

"Yes. Pinsetters."

"Pinsetters?"

"The automatic pinsetting equipment for bowling alleys. I'm with AMF—American Machine & Foundry."

Always interested in learning how different businesses actually work, Glavin was curious. "Everywhere I go, I see new bowling alleys. Tell me what's going on in the bowling business. Are you and your pinsetters making all this happen?"

"We've transformed the whole bowling industry. Of course, it's not just AMF. Brunswick makes pinsetters, too."

Both men worked in sales and marketing at companies with new products, both were in their early thirties with young families, and both felt like unwinding after another long day on the road. So both were soon enjoying their conversation. During the next hour, over drinks and then dinner, they talked about marketing and distribution; compared experiences in recruiting, training and supervising salespeople; discussed pricing and advertising; and then Glavin asked about the working relationships AMF had with the people who ran the bowling alleys.

"We do a lot for the operators because most of them have no past experience in bowling operations and need to be shown how to do it really right. We do all sorts of things to help them succeed. We analyze the potential demand in each market and make a judgment on the right number of lanes to build. We design the layout of the alleys. We advise on the right number of parking spaces, food services, how to organize bowling leagues, and how to advertise. You name it. We do everything to show the operators how to make a success for themselves *and* how to maximize the utilization of our pinsetters!"

"With such complex equipment, downtime must be a big concern."

"A breakdown *is* a big problem when it happens. And it's always urgent because any down pinsetter earns zero money for us or for the operator. But the cost to us at AMF is *not* big. It's actually quite small."

"Why? If it's a big problem, I would have thought solving it would cost a lot."

"Most of the cost is paid by the *operators*. We've learned that if you have a product that's important to your customers, particularly a new and different product that needs a lot of minor repairs to keep running, customers are more than willing to learn how to make those repairs themselves. That's the way it was when automobiles were first introduced. And that's why we train the operators how to do all the normal, minor repairs so they can make them themselves. This saves us a lot of expense and downtime when the pinsetters aren't working and producing revenues. Of course, we do all the major repairs, but routine preventive maintenance and normal repairs can be done by the operators if we just train one or two of their people—people who are 'mechanical' and have an interest in this sort of thing. Actually, these minor repairs are 80 to 90% of the total and the operators do *all* of them with their own people and at their own expense. It means huge savings for us and works much better for them because all those minor repairs are made immediately."

Glavin recognized that this same approach could be the solution to his company's servicing problem with its new copiers. Most stoppages *were* easy to fix. With a little training, the customer's own employees could fix most of the 914s problems—and fix them right away—while any major problems would be handled by Haloid's skilled service specialists. For customers, learning how to make most 914 repairs quickly proved to be easy for the mechanically adept and enthusiastic "Key Operators," and this sharply reduced the twin costs of machines being down and unproductive travel time of service reps.

Three days later, Glavin was at his desk in Rochester, trying to work out the right pricing strategy for the new 914, playing with various ideas and possibilities. The classic "sell razor blades" strategy was being used by most companies in the copier industry, but it clearly wouldn't work for Haloid and the 914. Competitors could sell their machines for a few hundred dollars and then sell these captive customers lots of high margin proprietary supplies. But Haloid clearly couldn't "sell razor blades" with the 914 because its costs were reversed: The *machine* would be expensive while the supplies such as paper and toner were cheap. Haloid needed a completely different approach to pricing, so it could make its profits on the *machine*.

"Then it hit me!" recalls Glavin. "We could *lease* the machines for a modest charge per month with a reasonable number of copies *given* to the customer for free until the copy volume accumulated to that monthly base fee. And then we could charge a small amount—say 5¢ a copy—for all the additional copies made over and above that monthly minimum. (At 5¢ a copy, Haloid's price per copy would be just one-third of competitors' price per copy.) With enough copies being made, those economics would work *very* well for Haloid. And we knew from our early users that copy volume was sure to work—really work—in our favor because everybody was making more copies than they'd ever expected."

Picking up the phone, Glavin called Wilson's secretary, Margaret Reddington, "Peg, I've got something that's *very* important and will only take a few minutes. Can I see Joe right away?"

"You're in luck, John. He's free for a few minutes right now. Come on down!" Quickly, Glavin got up from his desk and went to Wilson's office.

Wilson listened carefully to Glavin's explanation of his thought process and to his conclusion: "Joe, let's charge by the *copy*! We could charge a basic monthly rental—say, less than $100—and give the customer 2,000 *free* copies for that base fee, and then charge 5 cents a copy for volume *over* that base amount.[1] If usage goes over the monthly minimum—and it sure looks like it will—the per-copy charges will really rake it in."

Wilson thought about it in absolute silence—for *one* minute—and then smiled as he made what would prove to be the key decision: "Sounds good. Go see if you can sell the idea to Kuhns in Finance and Hartnett in Marketing."

As deliberate and careful as he was in analyzing decisions, Wilson was unusually able—because of his extensive preparation; his understanding of finance, people and technology; and his remarkable capacity for swift analysis—to make very quick decisions, even on major issues. He did this several times in Haloid's negotiations with IBM, RCA, and GE; when buying large acreage in Webster; when recruiting McColough, Clark, and Rutledge; and most obviously, when committing Haloid to electrophotography. However, not everyone could keep up with him.

Jack Hartnett was on board quickly: "It's OK with me, if it's OK with you."

But Harold Kuhns, after many years of carefully pinching pennies so Haloid could survive, was absolutely opposed: "You've gotta be out of your cotton pickin' *mind!*"

Deeply concerned, Glavin went back to Wilson, who counseled: "That's just Kuhns. We'll keep working on him. He'll be OK."

Glavin knew the remaining problem *and* he had a solution. The 914 would need an accurate, tamper-free meter to count the copies. Glavin knew that the Pitney Bowes postage machine needed a meter to count stamps, so the 914 would need a meter as good as the meters on postage machines. The original meter for the 914—which

[1]Original as it was, Glavin's concept was made easier to accept by Haloid's prior experience with the Copyflo. Priced at $1,200 per month for the first shift and $800 for each additional shift, it was making little or no profit until Peter McColough decided to meter the linear feet used and charge by the foot, just one step short of charging by the copy.

cost only $3.50—was just not up to the task, but a $15 item worked out well.

To make the decision to install a 914 as easy as possible and to show the company's confidence in the 914 as a product, all service and replacement parts were included within the basic charge and installation was free. In addition, Wilson and Glavin agreed to use a very simple one-page lease agreement that the customer could cancel at any time without penalty on just 15 days' notice. By comparison, IBM's lease agreement was formidable: Page after page of legal language and cancellations required 90 days' notice. The difference sent a strong message: Every aspect of the 914 was deliberately "user-friendly."

At 5¢ a copy *anyone* could afford to try a 914—and no one could afford *not* to try it. Charging just 5¢ a copy was a long, long way from the estimated $25,000 purchase price and its sticker shock. "Just 5¢" made trying a 914 an entirely different kind of decision. For a customer, the decision to give the 914 a try was now easy, and the decision to use the new machine *very* easy. "Nickel a copy" was catchy and compelling. Salesmen were soon sporting cuff links made of buffalo nickels. The *real* decision would not be to use the 914—it would be to use it again and again and again.

Of course, the solution to the marketing problem would compound Wilson's problem in finance. The only way to charge by the copy would be for Haloid to own all the machines. The capital required by 5¢ a copy leasing could be overwhelming. It would require truly enormous amounts of capital—particularly if the business were successful. If machines cost $2,400 to build and Haloid placed 5,000 of them, it would need $10 million. Wilson had only $1 million.

Scale was only one dimension of the financial problem. Risk was another. How could Haloid, all by itself, take all the risk of technological change? If, after three or four years of getting its machines out on lease, any one of a dozen corporate giants, all with keen interest in getting into copiers, made a technological breakthrough that made the xerographic machines obsolete—or even just less desirable—Haloid would be horribly overexposed.

In 1958, concerned by the estimated costs of tooling for and production of the 914s, Wilson again opened the possibility of joint venturing with either IBM or Bell & Howell. However, IBM wanted an exclusive arrangement, and Bell & Howell engineers, after seeing a demonstration of the 914, found so many design problems they were sure could not be corrected—such as a moving lens that Bell & Howell engineers were certain would cause vibrations and spoil results—that discussions fell apart. So once again, Haloid would have to go forward on its own.

Still worried that Haloid didn't have enough money to carry through the whole 914 program, Wilson was again thinking of going to IBM for help in late 1958. He asked 20 Haloid managers to write position papers on whether Haloid should go it alone or go into partnership with another company such as IBM. He then shared all the position papers with everyone in the group. Only one out of twenty was a doubter, and the doubts he raised were many. All others were positive. In the end, Wilson asked for and got one memorandum to which all had contributed. It argued that Haloid could—and should—manufacture and market the 914 on its own.

As Joe Wilson entered the meeting room where all of his colleagues were gathered, it seemed clear that his company and his companions had overcome the long years of uncertainty, doubt, and personal conflicts that he had worked so persistently to manage and subdue. He had led them through those wilderness years, and now they wanted to follow his lead into their future. In reality, the commitment decision everyone wanted had already been made by the entire group: Haloid should go ahead on its own and bet the company. Preproduction models would be needed as soon as possible for field-testing.

IBM's corporate motto was THINK, and Tom Watson was again thinking that Haloid and IBM, which had great strengths in both machine production and selling, should get together to manufacture and market the 914. Once again, Watson called Wilson to propose the link-up. On one level, Wilson was very pleased: He admired

IBM, and he liked Tom Watson. And such a combination was, of course, what Wilson himself had been seeking just one year before. But that was then. Now, it was too late to change strategies. Wilson told Watson that Haloid was committed to producing and selling the 914 on its own—assuming it *could* be produced and Wilson's company did not run out of money.

19

THE 914

"**Y**ou've gotta be kidding!"

Horace Becker was looking with dismay at Haloid's pride and joy: still called E-100.

Becker was "all Brooklyn" with a quick wit, and a short, blunt tongue[1] and deeply rooted irreverence toward Big Shots. Anxious about Becker's abrupt manners, John Dessauer had sought back-channel references before hiring him from Mergenthaler Linotype Corporation. Mergenthaler's vice president of research praised Becker to "hell and high water." But Dessauer worried whether such praise was too much for credibility. Were they maybe hoping to unload Becker? So he got a second opinion from the Vice President of Manufacturing, who said he had worked with Becker "more than he

[1]Haloid ran an ad in a graphics magazine for a manufacturing engineer, which was answered by Paul Catan, then Chief Engineer at Mergenthaler Linotype Corp. He began working at Haloid on what would become the 914. Even more important than joining Haloid himself, Catan called Horace Becker, another Mergenthaler employee who was worried about that company's planned cutbacks in R&D. After graduating from the Drexel Institute in Philadelphia, Becker had worked for five years at Royal Line Paper in Brooklyn. In 1953, he took the position of Chief Engineer at Davidson Printing Press, a subsidiary of Mergenthaler. Becker had heard about Haloid's xerographic plate masters while working on a short-run duplicator that made fewer than five copies.

ever wanted." Becker had a big mouth, and he was glad to see the SOB go. Then in an offhand remark, he assured that Becker would be hired: "One exception: Becker has never, ever been proven wrong—even in hindsight."

On his first visit to Rochester in 1958, Becker knew one thing: He was *not* impressed by Copyflo—and he had not yet seen the prototype for the new office copier that would become the 914. Even with 20/20 hindsight, Becker's caution about joining Haloid was understandable. After all, John Rutkus, whom Becker calls the "Father of the 914," and his team had barely completed the design of the 914's predecessor called, because of its color, the Green Machine.

Still, Becker sensed something exciting was going on at Haloid, so he agreed to return. Bill Asher advised him to wear a suit instead of a sports jacket on his second visit: "They get very nervous up here about sports jackets!" (The initial luncheon meeting had been held at the Rochester Club, where sports jackets were considered inappropriately casual.)

"Why?" parried Becker. "Are they looking for an engineer—or a salesman?"

Becker had a blunt reaction to the six-foot-high "breadboard" prototype for what would eventually become the 914: "You've gotta be kidding! You're going to make a machine out of *that*?" For Becker, the 914 prototype looked like "a lot of subassemblies hanging off an enormous face plate." The drawings had no specifics on manufacturing tolerances. The number of different parts that would have to be made to exacting tolerances was huge. And fitting all of them together in a high-volume production process was far beyond the experience of anyone at Haloid. Adding to the challenge, Joe Wilson had decided that Haloid itself would manufacture all of the most difficult parts—those that suppliers *couldn't* make.

Most distressing to Becker was that neither Haloid nor its local suppliers had enough experience with the tight tolerances—two millimeters or less—required for assembly-line production with truly interchangeable parts. The whole concept of interchangeable parts assembly was new to Haloid, and it was not at all clear where all those parts would be made. Small vendors saw Haloid's small orders as good business, but didn't understand the importance of tolerances. Large vendors understood the importance of meeting tolerances, but didn't see Haloid's small orders as good business. The necessary standards were far stricter than had been needed for the one-at-a-time, file'n'fit assembly of Copyflo machines. "Haloid was built on everybody being very pleasant," says Becker. "If an outside vendor's part didn't fit, you'd fix the part. But with high-volume production, that approach would never work."

Still, Becker was intrigued by an earlier engineering model of the copier, which was kept in the drafting room where Haloid people would fight to use it. Becker sensed that Rutkus and his design team had worked a miracle: "There was a great feeling around the company. You could smell it: It was a fantastic, vitalizing type of feeling. More and more Haloid people were coming to understand that they were breaking away from the old photographic business—Kodak's business—for a new and different business. It was exciting. And where I was had no future. Mergenthaler was planning cutbacks in R&D."

Becker's wife Gloria was clear-minded and clear-spoken: "I think it's an opportunity. I think we can handle it."

As an engineer, Becker was convinced: "This was clearly the greatest opportunity of a lifetime. After our second meeting, they asked what it would take to get me to move to Rochester and work for Haloid. I gave a number—and three days later, it was accepted by telegram."[2] Becker moved into the Rochester YMCA in March 1958, leaving his wife and three children on Long Island. Before committing his family to the move, he took six months to decide that the 914 was for real and would make it.

---

[2]That was February 1958. In 1978, Becker was elected a corporate vice president of a $2 billion corporation.

Joe Wilson had inspired John Rutkus and his team of design engineers to strive toward realizing a Dream. Despite always being strapped for money, working in makeshift facilities, and being frustrated again and again by the stubborn tenacity of the problems they faced, they had made great, if irregular, progress.

In their persistent, determined struggle, they kept finding clever ways to solve problems. For example, Rutkus found the answer to one stubborn design problem in his garage at home. The problem was figuring out how to remove sheets of paper adhering electrostatically to the selenium-coated drum without damaging its thinly coated surface. The selenium drum was too fragile to remove the paper mechanically because *any* scratch would show up as a dark line on *every* subsequent copy!

As Rutkus explained, "One day in 1958, I was fooling around in the garage with a bicycle. I had laid some papers on the hood of the car and one sheet got stuck. So I took the bicycle air pump, forced air under that sheet of paper—and off it came. Then I started to think about the 914 and using a whole bunch of nozzles to clear the copy off the drum with air. I went back to the lab and tried slits, then needles—hypodermic needles—and finally got a blast of air that was short enough in duration not to disturb the image. *That* was the solution." The famous puffer—an essential part of the 914—gently removed paper sheets from the selenium drum.

Clyde Mayo, head of engineering, was also vital to the 914 concept. He developed a crucial scanning system based on work he had done for the Army Signal Corps 15 years earlier. He also designed an optical system that could print from opaque originals instead of microfilm. "That recognition of the right way to go is why Clyde Mayo's name is on the original 914," said Merritt Chandler, a key manager for the 914 program.

The document was scanned at a velocity synchronized to the velocity of the rotating selenium-drum surface through a lens that was moving at exactly *half* that velocity, because the lens was located at half the distance between the drum and the document. Another problem was with the paper flow: The speed at which paper moved had to change from *faster* than the selenium drum's rotation just before transfer to *slower* just after. This was achieved with a slipping clutch so clever in design that in a subsequent lawsuit, IBM somehow asserted it couldn't work.

The key to success with the 914 program was the climate of creativity and innovation that Joe Wilson fostered in every area of the company: production, marketing, pricing, leasing, financing, and customer service. He also encouraged in his team the determination to achieve the entire transformation. Wilson needed Becker—who later described himself as the "midwife" to the 914—and other experienced engineers to transform Haloid from doing a little job shop assembling alongside its traditional business in coated papers, into a high-volume manufacturer of complex machines that required tight tolerances. This would be an enormous conceptual and operational change from the old file'n'fit approach of the past that had been used to assemble a few Copyflo machines. This is why Haloid needed a very different kind of engineer—a *product* engineer like Horace Becker.

Since there were no cost estimates for the 914, Becker did one. The required tooling for the 914 would cost $2 million, including $200,000 for one particular drill press. Cost-sensitive old timers like Harold Kuhns were more than upset by these huge cost estimates: They were distraught. For Haloid, the costs were high—which is one reason why, at the last minute, Wilson reached out once again to IBM and Bell & Howell.

If anyone expected Becker to fit in, they chose the wrong man and gave him the wrong assignment. (In Japan a few years later, Becker's personal identification badge—unbeknownst to him— would read "Typhoon" in Japanese.)

According to Becker, "I was pushing and pushing all the time. I was *so* abusive, I thought I'd probably be dumped—and thrown out onto the street. There was blood all over the place! So, it was not entirely surprising to hear one day that Joe Wilson wanted to see me in his office over on Haloid Street.

"It would be our first meeting. I felt sad to be starting with him this way—in serious trouble. At least that's what I was expecting. But to my surprise, in that initial meeting, we didn't talk about my pushing. And we never talked about business—or Haloid. We talked about family and children. Joe wanted to know about our family's housing and how we felt about settling into the community. Were we comfortable? At the end, he said simply, 'I'm glad I met you.' I was so surprised."

Becker walked back to his workstation totally bewildered. When he shared his surprise with the other engineers, they said they weren't surprised at all: "You've just met Joe."

Becker wasn't the only man to be surprised that year. Wilson, the visionary and long-range planner, surprised all of his colleagues by telling them to ignore his previous requests to prepare careful one- and five-year plans for that year's annual planning conference. Instead, Wilson wanted everyone to focus on just the next two years and on only three products: "We are about to give birth," he wrote that August to his division heads, "either to our greatest success or to our greatest failure—the 914. This program will be followed immediately by equally important ones. After much soul-searching, I have come to the conclusion that all considerations, other than the short-term ones of accomplishing these programs, should be subordinated to them." Wilson's announcement was just the right message at just the right time. He put into words what everyone was feeling, and validated all their individual commitments to the 914 by making them everyone's.

The consensus of those who worked most closely with him is that Joe Wilson was not a great operational manager, but he was a great leader of people—a very unusual and quite natural leader who had remarkable ability both to develop a great vision *and* to bring others to share that vision as their own. And he devoted himself resolutely to his great work.

"Joe had three great qualities as a leader," said Peter McColough. "Vision, never ever giving up, and getting people—by inspiration, cajoling, and encouraging *or* by tough decisions—to *do*. In conventional terms, Joe Wilson was not unusually able as a business manager. He was much more interested in research than in the nuts and bolts of manufacturing, because research fit with his very long-range vision of his company and where he had wanted to take it."

"Wilson was a visionary and a prophet with the great good fortune as a leader to see his Dream come true," said Glavin. "Wilson was an effective inspirational leader because he had the imagination to visualize the potential impact of a great technological change; the ability to inspire others; and the persistent determination of the great explorers."

"Recognizing and knowing an opportunity when you see it," said Glavin, "that's what really separates the sheep from the goats in corporate leadership. Joe had that unusual capability—and he had it to an unusual degree."

Wilson constantly drove himself and his company forward, and he expected a lot from himself and from the others who worked with him. (His secretaries knew he had no patience with typing errors and was quick to point them out. He found it hard to accept mistakes, particularly repeated mistakes. Certain kinds of detail had to be correct.)

As his friend Jack Hartnett said, "He was very impatient with people who were slow-minded. You had to be on the ball when you were with him."

On the other hand, Wilson was a realist who always accepted and often celebrated the best efforts of others. "He was not the genial, laid back, jovial sort who was always taking things in stride," said Linowitz. "He wanted things done and done on time. He was not an easy person to develop a fully open relationship with. He held himself uptight."

Yet, as Jack Hartnett recalled, "Joe was a disciplined person himself, but he didn't impose strict discipline on other people. He wouldn't dream of doing that."

Even when world famous, he wanted people to call him "Joe," and not "Mr. Wilson." Those who knew him very well said that while many people felt he was close to them, almost nobody got really close to Joe Wilson. His personal discipline led Wilson to follow a repetitive pattern of carefully thinking through all aspects of each important challenge, determining the most rational approach, defining his own role responsibilities, and carefully adhering to those role responsibilities. He seldom showed anger and was remarkably affable and thoughtful of others while maintaining a personal balance of warmth.

"He was always reaching for the stars and believing the right things were going to happen," Linowitz said in describing Wilson's persistence. "He was forever having a deep feeling for the future. He felt something had been placed in his charge and that we had a great potential. If he wasn't always doing those things the way he did, there might never have been a Xerox." As his secretary, Gloria Chapman explained, "Mr. Wilson had an inner glow or luminescence. He attracted others who got the bug and wanted to be a part of it. He had a tiger by the tail and could see the great potential ahead, so he would naturally want to see how far it could go." Tenacity and persistence, combined with optimism and the ability to engage with and inspire others, were hallmarks of Wilson's personality as a leader.

"Joe pushed Haloid and then Xerox forward," said McColough. "He was constantly pushing. Even on vacation, Joe would never be able to keep his business and his private interests separate."

Wilson made it very clear to his colleagues that he wanted them to reach and stretch—to be risk takers—so their company could break out of the pack. For Wilson, failure was acceptable—even celebrated—*if* you were really trying. Not trying hard enough was *not* acceptable; repeated mistakes *never* were. Wilson inspired his colleagues with his own compelling commitment, shared excitement, and sense of adventure. He related to each person individually and was habitually very complimentary, urging everyone to reach high and reminding: "You have to do well to be able to do right."

"What made the company so stellar as a business," said Merritt Chandler, "was Joe Wilson as a person." Chandler was working in Chicago for American Bosch Arma when a headhunter he knew and liked called.

"How big is the company?"

"$18 million in sales."

"I've got that much in my *division*. Why should I be interested?"

"This is a *very* unusual company."

"Call me back so I can think about it—which I'll do because I value your opinion."

"They'll want you to visit Rochester—soon."

"Well, I'm going to Washington for a meeting with the military. I could stop in Rochester on the way back."

When Chandler got to Rochester, Haloid people showed him the Model A and talked about the 914. Chandler agreed to return *if* he could meet with the president: "During my meeting with him, Joe Wilson talked about 'this engineering marvel' and its great promise. He believed they would sell 2,500 of their new machines."

"I didn't accept that number. I said, 'I think you'll sell many, many more. I think you'll sell 200,000!' To this, Wilson responded with a warm smile, 'Well, I do appreciate your enthusiasm. You may be right. But I doubt it.'"

Chandler pressed right ahead, saying: "But if I *am* right, are you, as president, ready and willing to take on the tasks of hiring all the people you'll need in sales and manufacturing, reorganizing your management team, raising the money—and do this with all the stresses and strains that are sure to come, too?"

In silence, Wilson was quite obviously thinking about that question and its many ramifications. After awhile, he looked directly at Chandler, and in his steady voice replied, "Yes, I am prepared for all that."

"If you offer me a job," Chandler responded, "I'll gladly accept."

Chandler started in July. In August, Wilson asked him what he thought so far. Chandler asked for time: Could he answer next week? Yes, if that would provide the time to explore important questions carefully. The next week, the two men met again.

"The most recent annual report described Haloid's huge expenditure on R&D; but if that much investment in R&D is really productive," explained Chandler, "an $18 million company would surely be too small to take full advantage of such an expenditure." Chandler urged Wilson to focus on the product that would become the 914. "You must concentrate on *this* product. If it proves to be anywhere nearly as successful as I expect, the profits from it will provide you with ample future funding for *all* the projects on your long wish list of new products."

A week later, Wilson stopped by to say, "Merritt, I've been considering what you said last week. Would you like to form a new corporate division to concentrate on developing our copier— everything from engineering to marketing?"

"No," said Chandler. "As an $18 million company, Haloid can't afford to hire a whole new team of managers for any one product— even for your very promising copier." Then noting that Haloid had three or four government projects in the works, each with a task force, Chandler continued: "But I would gladly head up a task force to lead in the copier's development and manufacture."

To build ten prototype 914s for field-testing, Haloid engineers went to one small machine shop after another, with the drawings for various parts in hand. Over and over they asked, "Can you make ten of these?" After reviewing the plans, the frequent reply was understandably blunt: "Can you pay in advance?"

"Joe was a master at keeping that flame going," recalled Horace Becker, "including talking to the wives when they didn't see their husbands very often. You did all you possibly could because you knew that he was giving all he had of himself—plus a quality that is hard to define: He was just a great guy to spend time with."

Problems with the 914 were not limited to the machine. Toner— later called 'black gold' because it was so very profitable—

presented a series of daunting problems,[3] and engineering ingenuity was required again and again. Toner was so hard to produce that Haloid expected the difficulties would prevent competitors from replicating xerography even after the machine patents ran out.

Toner has two critical temperatures: one at which the toner fuses physically and permanently into the fiber of the paper and another at which it blocks or sticks to itself in clumps. Ideally, the fusing temperature should be low and the blocking temperature high. Toner also needs to be sufficiently brittle so that it can be attrited to the desired particle size for good resolution and copy quality—five microns for a 914—*and* be tough enough not to disintegrate into useless dust. Finally, it must have a long shelf life.

Even with all of these complexities, Mike Insalaco, who was in charge of developing toner, promised to develop, produce, and have "on-spec" toner available by a specified date several months out in the future. This meant John Rutkus and his team would be developing an expensive machine that absolutely depended on a nonexistent toner that would not be delivered until late in 1958, *after* most of the preproduction engineering models had been completed and they were near the end of product development. In fact, the 914 was well into production design before the complex toner problem was fully solved,[4] meaning that the toner was brittle enough to break up into fine particles, but not soft enough to smear and not hard enough to hurt the photoreceptor. The only way to determine the right characteristics for all of these often mutually conflicting variables was by trial and error through hundreds of trials.[5]

---

[3]A combination of carbon black and resin, toner cost only 10 cents per pound to produce—less than the cost of the package it came in—and sold it for $3 to $5 per pound. The profit margin was well over 90%. (People left Xerox to make and sell toner. And to salvage old toner, scavengers were cutting open the filter bags that collected used toner in each machine.)

[4]Pell, page 94.

[5]Insalaco's "low melt" toner patent later played a *crucial* role for 20 years in minimizing competition.

Cleaning the granules of toner *completely* off the drum so it was ready to begin the next copy *and* doing it with perfect timing during the automated sequence of operations *and* ideally with a single sweep could have been a major challenge. For Haloid, it was as easy as walking downstairs to the first floor to the shop of a furrier who gladly helped locate the most effective natural fur. The answer: a New Zealand rabbit's fur with density so unusually constant that the selenium drum would be cleaned consistently. (For later generations of machines, the worldwide supply of these particular rabbits would prove too small, so synthetics were developed.)

The next challenge was how to clear the toner out of the rabbit fur. The key to this was controlling the length of the nap of the fur, which had to be cut to a tolerance of ¹⁄₆₄". In the fur trade, ¼" was considered close and ⅛" was very tight. A tolerance of just ¹⁄₆₄" was "out of sight." But a glove maker was found in Gloversville who had the necessary know-how to cut the fur to the ¹⁄₆₄" tolerance.

M ost, but not all, of the parts suppliers produced good work. Becker knew from experience at Mergenthaler exactly how to deal effectively with those who did not meet specifications. Any supplier who couldn't keep up in volume *and* meet quality specifications was dropped. Inspect first, pay later. Simple as that.

Maybe so in Brooklyn, but not in Rochester! For Harold Kuhns, the Controller, this conflicted with his standard practice—established during the lean years of the Depression and the War to reach for *any* way to add to meager profits—of paying immediately to get the discount offered for quick payment. The resulting tension between Becker and Kuhns exemplified the tensions that erupted over and over between the new guys and the older Haloid men. Wilson defused the mounting tension between Becker and Kuhns in his typical way: He reframed the issue by adding staff to speed up testing. This helped significantly, but did not solve the problem of rejected parts from suppliers.

For parts suppliers all around Rochester, if there were a problem, then the problem was not with the work done by their machine shops; the problem was with that guy, Becker! The owner of a local machine shop with rejected work would simply pick up the phone and call: "Joe, will you please *talk* to that guy?" And the calls were soon coming in faster and faster. So, Becker got a call, a very distinctive kind of call. Joe Wilson's secretary was on the phone. "Joe wants to see you—in his office—*now*."

Becker had been around. He knew this was no ordinary visit. The tone in her voice, being called off the floor, going to Joe's office, and being asked to go *now* were all strong signals.

Wilson was clearly upset: His voice was even quieter than usual; his sentences more carefully completed. He reviewed, one after another, all the calls he'd been getting from parts suppliers. As usual, Wilson had done his homework carefully and was well prepared. Now he was laying it all out.

Becker was ready too. He knew every aspect of the manufacturing problem; he knew what must be done to complete the mission; and he knew how important it was for a unit commander to have a CEO's full support during difficult times. Becker was about to lay it on the line with the classic yes or no question of authority: "Joe, are you running the 914 program—or am I?"

But, before he could ask his question, Wilson stopped talking and looked him straight in the eye—clearly struggling to maintain composure—and then, after a period of silence, pre-empted Becker's drawing the line in the sand by saying, "Horace, please don't ask me who is running the 914 manufacturing program. That's not what we want to talk about today. Right now, we want to address one question: How we can make our production objectives? Is there any way we can *fix* these parts instead of just rejecting them?"

As he would do so often, Wilson sought to avoid confrontation by identifying a purpose that could be worked on *together*. But since Haloid operated without a machine shop, there was no alternative this time. After some tense give and take, Wilson and Becker came to an agreement: The suppliers would have to be taught to produce to exact specifications.

Becker knew the moment of truth had come—and had passed—but he had gotten much too close to the edge.

"Horace," Becker said very quietly to himself while walking back to his area, "You very nearly crossed the line!"

He had forced Joe Wilson into a corner. Only through a very deliberate act of personal will had Wilson kept the meeting from going off the rails and into a confrontation that could have dealt grave consequences for the 914 program *and* for Horace Becker. (In such a confrontation, of course, Becker would soon be nothing more than "that difficult SOB from Brooklyn who *used* to work here.")

Becker had understood his manufacturing problem before, and now he understood Joe Wilson's business community problem. The quality standards for parts suppliers would have to be held high and manufacturing the 914 was Becker's show, but something—something other than just rejecting inadequate parts—would have to be done with the suppliers. On his way back to the production floor, Becker still talking silently to himself, he made himself a promise that he would never again put Joe Wilson in a corner. Then he muttered to himself, "And next time, don't say to some supplier: 'Take this God-damned scumbag work back—and make it *right!*'"

Wilson decided on a better way to approach the problem: Put on a convincing demonstration for the parts suppliers. "They are part of the Family and it's important that they each understand the position we're in and what we're trying to do together."

In a few weeks, with a record snow falling outside, the Orchard Street lab was jammed full of people. These people were getting a strong "sales pitch," but they were not customers; they were suppliers. They had come from 200 different companies at Wilson's invitation and the sales pitch was being made by Wilson and Becker. They had one purpose: to demonstrate to these parts suppliers how very complex a machine the 914 was; how many parts it had; and why each of those parts needed to be precisely made and produced to high standards *or* the whole machine could not work and everyone would be hurt.

Wilson began the presentation with a few words about the exciting potentials of xerography and his company's commitment to
this remarkable new technology. Then he introduced Becker, who
showed how the 914 was composed of 1,200 different parts. He then
explained how very important it was to have *all* the parts made to
exact tolerances for the machine to work properly. The presentation
concluded with a demonstration of the magic of the 914.[6]

The meeting was successful: Understanding the production
problem, the suppliers agreed that parts had to be made to exact
specifications.

But there were other problems. Gearing up production of 914s
revealed a host of serious problems that could have been prevented if there had been time enough to build models, test them,
and make design changes and corrections before launching full-scale
production.

Without money for modern equipment, Haloid's workers improvised. The early production models were built on wooden pallets
with wheels and were pushed by hand from one station to another
as parts were added. To get parts up to the third floor—accessible
only by two elevators that couldn't handle heavy loads—a covered
conveyor belt was rigged to take parts from the warehouse to the
assembly area.

Improvisations were needed again and again. Initially, it took
eight weeks to build one machine. (At full volume, production eventually reached 100 machines every day.)

In one case, an internal electric fan caused serious vibration. At
first, the fans worked well, but when the manufacturer increased
production volume, the fans caused so much vibration that the 914s
could not be completed—until one of Haloid's engineers designed a
simple bracket to isolate the fan's vibrations from the other parts
inside the machine—and the 914 production could go ahead.

[6]McKelvey, page VII-26b.

Meters to count copies were another problem in the beginning. Some jammed. Others miscounted with some registering too few copies and others counting 10 copies as 100. The 914 was so complex and had so many different parts that it was nearly impossible to figure out what was causing some of the problems. For example, early production 914s were failing after just a few copies. A scramble to figure out what was causing the never-before-seen problem finally isolated the culprit: a new kind of paint being used on the developer housing.

Through all of these frustratingly difficult problems, Joe Wilson was very much in charge when the managing group met every Monday morning to coordinate the disparate needs of the many different disciplines. The meetings, lasting half an hour with 10 to 15 people participating, were sometimes stormy. In these cases, Wilson would decide, "This ultimately is George's responsibility so we'll all go with George's decision."

When it came time for a new man's turn to speak at a workout session and he said: "Sorry. I've been too busy. I've had no time to fix that," Becker cut in: "My God, he ain't got the word!" But the new man was not alone: Joe Wilson and his company were running short of time *and* money in the scramble to produce the 914.

The meetings were deliberately kept very open. As Donald Shepardson described the sessions: "Joe was so skillful in working with people [that while he] used a lot of pressure, he did it in such a nice way—never personal—and handled it so well. The pressure we felt was really something. I almost drove my car off the road a couple of times on the way to those meetings, thinking about how to solve our problems."

Such intense emotional engagement in making the 914 successful spread throughout the company, thanks to one of Wilson's characteristics as a leader—his ability to connect with people and to inspire them to make strong personal commitments. Everyone came to think of the 914 as their *own;* it was a collective personal obsession.

20

GO!

The early 914s were more handmade than manufactured. The first 10 were put out on test with local companies. After a few weeks of use, they were to be taken back to Haloid and disassembled to see how they could be improved. All ten test users were reluctant to let the test machines go, and Nisner's 5 & 10¢ flatly refused.

"But it's *ours*," protested Becker.

"I don't care!" said Nisner. To get Nisner's reluctant OK to take the test machine back, Joe Wilson had to promise one of the very first production units. Nisner wasn't the only resister.

Clyde Mayo wanted more time to get the machine design really right: "Wait a year and we'll have a much better 914." But Wilson was under increasingly great financial pressure to go ahead with the 914, even though the machines were not perfectly manufactured and were frequently breaking down in the field—because his company was running out of money as inventories of machines piled up with just one part missing. With Becker, Rutkus, and Shepardson urging going into production, Wilson was ready to decide he would have to go ahead with 914 production and work out the myriad unsolved problems on the run.

Mayo was out one day when Becker saw an unsigned purchase

order on Mayo's desk. Becker signed the production order: "Clyde Mayo/HB" and Joe Wilson said, "GO!"

Mayo, as head of engineering, was outraged by Becker's signing off, using Mayo's authority. "Horace, you have a *problem*. That was very high-handed. We needed a year more, but you went ahead. If it had failed, you'd have been in big trouble. It worked out OK, but your conduct was *unacceptable*."

"Screw you!"

Joe Wilson reprimanded Becker. "Horace, you really shouldn't have spoken that way to Clyde," but Becker was sure Wilson felt he'd *done* the right thing. To learn more sophisticated and gentlemanly behavior, Becker was later sent to Harvard Business School's 13-week Advanced Management Program. The 13 weeks at Harvard was Wilson's way of rewarding Becker. (Mayo got his revenge on the signing of the purchase order by refusing to give Becker a raise. Wilson wouldn't override Mayo, but he was determined to reward Becker.)

Becker's summation: "At Hahvahd, I learned to say 'Incredible'—and the other guys learned to say, 'No shit!'" Looking back, Becker would later say that "Clyde Mayo was absolutely key to the concept of the 914."

The complexity of the 914, combined with the urgency to increase production volume was challenge enough for an organization that lacked experience in precision manufacturing. In addition, Haloid was depending on many new people who had to work in close teams, but who were just getting to know one another and were unfamiliar with the work to be done. Meanwhile, production and design change orders were coming in almost daily, bringing tension with them, as product and process improvements were developed. In those days, tensions were a constant at Haloid. Highly committed executives and workers, most of them relatively new to the company and to each other, were all experiencing rapid changes in their jobs, and most were working very long hours. And all felt the excitement of having a major challenge they didn't yet know how to beat. The tensions caused by change after change were everywhere. Tooling was originally set for up to 10,000 machines, with expectations for total production over the whole life of the 914 program being *possibly* as much as 15,000. This volume target would be raised again and again.

Meanwhile, production problems with the 914s continued. Running out of a particular part, two engineers tried to fly to Chattanooga to get extra parts, but got caught in a snowstorm and were forced to land in Washington, where they borrowed money from a friend at a company branch office because the railroads wouldn't take their airline tickets for credit. Arriving late in Chattanooga, they got caught in an ice storm. The cab driver didn't know how to drive on ice, so the men from Rochester took the wheel and drove to the factory. There the owner said he couldn't make the part, until the Rochestarians showed him exactly how and got the parts made. To be certain the parts got to Rochester, they divided them into two bundles and headed home by two different routes to be sure of making a good delivery. By the time the two engineers got to Rochester, they'd been on the road three days, eating peanut butter and jelly sandwiches, and had not had a chance to shave. They must have felt as bad as they looked, but they were so fired up they didn't go home to rest. Instead, they delivered the parts and went right to work.

"In late 1959, we needed suppliers of consoles for the 914 and I was delighted when a supplier I knew well won the bidding," recalled Chandler. "That winter's snow was unusually heavy and the drifts were very deep. Even so, that supplier delivered right on schedule: one perfect console *every* day. When a company representative went to Long Island to congratulate them on a job well done, he was told, 'It's great to have your nice words, but we should have bought your stock instead! Besides, we lost money on your contract.'"

"How much did you lose?"

"$135,000."

Joe Wilson's reaction when the facts were reported to him was immediate: "You're going to cover that loss, aren't you?" And then, typically, he added, "I'd like to meet him." Chandler continued, "We later learned that it had been our fault: The drawings for the 914 cabinets were incorrect. The supplier had redesigned the cabinet *and* done the job—at a loss. Joe insisted that no mention of this mistake be made at the company because there was no use in finding fault with either purchasing or design."

Wilson's repeated calls for accelerating the 914 program finally brought an emotional outburst from Becker at a morning session. "I will *not* keep asking my engineers to work time-and-a-half shifts in a hot, stuffy building behind closed windows that cannot be opened because of the stench from pig cars in trains frequently parked for hours on a siding right outside!"

Wilson eyed Becker briefly in astonishment and remarked coldly, "We'll have to make one more trip to the well." He promptly dismissed the meeting and followed Becker to his cubicle. After a silent eye-to-eye confrontation, Becker noticed the red color around Wilson's collar was slowly diminishing. Wilson, in an obviously carefully restrained voice, told Becker his timing had been all wrong—and completely inexcusable. If he had complaints to make, he should bring them in for a private consultation beforehand and not disrupt a group meeting. As Wilson turned and left, he told Becker, "Now, get on with the job."

Years later, Becker described his thoughts and feelings: "Joe Wilson was a man of steel. Don't ever mistake that. I did not see it myself at first, because he had infinite patience, at least with young guys like us. He was also a very strong man who would get his own way—completely apart from the fact that he was the president of the company. He just knew how to control us and motivate us. He knew how to draw you out very quickly and get to the facts. And he also took the time to come to you and find out the real story.

"But dedication was the main thing. I had never seen that kind of dedication in a group of people before: the hours we worked; the productivity of those hours; the absolute joy of it. Joe Wilson told us we were going to make it and we believed him. That was the attitude from top to bottom 'We *can* do it.' We all felt that we could do the impossible."

It was rumored that if a billboard were placed near the company, which said only "Dangerous mission. Low chance of survival. Led by Horace Becker," most of Becker's engineers would sign up without asking for further details.

But there were still plenty of tensions. One involved tiny fire extinguishers. If a fire started inside a 914 and a customer used a conventional water-based fire extinguisher to put out the fire, serious harm could be done to the high voltage power supply in the machine *and* to the person holding the extinguisher. So a small CO_2 fire extinguisher, with instructions on when to use it, would be needed in each 914.[1]

"No way!" protested Don Clark, the Product Manager[2] widely regarded within the company as the Godfather of the 914 because he was so effective. "I can't sell a machine so likely to cause a *fire* that it has a God damned fire extinguisher built right into it!" The engineers explained that the 350°F heat needed to fuse toner to the paper could cause paper, if a sheet got stuck, to burst into flames. The argument itself got heated and threatened to produce smoke of its own, until Clark had an inspiration and offered a compromise:

---

[1] Not everything was serious engineering. High heat was essential in fusing the toner to the paper—and high heat plus thin sheets of paper can mean fire, particularly when, because of a paper jam, a sheet of paper is exposed too long to the heat needed to make the toner fuse. At a 1959 demonstration in Washington—fortunately with more than one machine on hand "just in case"—a quick-witted and quite statuesque female demonstrator noticed a fire. With great presence of mind, she bent very low to hold her audience's attention and, smiling warmly said, "Now watch me *very* closely and follow me over to this other machine" and then whispered to a male colleague that his help was needed *fast*: "The God damned thing is on *fire!*"

[2] After graduating from Wesleyan, Clark worked at General Electric where he learned market research. Clark, others have said, "did a lot of good work that others take credit for."

"OK, let's call it something else. Something less scary than a fire extinguisher. How about 'scorch eliminator'?" When Joe Wilson heard the story and the suggested name, he let out a cheer. And soon, every 914 had a small "scorch eliminator" installed.

Chandler told Wilson they should be producing 914s by January: "We built a dozen machines for use in test operations so we could determine the right design for long-term, high-volume manufacturing. But experience soon proved that suppliers' components for the 914 were not up to standard. So in November, I had to tell Joe we would not make January—but we *would* make February. And we did produce four 914s in February."

Testing the finished machines became a test in itself. During Rochester's long, cold winter, the landlord shut off the heat in the rented factory at 5:00 in the afternoon after which the inside temperature dropped hour by hour. By midnight, it was cold, and it would get much colder before the heat came back on in the morning. The testers rose to the challenge by wearing winter parkas, not shaving, and hanging large sheets of canvas over their work areas so the heat from the machines they were testing would help protect them from the winter cold.

With everyone so committed and working such long hours, production continued to accelerate. By August, cumulative placements of the 914 broke 2,000 units—the expected volume for the whole year.

Then Wilson suddenly got very bad news: The $36 power supply was failing in more and more of the machines already out in the field. Eventually, they would *all* fail. Three successive redesigns were required before success seemed assured. By then, the shortage of power supply units was aggravated by Tech Reps stocking private, "safety cushion" inventories of power supplies so they could be sure to have one on hand if any of their own customers needed a spare unit.

"We called GE," Becker explained. "We told them we needed lots more power units right away to keep up with production *and* to replace the ones that were breaking down *and* to replace the replacements which would soon be breaking down."

How many? Enough to cover all the needs until the engineers could redesign the power supply and GE could produce new ones. Power supply units were failing in just four to six months. Worse, the interaction of components made it very hard to tell exactly what was causing the problems. There was not enough time for testing the new power supplies because a thorough test would take at *least* three months. So, in yet another compromise, after six weeks of testing, it was decided to go ahead with the new units.

"We had no choice." said Becker. "We were shipping machines we couldn't install. I was so upset, I had diarrhea *and* was vomiting. Without the essential power supply, 914 machines were piling up in the factory *and* in warehouses. It was pandemonium. We were out of control. And that's when Jack Rutledge took out a second mort- gage—on his mother's home—to buy more stock, saying: 'Horace, I *know* you will solve this problem!' Fortunately, the third power sup- ply design proved OK."

Still deeply concerned about cashflow, Wilson was determined to balance production costs to machine placements and insisted on the discipline of basing orders for parts, particularly expensive ones, on marketing's estimates of demand. Chandler went to Wilson to protest: "Low estimates like those you're receiving from marketing," he protested, "restrict the orders we place with suppliers for future needs. They limit our budget for motors, cabinets and everything else. In my opinion—and others agree—we should be prepared to make and lease at least fifteen *thousand* copiers in 1961. And we've got to order ahead on that assumption if we plan to be ready to meet the demand."[3]

Wilson looked at Chandler thoughtfully. He had great respect for his opinions, but planning for 15,000 copiers in 1961 seemed a wild flight into astronomical numbers. Purchasing materials for such a large volume meant committing the company to heavy debt. Wilson toyed with a pencil as he did some serious thinking.

[3]Dessauer, page 139.

Chandler added, "If we can't make it big with the 914, we're fooling around with the wrong product."

Wilson briefly discussed the estimates with Glavin and McColough *and* the balance of risks of having too much inventory versus constricting sales if demand were very strong—and Chandler was soon authorized to prepare for 15,000 machine placements.

Orders for the 914 poured in. The White House wanted four machines. Production accelerated from 50 machines a *month* to three machines every *day* to 12 a day, then 24, and then over 50—and eventually over 100 machines *every* day! As volume accelerated, less and less time was available for testing. Engineering change-orders to modify the 914 were frequent—and many were made on the factory floor, right up to the time of shipping. (Becker later counted the total number of change orders. It was in excess of 10,000!)

For two very different reasons, placements of the 914s were concentrated in four major metropolitan areas: New York; Washington, DC; Philadelphia; and Chicago. As J.P. Morgan once said, there are usually two reasons for a major decision: One is recognizable as a *good* reason; the other is the *real* reason. The good reason was that demand was so very strong that such a concentration enabled the company to serve the largest number of customers. The real reason was that the machines had been produced as rapidly as possible with on-the-run design changes, but without time for the requisite testing of parts design or the manufacturing process, so the early 914s needed many repairs. Early 914s required, on average, one service call every 2,000 copies or, at seven copies a minute, once every 300 minutes of operation—less than half a working day at a large law firm where copying was virtually continuous. If repairs were made quickly, the customers didn't mind much because they only paid for actual copies. But machines that were down were costly to a company that needed to focus on cash flow. By concentrating placements in a few major cities, the logistics of service and timely repairs were made manageable—even in that first wild year.

Eventually, the total number of new machines built for the 914 family was 200,000. (The number of machine *placements*—including old 914s that were rebuilt and converted to faster versions—was a much larger number: 600,000! These converted machines included the 720, which increased the speed from 7 copies per minute to 12 and then, the 1000, which made 17 copies a minute.)

"The enthusiasm for the 914 is unbelievable," said Joe Wilson in a report at the business equipment show in Washington. "We have shaken this industry, and can achieve great success if our manufacturing and marketing organizations meet the challenge."

After that first stressful year, 914 machine quality improved so much that it enabled the company to take all the risks of downtime *and* confidently offer customers a short 15-day notice for cancellation. The anxious sales force called this "The Sword of Damocles" policy, until they saw how well it actually worked. Then they loved it because it made prospective customers feel very safe in committing to the 914. (The son of American Photocopy's CEO saw the 914 demonstration at the show in Washington, DC and bought a *lot* of common stock in Wilson's company. Even though he was treasurer of a major competitor, he knew the 914 would be a real winner.)

Wilson's company was placing many more 914s than expected, and each machine was being used to make many more copies than ever expected. Designed to make 10,000 copies a year, many 914's were producing 10,000 copies every *month*! With this multiplication, copy volume simply exploded. Profits on the unexpected volume of demand helped pay for the service organization that became a protean strength of Xerox. (At major users, a full-time service representatives was assigned.) The product nobody wanted became the product *everybody* wanted. As *Fortune* expressed it: "The company has about the most delightful economics around these days. It makes a unique office-copying machine for some $2,500 and rents it out for an average of $4,000 a year."

The 914 was the most profitable machine ever manufactured in the United States.

By this time, Glavin's estimate of actual machine placements had been increased to three *times* the Arthur D. Little estimate. He now projected 15,000 placements of 914s over the next five years— followed by 30,000 placements of 813s. And McColough argued that the company had the chance to establish its name as *the* leader in the market: "If we take IBM's strength and success in office equipment as our ideal and model, it's very clear that they did not give up on any promising products of their own development and as a consequence, IBM has become a great and highly profitable company of almost unrivaled strength."

Timing—deciding *when* to take action—is often far more important than deciding *what* to do, particularly when the crucial variable is as fluid and interactive as a free, competitive market. The spirit and commitment of the whole Haloid organization had been brought to a vibrant, high intensity. Wilson must have wondered how long that spirit of commitment could be sustained without people cracking. And if stopped or suspended for half a year, how could that spirit of commitment be reignited? And at what cost?

Market anticipation was another major consideration. There *is* a tide in the affairs of men and the publicity campaign had built up market expectations: A deferral of several months could break the momentum. On the other hand, if the machines broke down too often, the 914 could get caught in a destructive sandstorm of errors, frustrations, and downtime.

Wilson had yet another problem: He was running out of money. For a company as small as Haloid, its financial capacities were being overwhelmed by the costs of building up the sales and service organization. Each new person cost $12,000 to train and new people were being hired in the hundreds. Collectively, these new hires were costing millions. At the same time, capital was required for the manufacturing facilities, plus the inventories of expensive parts, and, most of all, for the hundreds of new 914s that would be installed in customer's offices without knowing how long it would take for them to become cash-flow positive. Wilson had already agreed with Merritt Chandler to delay 914 shipments from October 1958 to March 1959, so inventories were absorbing scarce capital, like so many giant sponges. Tensions were understandably high. Haloid was rapidly running out of time and money.

The whole concept of copiers and copying was changed by the 914: Copies went from wet to dry, costly to cheap, messy to easy, and from nuisance to convenience. Copying morphed from one copy of one document to several copies of many documents to many copies of *all* documents. To save time looking through central files, copies were made by branch offices of corporations, departments of government. Even individuals made copies for their own files. Not only were more copies being made; they were made for new kinds of reasons.

Only after office work habits had changed, and changed quite profoundly, would the considerable economic advantages of the 914 become obvious. First, people had to change from making only a few copies with carbon paper to making several or many copies of all sorts of documents. Imagine a 30-page memo and estimate how many copies would be made with carbon paper. Four? Two? One? None? With xerography, why not make ten copies and why not make ten copies of each *draft*? If four drafts were completed and distributed for comments and changes before the final version of the document was printed, that could be 10 copies of four drafts and a final copy of those same 30 pages. This multiplies out to 1,500 copies. Compare that with, perhaps, no copies at all with carbon paper. What everyone overlooked would become, with the remarkable convenience of the 914, the largest category of copy demand: *copies of copies!* Before xerography, copies of copies were impossible. Now, copies of copies, often made far from the point of origin, would generate much more demand for copies than copies of originals. The whole concept of "copies" was revolutionized by the 914. And the 914 enabled Joe Wilson to revolutionize his company.

Wilson's company achieved results beyond all expectations,

changing more in sales and profits *and* in strategic position than any major company had ever before accomplished."I keep asking myself," mused Wilson, "when are you going to wake up with the dream over? Things just aren't this good in life."[4]

For Joe Wilson, the 914 opened up a whole new realm of opportunities in corporate leadership and public service. For Chet Carlson, the astonishing success of the 914 meant that the great work of his life was complete. Before the 914 copier, Carlson came in once or twice a week, but after the 914 was in production, his involvement steadily declined. Carlson gave away most of his large fortune,[5] usually anonymously,[6] to ethical and educational organizations. His financial reward may have totaled well over $100 million, about twice the reward earned by Joe Wilson. But neither man really cared. Both

---

[4]*Fortune*, July 1961, page 51.

[5]Dorris Carlson once observed that if Chet had kept everything he had earned, his personal fortune would have exceeded $150 million. However, she reported that he had given away what would be worth $100 million to 16 major beneficiaries—including Cal Tech and other educational institutions, the Center for the Study of Democratic Institutions and other peace groups, many organizations working for civil rights, and organizations promulgating Zen Buddhism, because that was Dorris's interest.

[6]In May 1968, *Forbes* identified Chet Carlson as one of America's 53 richest people, all with estimated assets over $150 million. In a letter to the editors, Chet explained that he belonged in the under $50 million category. Silently and anonymously, he had begun his major philanthropic giving. In 1986, Dorris Carlson wrote to Time, Inc., requesting a correction in the company's morgue or subject files and saying: "A few years ago, in a brief article in *Time*, Chester Carlson was described as 'penurious.' He was the opposite of this. This was a man who gave away almost his entire fortune for humanitarian causes and to further peace in the world. Most of his gifts were anonymously given, in character with his generous and unpretentious nature. To describe him as 'penurious' is a disservice and gives a distorted image to people around the world which can never really be erased from their minds. Will you follow through in correcting your files so that others, who write articles in the future, using previous material as informational sources, will not repeat these false statements. May I hear from you regarding the steps your magazine has taken to correct your files?"

were engaged in something they thought was far more meaningful and important than making money.[7] They were deeply committed to a great adventure and the chance to effect major change in the world and how people live.

In the two decades from 1946 to 1965, Joe Wilson organized and led the business enterprise that drove a major technological revolution and created its own future through complementary innovations in technology and marketing. It became one of the world's most successful and most admired international companies. And it changed the whole concept of office work, improving the working lives of millions. Simultaneously, Wilson's creative commitment to social leadership included innovations in labor relations; commitments to advancing education; distinctive aesthetic style in product design, graphics, and advertising; pioneering public-affairs programming on television; and effective early initiatives in race relations.

As he often said, modern corporate leaders owe it to their companies, their communities, their nation, and themselves "to set high goals, to have almost unattainable aspirations, and to imbue people with the belief that they can be achieved." Wilson understood that financial rewards are secondary to the real reward for leadership: the fulfilling experience of building a company to greatness—measured externally by value delivered to customers and society, and internally by career satisfaction and personal fulfillment of many individual people. Wilson wanted to understand what *could* be done, because he believed knowing what could be done often defined what *should* be done. This would define his personal responsibility as a leader.

For most of his life, Joe Wilson carried a blue index card in his wallet with a set of aspirations that he referred to regularly. His friends always believed he had written what it said: "To be a whole man; to attain serenity: Through the creation of a family life of uncommon richness; through leadership of a business which

---

[7] Ironically, the machine shown in the Chet Carlson commemorative postage stamp is a model that *never* worked.

brings happiness to its workers, serves well its customers and brings prosperity to its owners; by aiding a society threatened by fratricidal division to gain unity."

The challenging simplicity of Wilson's personal aspiration, like a compass, guided his thoughts and energies as a leader just as an inspiring communication program would position Wilson's company and its products in new and inspiring ways.

21

GETTING ON MESSAGE

The marketing revolution that converted Haloid into Xerox was both conceptual and organizational. Time and again, Joe Wilson took the lead in either conceptualizing, encouraging, or endorsing a change in the way his company was seen—both from outside *and* from within. He knew that enduring external change could only be achieved with strong support from within.

Wilson's interest in using public relations to create greater awareness of the benefits of xerography was stimulated when he received a letter from Paul Garrett, retiring Vice President for Public Relations at General Motors in 1955: "I've been following your company and am really interested. I'd like to take a major position in your stock and try to help." At the same time, Dave Curtin, a popular radio personality in Rochester, joined Haloid to head up public relations. He was keen to work with Garrett.

"Paul took me by the hand to see *Business Week*," says Curtin. A few weeks later, when Sputnik was on the cover of every *other* magazine, Joe Wilson was on the cover of *Business Week*."[1] The four-page

[1] September 19, 1959.

cover article was a fact-filled feature on Wilson and his company and an overall review of the copier industry—a major publicity coup. Noting that the copying field was crowded, with more than 30 companies already competing, the article also explained that copy volume was rising "like a guided missile." Industry sales had multiplied 370% in less than a decade, surging from $60 million in 1950 to $224 million in 1959.

The *Business Week* article included a picture of Wilson, Dessauer, Linowitz, and Glavin sitting together and discussing a marketing report on the number of copiers in the world and prospective growth in demand. At the photographer's request, Wilson was leaning forward to look closely at the report. With a nearly photographic memory, particularly for numbers, he noticed that the report cited numbers for Eastman Kodak's machine placements that were higher than the figures Glavin had used in his recent planning presentations. Wilson wanted to know why. Glavin protested he had only just received the report himself, and had no time even to look at it before this moment, so he didn't know exactly how they were put together. Wilson would not be put off. He wanted to know and pressed Glavin for a straight answer. Glavin protested. Wilson insisted. The photographer kept shooting.

"In fact," Glavin recalled, "Joe was asking one question after another, hammering away at why the numbers in that report differed from some of the numbers we'd been using. With all those questions, I got so steamed up that as soon as the photo-shoot was over, I stormed out angry as could be. Refusing to take that kind of crap, I was set to *quit!*"

But, Glavin quietly admitted, "after 10 to 15 minutes, I began to calm down. It was just too hard to stay angry with Joe Wilson."

A major component of Wilson's overall communications strategy was public speaking, particularly to groups of lenders and an interesting new group of investors that were managing more and more money in mutual funds and pension funds: the so-called institutional investors.[2] One way of reaching these investors was by speaking at luncheons and dinners that brought together dozens of financial analysts. The analysts were particularly important because they were "message carriers" to the rapidly expanding community of institutional portfolio managers whose large-scale trading increasingly determined the price of a company's common stock and therefore its cost of capital.

Wilson was particularly effective in these presentations. Not only did he know the numbers thoroughly and have an exciting story to tell, he had a unique style of presentation, frequently and comfortably incorporating inspiring quotations from great philosophers and historians.

"Wilson sounded more like a college professor lecturing a fairly advanced class rather than a salesman making a pitch," reported the *New York Times* on Wilson's 1962 presentation to the New York Security Analysts. "He quoted at considerable length from Lord Byron's *Don Juan* and reminded his forum of various perceptions of Dostoyevsky and Montaigne."

Having carefully selected quotes and phrases to match the specific moment—and having delivered a dress rehearsal that same morning via telephone through a loud speaker system recently installed in company plants—Wilson gave his formal presentation without any notes, appearing to speak extemporaneously. He did this often and it always made a strong impression on his audience. But he never got over the inner tension, an almost paralyzing fear that he had to master—and then use as energy to give zest to his presentations.

---

[2] In the 1950s, institutional investing, as we know it today, was just beginning. Trading on the New York Stock Exchange was small, averaging fewer than 3 million shares a day (versus 1.6 billion a day now). At less than 10%, institutional trading was a very small fraction of daily trading volume. Today it reaches 90%. No brokers specialized in investment research. Quotron and other electronic devices to report stock prices on demand had not been invented. The growth in pension funds and mutual funds and the increasing competition for investment performance that transformed the capital markets did not arrive until the 1960s and 1970s.

I nstitutional investors were an important audience for the company's outstanding annual report. Wilson's sense of humor and
his ability to rise to an occasion came together when he accepted
the Gold Oscar for the company's annual report. He had just learned
that his audience included C. Northcote Parkinson, the author of a
popular spoof on the foibles of management that included, as Parkinson's Law, the proposition that work expands to fill the time
available. Smiling, Wilson improvised his introductory remarks
good- naturedly.

"Like almost everyone else, I suppose, I've read Professor Parkinson's little book called *Parkinson's Law and Other Studies in Administration*.
The propinquity of Professor Parkinson and our people at this dinner," he declared, "might well be marvelous irony. We, after all, benefit from Parkinson's Law because our business is paperwork. Dr.
Parkinson once said that 'work expands so as to fill the time available
for its completion.' There is no authority on earth powerful enough
to halt the inexorable force of this principle. It's like gravity. In addition, we have found that our customers' demand for copies grows
faster than their expanding work, a kind of compounding of Parkinson's Law, an extension not unwelcome to our shareholders or those
of us with stock options."

Deftly shifting to a serious tone, Wilson declared, "Businessmen
today . . . must think of functions beyond profit . . . must expand
their vision beyond the limits of making maximum profits. . . . Each
one must help solve, if he can, the social problems that wash the
edges of his island."

Quoting Alfred North Whitehead on a great society, he concluded: "Making profit is a great function, but not the only one. And
some of us would not be caught dead in this profession—if I may use
the term—if its goal could not be expanded to encompass those
other affairs, even though to do so might give revered old Adam
Smith a nightmare."

In addition to public speaking and public relations, Wilson knew advertising would be essential.

As part of their marketing revolution, Wilson and Don Clark, product manager for the 914, agreed that Haloid should change ad agencies. Advertising and sales promotion had been small: Their combined annual budget was less than $50,000 and for that small an amount, a local Rochester agency had been able to give better service than a big New York agency. But, in 1961, with plans for a substantial national advertising campaign that would multiply the annual advertising budget 10 to 15 times, most of the advertising business would have to go through a major agency in New York City, one with real clout. The local Rochester agency suggested a hot new Manhattan agency: Papert, Koenig & Lois. Innovative advertising became a powerful part of Wilson's comprehensive communications strategy, but as important as advertising would be, paid advertising could never have as much credibility and impact as editorial coverage.

Getting good editorial coverage is never easy. Journalists have lots of alternatives because many, many people want *their* story told, *their* picture printed, *their* product featured. And while many stories are true, some others are not true—or are only partly true. Spin is not new. So journalists must make choices, and the easiest choice is to do nothing, just as the second easiest choice is to report repeatedly on a running story.

Being first with a big, new story is obviously desirable, but being wrong and in print really hurts. So when Joe Wilson went courting the journalists, they were as always, professionally skeptical. For example, Jim Michaels, the editor of *Forbes*, told how he and his editors missed the boat in July 1957:

The 47-year-old president of a promising technology company talked for about an hour of the great plans he had for his company and the fantastic process it owned; described his decision to go it alone rather than accept any of the favorable merger offers he had received and told how he was determined to avoid diluting his common stockholders' equity. The theme running through everything he said was: 'We're not just bringing out new products; we're founding a whole new industry.'

The *Forbes* men were impressed. The president was a sincere, enthusiastic, extremely articulate man. He believed in what they were doing. He had the facts and figures right at his fingertips. He understood finance and he understood technology. The president handled all our questions beautifully, professionally.

And what did *Forbes* do with the story? Nothing—partly because the company was well below the minimum size we had set for a company story and partly because its high stock price seemed to discount all the possible good news for the next ten years."

The company's name is Xerox. The speaker was one Wilson, its president then and now. That $24-million-a-year operation is a $500-million-a-year one today. Its earnings, then eight cents a share on the present stock, will hit $2.75 this year. The stock which looked ridiculously high in 1957 has since gone up over 4000%; an investment of $1,000 at that time would be worth better than $40,000 today.

That omission taught me a valuable lesson: It was to trust my instinct even if this required overcoming my inbred skepticism. Among the things that impressed me was that Wilson came unaccompanied. Most corporate executives arrive accompanied by a retinue, usually including at least one PR type. Wilson obviously felt the message he had to deliver could stand on its own without embellishment—and it did.

Over the next year or so, Joe Wilson was on the cover of virtually every business or financial magazine. As one cover story after another featured Wilson as "Mr. Xerox," almost everyone at Haloid felt terribly proud of him and glad to see him being recognized for all he had accomplished. However, there were two exceptions, and one was Joe Wilson. Over and over, Wilson insisted on recognition for his associates—particularly Chet Carlson, John Dessauer, and Sol Linowitz, but also Homer Piper, John Glavin, Horace Becker, and Merritt Chandler. And the other exception was Sol Linowitz who complained that the attention focused on Wilson was "just not right," that Wilson "should have shared the recognition more with the others."[3]

S elling the 914—and the concept of xerography—as a fast, clean, simple process to large numbers of business customers through a direct sales organization would clearly be essential and could never be sufficient, particularly in the few years of the 914's product life. Direct sales and service with frequent customer contact would, of course, be the largest, most costly and most effective part of the overall marketing strategy. But the 914 was *heavy*. It weighed 650 pounds, so salespeople couldn't haul a demonstrator to prospective customers' offices. Prospective customers would need to see the 914 for themselves *outside* their offices. Relying entirely on "push" marketing would be too slow, too hard with a 650-pound product, and far too costly: "Pull" marketing would be needed, too.

The concept of xerography and the credibility of the company had to be strongly validated *before* the sales call in order to create the buying consensus within each prospective customer organization that the 914 was a really good idea even with its new technology, its large size, and its unusual pricing-and-leasing arrangement. At most companies, this would be a *group* decision with executives, secretaries, office managers, and cost controllers all having a say. With such a broad spectrum of different people involved in making the decision, a saturation medium like TV, despite the expense, was clearly needed. Developing the "I want one!" desire for a 914 would be a crucial part of the major marketing success needed to achieve

[3]Jack Harnett interview with Blake McKelvey.

the sales volume that would enable his company to become the new kind of business organization Joe Wilson dreamed of creating.

Changing basic perceptions—the way people habitually think about anyone or anything, is notoriously difficult. Wilson needed to change the way people—lots and lots of people—thought about copies and copiers and about the 914 *and*, even more importantly, how they thought about Wilson's still unfamiliar company. Wilson appreciated that TV had to be an important part of his overall strategy to achieve the transformation of his company from a virtually unknown Haloid in upstate New York into an international corporation with strong, worldwide recognition and acceptance. Other parts of Wilson's overall positioning strategy included industrial product design excellence; distinctive graphic design for signage, stationery, annual reports, and the corporate logo; attention-getting public relations; public speaking; and clever media advertising. As usual, Wilson took the initiative in specific ways and retained expert advisors.

Dave Curtin pointed out the obvious: Graphic design at Haloid-Xerox was a hodge-podge of ideas, typefaces, layout and design—and none of it was very good. "Joe, we look like hell!"

So, in 1958, Gordon Lippincott of Lippincott & Margolies was brought in from New York to help. Lippincott & Margolies created the Xerox logo and then added a decorative extra: a series of tiny blue flags. While this design was being considered, company executives who were eating at a local restaurant looked at the restaurant's paper doilies and saw the very same decoration. The L&M team had "borrowed" the idea from that same restaurant and then charged the company high fees for "creativity." After this, the relationship went downhill rapidly and was soon terminated.

Other initiatives were more successful. Al Zipser, a *New York Times* financial writer, was hired by Curtin to develop coverage in leading newspapers and magazines, and his efforts resulted in a major feature article. Jack Hough organized a small design department and hired Chermayeff & Geismar for graphic design—annual reports, stationery, and all the many other ways a fast-growing company appears to its many publics. Their challenge: Provide Xerox with a consistent look that was attractive, contemporary, universal, and distinctive. (Welton Beckett and Associates were retained as architects to make Xerox's buildings—both the new factories at Webster and, later on, the office tower at downtown's Xerox Square—structures in which Xerox employees and Rochester citizens could take pride.)

Dramatic events and imaginative demonstrations that would capture the attention were needed to get people thinking differently about the company and the 914. So Don Clark, with strong encouragement from Wilson, went looking for ways to get people talking to each other about xerography and the 914. Where could Haloid-Xerox target very large numbers of people, particularly the most influential people, to stop, look, and listen long enough for a demonstration of the 914?

Grand Central Station! The company leased an exhibit area in Grand Central, New York City's biggest railroad station, so everyone coming or going would see it every time they went through. A fact-filled, 12-minute demonstration was produced that explained the xerographic process. The show was a real hit. Repeated over and over again, every 12 minutes, it ran for two straight months.

The company's advertising budget was far too small to compete for share of mind against such marketing giants as RCA, IBM, Eastman Kodak, and 3M. With no hope of competing on *reach*, Wilson's advertising campaign had to compete on *intensity*, so he and Curtin concentrated all advertising in a few major business publications. And to get the greatest impact, those ads would have to be innovative attention-getters.

The ad campaign to introduce the 914—concentrated in *Fortune* and *Business Week*—was almost as revolutionary as the 914 itself. One ad was a six-page, four-color gatefold, with a die-cut opening that enabled the reader to see right into the works of the 914. *Fortune* had never before run such an ad. The impact on readers was great; the surrounding buzz in conversation and in editorial copy was even greater.

For another *Fortune* ad, actual xerographic copies were inserted into the magazine. (200,000 copies were made at the rate of 7 copies a minute, or 420 an hour: The total number of inserts needed took 500 hours to produce.) The second ad in *Forbes* took 500,000 xerographic copies that were individually glued on over the original page—so readers could lift up the copy, look at the original and see the quality for themselves. (Making the xerographic copies took 2,000 hours—the equivalent of one person working full time for a year.) The text of this ad was written to catch a reader's attention: "We knew you wouldn't believe we can make copies on ordinary paper, so to prove it to you. . . . we did it!"

But were the claims valid or were they exaggerations? A skeptical inquiry came in a stern letter from a government official challenging the advertising claim that said, "Our machine can copy on *any* kind of paper!" Don Clark handled this inquiry easily, turning to his assistant. "Copy that letter on an ordinary paper bag and mail it back—without comment—to the man who wrote that letter." Later, Clark used the idea in public: He ran another ad using a copy made on a brown paper bag.

Picasso's picture of an owl was shown in a series of advertisements in *Fortune*, *Business Week*, and *U.S. News & World Report*. On one side of a two-page spread was the quite valuable original engraving, and on the other side, a xerographic reproduction. One was in a $1,000 frame. Readers were invited to identify which was which, and were promised a copy suitable for framing if they could correctly distinguish between them. Over 16,000 readers wrote in. The "vote" was evenly split. That was perfectly OK: Even if readers guessed wrong, they got a copy suitable for framing—a xerox copy—with a note saying, "We are happy you guessed the xerographic copy was the Picasso original!" (Later, when taking it around the country for in-person demonstrations, the Picasso was supposed to be locked up at night. But even the Xerox team couldn't tell the difference: They were locking up the xerox copy!

Television was a vital part of the systematic program that would be needed to establish Xerox and its products as truly global leaders. Carl Ally, the account executive assigned by Papert, Koenig & Lois to manage the Xerox account was persistently urged by Wilson to strive for excellence. So Ally, in turn, convinced Wilson to focus on TV ads in promoting the 914. Print ads, even when asserting quite legitimate value claims, would always *seem* exaggerated. But seeing would be believing, and ads on TV could be stunning. So, if the TV ads were cleverly designed, the impact on viewer's perceptions would be well worth the daunting cost.

The first ads were clever, fresh, and charmingly original. They were fun, had impact, and were directly "on message." In one ad, a little girl with a rag doll was the operator of the 914. A man in a three-buttoned suit turns to the girl and says with a warm smile, "Honey, please make a copy of this"—and off she skips, with her rag doll to a 914, where she quickly and easily makes a copy and then skips back to her father with it. So quick. So simple. So easy. Even a grown-up could make copies on a 914!

Dad looks at the copies and asks, in wonder, "Which is the original?" The girl isn't sure. She tilts her head and with a shy smile says, "I forget." It was unique, fun, and had one clear message: Making excellent 914 copies is *easy* and *quick*. (Don Clark's wife made 25 rag dolls, which were sent out to the branch sales offices. They were easy to copy and they, too, made an effective demonstration.)

The second ad was just as clearly "on message." In this ad, the operator was not a child, but a chimpanzee. The chimp goes through the same routine as the girl had done—except for the addition of scampering up over a group of office chairs on the way to the 914. As the chimp hands in the copies, the executive asks the now familiar: "Which is the original?" The chimp furrows his brow, scratches his head and makes a sound a lot like "I forget." People loved it.

But not *everyone*. Some, particularly some secretaries, were offended by the comparison. (Wilson was personally uncomfortable with the chimpanzee, fearing it might upset people, so it ran only once.) Then, bananas—whole bunches of bananas—started showing up on secretaries' desks. A newspaperman wrote a humorous article about the banana placements as an interesting sociological phenomenon. His paper got so much reader response that he turned his initial human interest feature article into a running series of pieces "defending the honor" of the nation's secretaries. Then, copies of the newspaper story on the chimp and the bananas showed up on secretaries' desks all over the country—like one of those instant fad jokes that sweep through America's colleges.

Don Clark was up to this challenge. He invited the newspaperman writing those articles to lunch at the 21 Club in midtown Manhattan. Their table was set for three. After Clark and the journalist were comfortably seated, in came the third party. A chimp. The chimpanzee jumped onto its chair and put on a bib. Good to go! Humor was a distinctive part of Xerox advertising, but not all Xerox TV used humor *or* advertising.

"Xerox Corporation is privileged to bring you the following major television event" was all that introduced a 90-minute television documentary on the work of the United Nations. During the next hour-and-a-half of prime time television, there were no commercials of any kind. The program closed with a similarly brief statement: "This program has been one of a series produced and telecast as a public service through funds provided by Xerox Corporation."

This minimalist innovation in corporate advertising—dignified, tasteful, and starkly original—was quickly and favorably recognized across the United States as "typical of Xerox." No other company had ever made such a major broadcasting commitment for such remarkably restrained recognition. Far from being popular entertainment, each program in this series presented dramatized, in-depth reporting on a major, difficult issue. The whole series of six 90-minute, prime-time documentary programs was expensive: *Twice* Xerox's entire advertising budget for the year 1964. Joe Wilson made the decision and called Don Clark and Dave Curtin to announce, "Boys, I'm going to spend $4 million you don't have in your combined budgets—on TV!"

As so often at Xerox, the first thread of connection had come through Joe Wilson. His work in labor relations and his respect for Cornell's School of Industrial Relations had resulted in acquaintance with Anna Rosenberg, a lecturer and labor arbitrator, and the wife of Paul Hoffman, the United States' first ambassador to the United Nations. As director of the United Nations Association of the United States, Hoffman was organizing the TV series. Simultaneously, Hoffman discussed the idea with an associate of his wife who knew television and also was a friend of Frederic Papert, head of Xerox's new advertising agency.

"Have you got a sponsor?" asked Papert.

"Don't be silly. Nobody can sponsor the United Nations!"

"I'm not so sure."

Papert and Rosenberg spoke to Wilson, who was intrigued with the possibilities. Soon Xerox made an imaginative arrangement: A special purpose foundation—the Telsun Foundation—was set up specifically for the TV series.[4] Xerox agreed to sponsor the series without any control over or even any prior knowledge of program content.

The United Nations had a strict policy: No nation within the United Nations, whatever its politics and whatever its record, could either be criticized or admired publicly, so the programs would have to be carefully nonpolitical. Ironically, however, in the early 1960s—shortly after the Joe McCarthy era and with the John Birch Society still flowering—this nonpolitical discipline to neither criticize nor

---

[4]Trustees included John J. McCloy, Eugene Black, Andrew Heiskell, Paul Hoffman, Sol Linowitz, and Joe Wilson.

admire would be taken as highly political among arch-conservatives who viscerally distrusted the U.N. Wilson was ready for hostile reaction, saying: "We are willing to accept that risk. In supporting this project we may create some enemies, but we also hope to win many more powerful friends."[5] Wilson recognized the risk that some organized right-wing groups would be upset—and he was correct. Deering Milliken's president, Rodger Millikin, an arch-conservative, who served on the Citibank board with Joe Wilson, cancelled all his corporation's contracts with Xerox.

"For the Corporation to forego its normally allotted commercial time in a TV series of this magnitude is, I gather, unprecedented," acknowledged Wilson. "Our eyes are wide open about it. It is part of our philosophy that the highest interests of the Corporation are involved in the health of the earth's society."[6]

ABC and NBC agreed to broadcast the series, but CBS refused, saying a dramatization must not serve as a political tract or as propaganda for a particular viewpoint and declaring that it didn't matter that Xerox had already agreed to sponsor the series "blind" and would have no knowledge of the content.

Still, Wilson was not being naïve. He wanted recognition and clearly recognized the possibilities of making a publicity "event" out of the act of sponsoring such a long, serious program on prime-time TV, and startling observers with such minimal advertising. The resulting newspaper publicity could be very valuable, and well worth both the cost and the risk. Success began with the announcement of the TV series at a formal luncheon at the United Nations in New York, where Secretary General U Thant shook hands warmly with Chet Carlson, and several dignitaries made speeches. Wilson's brief talk concluded: "It is part of our philosophy that the highest interests of a Corporation are involved in the health of the earth's society. We are proud to be part of this enterprise which, as we all know, is making history."[7]

[5]Dessauer, page 194.
[6]*Business Week*, April 18, 1964, page 82.
[7]Dessauer, page 192.

The series attracted stellar performers, such as Peter Sellers, Eva Marie Saint, Ben Gazzarra, and Sterling Hayden; such major producers as Otto Preminger, Stanley Kubrick, and Joseph Mankiewitz; and such musicians as Richard Rodgers, Henry Mancini, and André Previn. All volunteered their services at minimum union-scale wages because Xerox was not running commercials. Press coverage of the high-minded concept, the courage of Wilson's convictions, and the dignity of the whole arrangement was unusually extensive and complimentary to Wilson and to Xerox. As Curtin gleefully recalled, "It was a public relations coup and all my contemporaries at IBM, GE, GM and others were green with envy. That's a fact!"

Wilson was particularly pleased by the gracious way Xerox's sponsorship was celebrated in Washington. He and Peggy were invited by Secretary of State Dean Rusk to view the inaugural program at a Sunday afternoon reception at the State Department, cohosted by Adlai Stevenson, U.S. ambassador to the United Nations. Guests included Peter and Ginnie McColough, Sol and Toni Linowitz, and a throng of U.S. and international diplomats.

The TV presentation was disturbingly graphic, and clearly not slanted to a U.S. perspective. At the end of the program, the room full of usually talkative people was silent. Across the screen came the discrete and silent statement, " . . . as a public service through funds provided by Xerox Corporation." More silence.

Then everyone seemed to want to speak at once. Some were offended. Some were chagrined by the blunt tone. Others, including Ambassador Stevenson, thought it was bold and vividly accurate. "Those problems *are* the reality. The challenges ahead *are* enormous. No, the U.N. has not solved them, but, yes! That's why the U.N. is so important and so needs America's support."[8] As Joe Wilson put it: "As an organization of human beings, the U.N. has foibles—but it's all we've got."

---

[8]After the reception, the Wilsons and Stevensons flew to New York for a dinner in the ambassador's honor at the Four Seasons.

Overall press coverage was highly favorable and international. The U.N. series served notice in a powerful way that Xerox was bold, original, and international; intended to be a real leader among corporations with a serious commitment to serving the public interest; and respected the intelligence of American viewers. Wilson explained: "Our objective is to help men better communicate with each other. Therefore, it is important for Xerox to be favorably known throughout the world as an institution that is willing to take a risk in order to improve understanding and will accept a challenge to its short-run position in order to buttress the long years ahead."[9]

Wilson was, on a major scale, affirming his belief that a corporation owed itself, its people, and its community a strong commitment to strengthening service institutions.

"People have come to understand," Wilson maintained, "that it is good business for a modern corporation to exercise a sense of social responsibility."[10]

But, while many agreed that Xerox deserved solid affirmation, others were angry. The John Birch Society mobilized a protest letter-writing campaign and got 12,000 missives off in an attempt to thwart Xerox. It didn't work; it backfired. One giveaway: Most of the letters quoted verbatim from the John Birch Society *Bulletin*. Xerox collected the letters, sorted them by location of sender, matched up duplicates, and announced that they had all been written by just 2,100 people. The "mass protest" was scoffed at in newspaper articles as the over-organized work of the Ku Klux Klan and right-wing weirdos. A public opinion survey by Elmo Roper found that Xerox had indeed *gained* more friends than it lost.

The U.N. series was followed by a steady stream of significant television programs on the Louvre and its great art collections, on Martin Luther King Jr., and on Jimmy Hoffa. Xerox brought to a national audience such shows as *Let My People Go, Death of a Salesman, The*

---

[9]*Business Week*, April 18, 1964, page 80.
[10]Dessauer, page 194.

Cuban Missile Crisis, The Kremlin, Hal Holbrook's *Mark Twain Tonight,* and *Of Black America.* Publicity for this last series was symbolized by two hands shaking: one white and one black. Most potential sponsors were scared of it, particularly because people in the South might react negatively, but Wilson and McColough both felt it was the right thing to do. Also, Xerox's selling directly to its customers—rather than depending on middleman distributors—made it easier to take stands on controversial issues because Xerox did not run the risk of distributors' protesting by refusing to carry its product line. Right on schedule, immediately after the first episode, one customer cancelled its Xerox copier: the Ku Klux Klan.

Another program, based on Theodore White's *The Making of the President—1964,* led Wilson into a different kind of controversy: Authors were increasingly concerned about the impact of xerography on copyrights. And in *The American Scholar,* Marshall McLuhan wrote that "xerography is bringing a reign of terror into the world of publishing."

Theodore White received angry reactions from author friends whenever he mentioned working with Xerox on the TV series, so he conveyed that problem to Wilson. Already sensitized to concerns about xerographic copies from the tension found in his earlier negotiations with the Wesleyan University Press, Wilson reached out to White and the Authors League, saying to his colleagues at Xerox, "I feel even more strongly that the attitude we expressed a year ago— that this is a problem for others and not for us— is extremely short-sighted."[11]

In early September, Wilson hosted a luncheon in New York City for White, the President of the Authors League, and several authors. Expressing deep concern for the protection of authors' rights, he pledged support for their proposed bill, HR 4347, and wrote a strong letter of endorsement to 40 congressmen and key editors. Asked to contribute to a committee to investigate copyright prob-

[11]McKelvey, page X-31.

lems, Wilson promptly sent $20,000, the largest contribution by any supporter.

Testifying before the House Judiciary Committee, Wilson said Xerox was flatly opposed to any special exemption from the copyright laws. While Xerox was also a publisher—via University Microfilm and American Education Publications—Wilson's main concern was assuring fairness to writers. He consistently maintained that what some observers considered a bold demonstration of corporate idealism was simply good business judgment. Over and over again, Wilson would see doing well as interdependent and mutually beneficial with doing good, saying: "We are determined to make this economic institution a socially valuable one as well. The time has passed when a great business . . . can be a vitally growing and successful enterprise unless it accepts fully the responsibility of good citizenship in every sense of that phrase."

Wilson's innovative advertising and TV programming in America were later matched in comparable media leadership by Fuji-Xerox in Japan. Recognizing that Xerox advertising and Xerox special programs on U.S. television were very progressive, Fuji-Xerox attempted to create comparable programs.

"At first, it was not possible for us to get prime time allocations," said CEO Tony Kobayashi. "Still, we decided to go ahead anyway. Our first TV special was on the opening of the Suez Canal. It received so-so reviews and audience reaction. We made no apologies for that disappointing reception, and continued on."

The second Fuji-Xerox special was dynamite: A tough and critical documentary on the war in Vietnam. This program was aired in prime-time at 10:30 PM. It won critical praise and an Academy Award. For many Japanese people, it was surprising to see a company with American ownership being critical of Washington, DC and of General Westmoreland even during the war period.[12]

----

[12]In 1971, in concert with the Osaka World's Fair, Fuji-Xerox launched a new kind of advertising campaign around the theme that the decade of the seventies would

Joe Wilson brought forward a different concept of communications in the same way he had led in the development of differentiating concepts of labor relations, financing, pricing, marketing, and production. He was, as we now see so clearly in retrospect, a leader who inspired many others to innovate because he created an atmosphere that made it possible for people to understand, trust, and commit to his vision *and* because, in Disraeli's felicitous expression, his mind was "in league with the future." And what a future it was!

---

be different. As Kobayashi explained, "The sixties had been the 'work hard' decade with the Japanese people being asked to make many sacrifices. So, we proposed the seventies were the time to revisit and rebalance—with a new emphasis on the *beautiful*. This campaign was extraordinarily successful."

22

XEROX: ZOOM-ZOOM

I n the 1960s, Wilson's major challenge was to succeed with success—really, to succeed greatly with great success—by sustaining the high growth momentum of Xerox. Deliveries of the 914
accelerated very rapidly: 2,000 in 1960; tripled to 6,000 in
1961; and went up again two-thirds to 10,000 in 1962. Xerox had
expected average usage across the total 914 population to slow
down as more and more machines were placed with lower volume
users, but this did not happen because usage rates among older
machines continued to increase.

Americans fell in love with copying and the remarkably inexpen-
sive, simple, speedy convenience it brought to many aspects of their
busy lives:

- Doctors copied X-rays for 5¢ instead of making another new one
  for $5.
- Police quickly photocopied the contents of suspects' pockets.
- Magazine publishers learned that xerographic copies of photographs made line engravings easy and cheap to produce.
- Realtors could make 50 to 100 copies of a preprinted translucent
  form with key data on houses up for sale.

- The FDA stopped typing copies of bottle labels. By rolling a bottle across the scanning glass of a 914 copier at the same speed as the scanning lamps moved, exact copies were easily made.
- Friends copied recipes for friends.
- Students copied pages from textbooks instead of making laborious copies.
- Kids made pictures of their hands—and dolls and other toys.
- Most importantly, office workers could quickly make 20 copies of a draft of any "work-in-progress" document for all participants. Each recipient could then make changes—and then make multiple copies of the revised copy with their changes on it.

While numbering just 2% of the nation's total population of copiers, 914s produced 75% of all the copies.

"Our first customer was Standard Pressed Steel in Jenkinstown, Pennsylvania," Curtin recalls with pleasure. "Right from the first, that machine made over 10,000 copies a month!"

Not every placement came so easily or worked so well, because not every customer saw things in terms of benefits. U.S. Steel was producing 20,000 copies a month and the Xerox salesman happily anticipated Big Steel adding another machine, but when he went to get the order, he was nearly thrown out.

"Another machine! I'm thinking hard about getting rid of this one!"

"Why?"

"My God, man, I used to have a copy bill of less than $200 a month. Now, my monthly bill is over $1,000 because *everybody's* making copies of *everything!*"

That's why the 914 was an extraordinarily successful product, often cited as the most successful new product in the second half of the twentieth century. Sales increased nearly tenfold in the five years from 1960 to 1965: By then, more than 60,000 machines had been placed. Since the 914 machines cost only $2,400 to build (in time, the cost was reduced to $2,000 per machine) and average annual revenues were $4,500, cash flow and profits increased even faster.

In 1963, Xerox hired more new people than its total employment had been just three years earlier, and in 1964, the year-to-
year increase in sales exceeded the total sales of 1961. In 1965,
the R&D budget, at $33 million, was almost as large as total sales
had been just six years earlier. To support and sustain such
growth, John Rutledge had more than 5,000 sales and service representatives working out of 130 offices in 1965—up four-fold
in just three years from the 1,250 sales and service representatives
of 1962.

In 1963, IBM's Birkenstock was back, but with a very different
proposition. Pleased and impressed, as he said he certainly was, with
all that Wilson had achieved with the 914, he explained with apparent sadness, an inevitable, but ironic twist of fate: Market dominance
now created serious anti-trust problems. Birkenstock went on to suggest that the best solution would be to license IBM to produce
copiers.

When Wilson's colleagues expressed genuine surprise and skepticism, Birkenstock cautioned that Haloid should get the objective
advice of outside counsel. Linowitz accepted the challenge and a
month later he had a judgment from Whitney North Seymour,
senior partner of Simpson, Thatcher & Barlett. Seymour evaluated
the company's position and rendered the opinion that it had no need
to license *any* competitor to make plain-paper copiers. Furthermore,
if it did license others, it should not under any circumstances give
IBM any priority over any other organization.[1]

Wilson did not limit his vision to producing one great product.
He was determined to create a great company: "When people
ask me what our company really wants to do, I say we want to render
values, usually new ones that people have not enjoyed before. We
want to be part of an industry that gives men something worth getting. We want to add new dimensions to the ways they communicate,

[1]Linowitz, page 81.

to make increasing knowledge more broadly available. We want to profit from these efforts. And we want those associated with us to be proud of what they are doing. To say we are in the communications business suggests, at least to us, an obligation to a world in which people can communicate. It suggests the need for freedom and peace—and demands the end of ignorance."

Much as he excelled at developing and articulating an inspiring vision for his company, Wilson's defining personal characteristic was always discipline. Exhilarating as the global growth of his company surely was, Wilson understood that to succeed with success—to reproduce success anything like the success of the 914 on a regularly repeating basis—would require substantial expansion in corporate management and huge investments in R&D to develop major innovations.

As Haloid grew into Haloid Xerox and then into Xerox, and zoomed ahead in pace and scale, Wilson was constantly challenged to redesign the company to keep its structure in harmonious support of its strategy and to reposition senior executives so their capabilities were matched appropriately to the challenges ahead.

Such changes are never easy: The future is always uncertain, as are the capabilities of individuals or combinations of individuals. And for each person, change itself—particularly change in status and stature, and of course, in compensation—would have unknown consequences. Wilson made changes that were large and wide-ranging, *and* well-accepted. Not once did Wilson lose good executives because they were disappointed: Because they trusted him, they always understood that change was important and well-considered.[2]

[2]The extensive changes of 1963, when employment jumped to 11,000, were representative. John Rutledge and Francis Pallichek, who had recently been hired, became Group Vice Presidents, which was a new title. Rutledge was made responsible for marketing (with four divisions) and Pallicheck was placed in charge of manufacturing (with five divisions). Both reported to Peter McColough as Executive Vice President for Operations, who also had five other divisions reporting directly to him. Product planning was under John Glavin, communications under Dave Curtin, and finance under Kent Damon. John Dessauer was also made

Xerox was in a remarkable position for a company whose earnings were growing so very rapidly: Xerox actually *knew* its
future. It knew what its future earnings were going to be for several
years out because with a meter reading the month-by-month usage
of each and every 914, the patterns of usage—particularly the rate of
increasing usage—could easily be analyzed and projected out into the
future. The usage of each particular 914 could be compared with the
past patterns of increasing usage of all existing 914s, sorted into
comparable groups by size of company, by number of employees, by
industry and adjusted for by such macro factors as changes in GNP
or inflation. With increasing accuracy in estimates for each machine,
the actual volume of usage for the whole population of 914s could
be forecast with remarkable accuracy.

In addition, Wilson used unusually conservative accounting
practices. Before 1962, 914 machines were depreciated over eight
years, but this was soon reduced to five years. This reduced reported
profits but increased cash flow, which was still Wilson's entrepreneurial focus. If accounting depreciation were compared to physical
depreciation—the actual useful lives of the 914s—it was clearly very
conservative accounting because the machines lasted much longer
than was assumed in the depreciation schedules. With accelerated
depreciation *and* the assumption of unusually short useful lives, the
company was substantially understating earnings. Xerox might *look*
like a high-priced stock relative to its current reported earnings, but
compared to its real economic earnings, its share price was not at
all high.

With costs known—machine-by-machine—and revenues uncan-
nily predictable and placements almost equally predictable, by the

---

an Executive Vice President with three research divisions. Sol Linowitz, as
Chairman of the Board, was responsible for international activities, patents, and
licensing. Only the three seniors within this group, plus Abe Zarem, would report
directly to Joe Wilson.

mid-1960s, Xerox knew its future cash flow and its future earnings. No growth company in history had ever before had such prescience, such ability to see into its own future earnings for years ahead.

As the sixties began, Joe Wilson and Xerox were not expecting anything like the zooming demand the 914 would create. Nor did they recognize the change that was coming to institutional investing and its importance to Xerox. Sophisticated as it was in many ways, the company's innocence was evident too. Five-year demand projections for the 914 had been laid out on five pages of paper, with those pages in full view for visitors to Kent Damon's office. They had been posted on a bulletin board with "company best estimates" underlined in red.

"They were overwhelmed by Wall Street," recalls Ernie Stowell, one of the leading technology analysts of the era.[3] "They were much too accommodating on sharing information."

In a way, it didn't matter because "insider" estimates were way too low. Damon's early and conservative figures put annual revenues, after five years, at $6¼ million. Total market demand for 914s was estimated at 5,000 units with usage per machine expected to earn an annual average of $1,250. Actual results would beat these estimates by a wide margin.

The leading analysts on Wall Street had much higher estimates for the 914—both in the number of machine placements *and* in the annual volume of usage per machine. Using insights gained from probing interviews with actual users, Wall Street analysts were soon developing a very different model of potential demand. The difference was astounding. One analyst had a friend at the leading New York City law firm, Cravath, Swaine & Moore, who provided him with meter readings of the number of copies produced. Recognizing how rapidly earnings must be rising, he bought call options and later reported: "I made so much money, I could live well without working for 25 years."

[3]Ernie Stowell of Faulkner, Dawkins & Sullivan, who earned recognition as the leading Xerox analyst, studied mathematics and accounting, learned to create formulae to solve highly complex problems, and then was a university math professor before heading East to Wall Street as an analyst.

Since the 914 was truly revolutionary, the leading investment analysts realized that the 914 would not only displace other copiers already in use: The 914 would create a lot of *new* demand. One estimate of five-year demand projected 50,000 placements—ten *times* the company's estimate—*plus* per unit usage that would produce rental fees of $3,500 a year—nearly three *times* the company estimates.[4] This compounding meant there could be 30 times as much revenue as the company was then forecasting. And this meant that profitability would zoom upward. Even Wall Street estimates would not be met: They too were beaten. With 49,000 placements and the average 914 generating nearly $5,000 a year, revenues mushroomed to $245 million—nearly 40 *times* Kent Damon's original internal estimate.

With rapidly increasing machine placements, Wilson and Damon needed to raise substantial new capital: $15 million in 20-year convertible, subordinated debentures in 1961 and then $25 million in a private debt placement with insurance companies, and a $30-million revolving credit facility with a group of commercial banks. While 914 usage and revenues were increasing and the cost of servicing machines was declining, Wilson approved an increase in the rate of depreciation, reducing the estimated useful life of machines from eight years to five years. This lowered reported earnings by $1,750,000, but increased cash flow.

In July, 1961, Xerox was listed as XRX on the New York Stock Exchange. Wilson and Damon went to visit Keith Funston who was head of the New York Stock Exchange, to request that Wagner Stott be appointed as the specialist in Xerox stock.

Funston said, "Now, wait a minute. That's a decision *we* make." And then he assigned Wagner Stott.

In August, Wilson initiated a tentative discussion of acquisitions and acquisition strategies, but insisted: "Any acquisition must have

[4]Customers couldn't buy 914s for many years, until required by the U.S. government on antitrust grounds.

promise equal to xerography. We will not dilute our management by making acquisitions that can create new problems."

Wilson saw into the future and looked for ways to improve it. With annual earnings up 151% in 1961, Wilson again proposed that Xerox contribute more to financing the growth of Rank-Xerox in exchange for Xerox taking control of all business in Latin America. After some resistance from John Davis, agreement was reached for Rank to increase its share of Rank-Xerox profits by two percentage points and turn Latin America and Fuji-Xerox over to Xerox.

23

FUJI-XEROX

I n 1953, Ichiro Sugi, a senior staffer in Fuji Photo Film's business development department, visited Haloid in Rochester and suggested his company might consider commercializing xerography, then limited to the primitive Model A machine.

In 1957, when Dr. Harold Clark went to Japan as a tourist, he was intercepted by Fuji Photo executives who convinced him to tour their plant. They had read a translation of John Dessauer's recent article, "Xerography Today." During that tour, they asked about a license to use xerography in photography, Fuji's main business, because an executive, Setsu Kobayashi, was impressed with xerography as a promising new photographic technology.

In 1958, Tokyo began importing Model A machines for plate making, but only at a rate of five per month. By 1960, several Japanese companies were working to commercialize RCA's electrofax technique, but with only limited success due to cost and quality limitations.

Later, when Fuji's engineers heard about xerographic copiers, they signaled a strong interest, but by then, Rank-Xerox owned the global rights outside of North America, so the call from Fuji to Rochester was referred to London. Since Rank had no technical people with expertise in xerography, Fuji's call was soon passed back to

Rochester. Organizational and legal problems were compounded by the significant cultural differences in office work. In Japan, the size of office papers was never 8½ × 11, and rice paper, which came in many different sizes and was thinner and more fragile than office paper used in the West, did not work in the 914. More importantly, most offices still relied on the Diazo process for copying because it was the cheapest. Furthermore, since nearly all informal writing was done by hand, carbon copies were used very little. (Typewriters for the Japanese language using Chinese characters were complex devices that only trained experts could operate. In the Japan of the early 1960s, there were many more Western-language than Japanese-language typewriters.)

Meanwhile, Rank-Xerox had hired a firm to identify possible partners for a joint venture in Japan.[1] Toshiba was at the top of the consultant's list of ten companies because of its capabilities in physics—and Fuji Photo was at the bottom. However, during a follow-up visit to Japan, after visiting all the candidate companies and meeting Setsutero Kobayashi, who had become Fuji Photo's CEO in 1960, Tom Law put Fuji at the top of his list.

It took two years of negotiations to work out the appropriate structure of the relationship between the companies—Fuji had wanted to operate independently under a license agreement, while Rank Xerox had wanted an integrated joint venture—and to obtain the necessary approval of the Japanese government agencies for the formation of Fuji-Xerox in 1962.[2] Then, after all the time consumed by bureaucratic red tape, the Japanese moved quickly and the final formal agreement was only four pages long. Just four weeks after signing documents, Fuji Photo had a team of technicians in

[1] Charles Rayden Associates.
[2] Xerox owned 50% of Rank-Xerox, which owned 50% of Fuji-Xerox, giving Xerox effective ownership of 25% of Fuji-Xerox.

Rochester to learn the specifications for manufacturing 914s. Still, developing the right working relationship was neither natural nor easy.

Motohiko "Fred" Nakamura came up from Fuji's New York City office to translate English into Japanese and vice versa. Nakamura had earned an MBA at Wharton and was greatly trusted by Fuji Photo's top management, including Setsu Kobayahsi, but he was not an engineer. So the blueprint-by-blueprint examination was going slowly: With several thousand pages of blueprints to work through— a 914 had over 2,000 different parts—the two teams completed only 20 blueprints on a slow day and just 40 on a fast day. After a full day's work, the Fuji team would huddle at their hotel and check to be sure they fully understood each blueprint and then bring their unresolved questions to the next day's meeting. The careful language translations—English into Japanese and Japanese into English—were particularly time consuming.

One evening, Horace Becker invited the Fuji team to his home to relax and have dinner. When his engaging wife Gloria came into the kitchen where Horace was fixing drinks, she cheerfully observed, "Mr. Iki is a charming man, and speaks English so very well!"

Startled at first, Becker saw an opportunity for a breakthrough: "Iki-san, you have hurt my feelings because you don't trust us. You don't need a translator! Let's send Fred home and conduct the rest of our meetings in English!"

After this, progress accelerated rapidly and in early 1963, Fuji-Xerox was producing 914s.[3]

---

[3]For several years, Fuji-Xerox had less than a few hundred people, all doing marketing under EVP Naebue Shono and Setsuturo's son, Tony Kobayshi, who was born and lived in England and studied at graduate school in America, so his English was both fluent and British. Manufacturing was subcontracted to Fuji Photo. Then Fuji-Xerox bought the factory from Fuji Photo, in part because of the stigma among the Japanese people of being "just marketing."

The well-known custom in doing business in Japan is to develop person-to-person relationships and shared understanding prior to developing a business relationship and the appropriate personal relationships are traditionally developed over dinner. Such dinners are traditionally long and elaborate—and costly. As usual, Wilson was interested in getting to know the people of Fuji Photo and developing good personal relationships, so a series of traditional dinners were arranged. But one such dinner didn't develop understanding; it caused a serious misunderstanding.

Wilson and his team from Xerox were surrounded by Japanese dignitaries at a gala dinner in an exclusive restaurant, while a flurry of geisha and *maiko* entertained each of the guests with the graceful, stylized pastimes and games of the Rion era. Course after course of artistically presented dishes were served. The room was filled with activities and bursts of laughter and the colorful gaiety of the occasion. As he was hosting this particular occasion, the evening's bill of fare was quietly and deferentially presented to Wilson. The room was rather dark, so reading the bill was difficult and required Wilson's total concentration. To assist, the hostess offered him a small flashlight so he could see the bill. As Wilson focused on the total charges, he was stunned. The total was surely *impossible!* The charges were *ridiculous!* This was way too much and must be all wrong! There was a mistake in Wilson's expectations, but there was no error in the bill.

Fortunately, such cultural misunderstandings were infrequent as Wilson and Linowitz soon developed quite favorable relationships, particularly with Setsu Kobayashi of Fuji Photo who, despite the substantial personal risks if the joint-venture was not successful, had decided to go forward.

In their home, Mr. and Mrs. Kobayashi quietly discussed the two wonderful Americans—Joe Wilson and Sol Linowitz—agreeing that among the many foreigners visiting Japan, these two seemed most unusual: They did not talk as much as most Americans talked and they always spoke softly. Kobayashi was a man of very few words, and, naturally, felt most comfortable with similarly inclined people.

As his son Tony recalled, "To my parents, I realized, the two Americans must be very special people because it was clear to me that both my father and my mother were quite impressed."

On a person-to-person basis, Wilson made much greater progress in developing real rapport with Kobayashi than with Davis who, Linowitz observed, was "rarely burdened by humility" and "cut through the air just as the bow of the *United States* had cut the water of the Atlantic Ocean."

Davis projected an imperial air of arrogance, both in person and in his letters, that others found hard to take. (Davis's personal life appalled Wilson and the Kobayashis. Divorced several times, Davis was openly living with Lady Aitken. Later, he married someone else.) One such letter seemed, in its demanding tone, particularly arrogant to Kobayashi who asked Wilson, "What kind of man is this to treat those who are supposed to be his *partners* as though they are only his *subordinates*?"

Wilson smiled knowingly, shook his head in wonder, and diffused the tension by saying: "All I can tell you is that he writes to me in the same manner."

On another occasion, Horace Becker was in London working with Tony Hargroves, Rank's Chief Engineer. They were walking up Pulham Street when they both saw Joe Wilson and John Davis coming the other way. "There's Joe," said Becker, "Come on, I want to introduce you."

But Hargroves, a former British Army Major, held Becker back cautioning quietly: "You wouldn't want to stop Sir John on the street just for a conversation. It just isn't done."

But it was too late: Joe Wilson was already coming across the street, nearly getting hit by a taxi because he hadn't looked the right way before stepping off the curb. Becker greeted his boss the usual way: "Hi, Joe," and Wilson, as usual, wanted to know how his man was doing on a personal level: "Are you in a comfortable hotel? Do you have all you need? Are you enjoying London? Do you have plenty of money? Are they treating you OK?" All the classic Joe Wilson questions and then: "Horace, come on. I've gotta introduce you to Sir John. He's a charming person!"

"This is Horace Becker, the man who put the 914 together!" announced Wilson. Sir John knew his rightful place and was, with quite evident difficulty, being tolerant. He certainly did not offer to shake Becker's hand.

After the four men parted, Hargroves spoke with wonder: "I cannot believe that that was *the* Joe Wilson! Frankly, he's beyond my imagination!"

"That's the way he always is," said Becker.

After the long negotiations required to establish the Fuji-Xerox joint venture agreement, Linowitz and Law were invited to attend a Kobayashi family wedding at the old Imperial Hotel in Tokyo. Yotaro "Tony" Kobayashi, a recent MBA from Wharton, was explaining the Shinto wedding ceremony to the foreign guests. After the ceremony, young Kobayashi was surprised to be rather casually invited by Linowitz to "come on up to my room for a cup of coffee." Receiving this invitation must be a great honor but, if the invitation were serious and important, why was it extended so casually? The same puzzlement came with Linowitz's subsequent invitation to "come over to Fuji-Xerox." If it were a serious invitation, why was it expressed so informally?

Kobayashi, knowing he was soon to be assigned to Fuji Photo's New York office and recognizing the personal risks of working for a foreign company or even a joint venture, consulted his father who said: "You must decide for yourself. As I told you, Linowitz and Wilson are the two finest Americans I have known."

Kobayashi decided to accept the invitation to join Fuji-Xerox—officially starting on his wedding day—and proceeded to spend one year in London at Rank-Xerox to learn this new business that he would later lead.

The initial five-year plan for Fuji-Xerox projected 2,500 installations by 1967. Yet despite early complaints from Rank-Xerox about the sales force, 12,000 units were placed within five years and the concept of renting had become increasingly accepted in Japan. These efforts had been supported by a clever series of full-page newspaper advertisements with catchy propositions like "Borrow the hen and keep the eggs."

The successes of Fuji-Xerox and Rank-Xerox helped transform Haloid into the leading international organization that we know today as Xerox.

24

CHALLENGES OF
SUCCESS

The only threat that might puncture Xerox's ballooning revenues and profits was obvious to everyone: an even better copier from a competitor. In 1962, that abstract threat became explicit. The Xerox annual meeting would be held at upstate Webster, but the real story of the day would take place in Manhattan. An entirely new competitor—a small, unknown, company from Canada called Racon Photocopy Corp., Ltd.— claimed a radically new principle in dry copying. Racon appeared to some to be just a promotion, but it was getting lots of publicity— particularly in Wall Street. As investment analyst Ernie Stowell told institutional investors, "If it performs as they claim, it could be very important. You ought to keep track of it, and I assure you we will." Racon announced that it would demonstrate an entirely new copier that was even better and cheaper than the 914. This could be the blindsiding event everyone had been worrying about.

Stowell was the widely recognized "dominating" analyst of Xerox, so institutional investors expected him to be on top of *all* significant developments, and a dramatic new competitor was a *very* significant development. The Xerox annual meeting would start at 11:00 AM in Webster; the Canadian's demonstration was set for 10:00 AM that same morning in Manhattan. Stowell felt he must be at Webster for the annual meeting, so he got his top salesman, Dan Murphy, to cover the Canadian company's demonstration in Manhattan. To be first in line, Murphy arrived early, but not early enough. By 9:00 AM, 40 people were already lined up waiting to be ushered into the demonstration room, one at a time.

Murphy wasn't Irish and a master salesman for nothing. He was engaging, nervy, and quietly aggressive. He might have 40 people in line ahead of him, but his job was to be *first* to see the demonstration and *first* to know what it was all about. He'd just have to work his way up to the front of the line. By 9:30, he was only 15th in line; by 9:45 he was sixth. By 10:00, Murphy was the first person through the door and the very first to see the new copier. Murphy was impressed, very impressed. The copies were beautiful: better than the copies made on the 914. And copies were coming out of the machine rapidly, faster than the 914.

Then Murphy noticed something even more important than copy quality or speed. He saw *two* copies come out—at the very same time. They were *identical*. This couldn't be real—and it wasn't. The copies had been made *before* the demonstration. The Canadian machine wasn't a new kind of super copier. It was just a new kind of hoax.

Murphy said nothing. Why blab and give the hoax away? Not a chance! Saying "Thank you," he left the demonstration room to get to a phone and call Stowell. Comfortably before the 11:00 AM start of Xerox's annual meeting in Rochester, Murphy reported by telephone to Stowell in Webster, who told Dessauer, who told Wilson, who reported calmly to his many shareholders: "Our friends in New York City tell us we have *no* direct competition," putting an end to any concerns about the mystery competitor from Canada.

In the five years from 1959 to 1964, Wilson's company's sales surged from $33 million to $250 million, and then on up to $385 million in 1965. (The 914 was first offered for sale in August 1964 for $29,000. Even after purchasing a 914, customers still paid 1.9¢ per copy for paper, toner, service, and spare parts.) By mid-

1965, production of 914s was catching up with demand as monthly output increased to 2,200 machines. Total installations increased to nearly 70,000. And as machines were built to ever higher production standards, the costs of servicing machines continued to decline. Initially, maintenance and service calls averaged one call every 1,700 copies. By mid-1963 that ratio had improved to one call every 4,800 copies. By 1965, the servicing ratio had improved to one call every 10,000 copies. Still, concern about the threat of an effective competitor—coming somehow from somewhere—was a continuing concern and provided extra motivation to keep increasing the speed and quality of copying. That's why most of Haloid Xerox's R&D expenditures in the early 1960s were focused on upgrading the 914.

Institutional investors were excited by the 914, but they were equally impressed and confident in Joe Wilson and the management team he was developing. As one investor explained, "Seldom does one find a brand new technology that can be utilized economically and on a large scale resulting in a rapid build-up of revenues and profits for the lucky company. Even less often can one find an opportunity occurring in a company where management is ready for the expansion and able to think big enough to utilize all their available resources and keep a keen eye on the long term profits. Such was the case with Xerox, and management can take full credit for the successful exploitation of their opportunity."[1]

With earnings rising rapidly and investors coming to appreciate the remarkable prospects for continuing large gains in future earnings, Xerox stock shot up–and up and up again. Xerox executives sold stock and Wilson got upset when executives sold. He didn't mind the large amounts of money they were getting by selling stock they had gotten from options and he didn't mind the stock sales. That was exactly what he had hoped for when he set up the stock-option program back in 1954. But he was outraged at the proposal

[1] Howard Schow, who was then at Capital Research and Management and is now at PRIMECAP.

from the compensation consultants at McKinsey & Co., who proposed that bonuses and stock options should be based on individual performance, *not* on overall corporate profits and the Xerox stock price. After years of working to build broad-based teamwork throughout his company, Wilson recognized that this switch could easily be seen as welching on a commitment. That was not Joe Wilson's way. "These people have been working their heads off for *years* to accomplish what is only in '61 and '62 actually coming to pass! I don't care a hoot about how difficult we make the ground rules for earning bonuses, but I do care enormously that this particular group of top people have the belief that they can earn substantially more [here] than [in] companies of much larger size, because, don't ever forget, we have a program which is lifting us to the level of companies several times our size at a pace which is most demanding upon executives. My fundamental decision is that no one will suffer."

In addition to his many progressive innovations, one important strength of Wilson's management was what was *not* done. Where other producers of copiers were proliferating various models of their machines—and losing the advantages of long production runs—Wilson stayed with one model of the 914 until the company could make a major new product introduction: the 813. (Wilson initiated the essential engineering work on the 813 before the first 914 had been shipped.) The 813 made six copies per minute and was aimed at the "middle market" where users made 30 to 40 copies a day. Below 100 copies, the 813 was cheaper; above 100, the 914 was cheaper. Xerox figured there were 50,000 installation points needing more than 100 copies per day and four *times* as many that needed less than 100 copies a day. Engineers at Battelle, working closely with Don Shepardson at Xerox, had reduced the size of the selenium drum for the 813 to just a 3" diameter. This meant a much smaller machine would work with just two very easily accepted adjustments; smaller carrier beads for the toner and a slightly slower machine.

The key to success for the 813 was clear: lower costs. But finding the right balance between cost and value was a design challenge that soon centered on cost versus machine strength. John Dessauer was on the verge of giving up on the 813 and wrote to Joe Wilson saying, "We probably will have to cancel the program," because he doubted the machine could stand up to the stresses of shipping.

But the can-do attitude Wilson always fostered came through again. Bob Ellis, one of Horace Becker's engineers, needed less than ten minutes to solve the problem by simply changing the design of the shock absorbers on the shipping pallet.

Xerox copiers created demand for two kinds of very profitable "incidentals": toner and paper. But selling paper took some adjustments. Xerox salespeople measured the number of boxes of paper sold. Paper companies sold paper by *weight*, so they wanted more moisture. But too much moisture prevented proper fusing of the toner by causing steam that impeded bonding. Some argued that Xerox should go into the paper manufacturing business, but were stopped by questions like: "Who wants to be a 'feather' merchant?"

The paper companies couldn't change their historically standardized practices enough to sell by the sheet. So the solution was to sell the paper under the Xerox label, with tight tolerances on the moisture content that were controlled by systematic sampling. Xerox soon became the world's largest seller of 8½" × 11" paper. The paper companies delivered the paper to United Parcel Service, where it was warehoused and distributed as needed to Xerox customers. As a result, the inventory turned over more than ten times every year, and paper became the single most profitable product that Xerox sold.

Still, there was one more necessary adjustment. The standard "guillotine" cutting of 8½" × 11" sheets caused the sheets to bond together—ever so slightly, but enough to impede sheets coming off separately inside the 914. So the Key Operators were advised to bend and riffle each package of paper so the "guillotine bond" would be broken. Nevertheless, paper jams were their top complaint.

Horace Becker decided to confront the paper suppliers on the matter and get them to riffle the pages *before* delivery. The paper companies agreed among themselves to refuse and hold onto their past practices. Becker took it as a challenge—a rather personal challenge. To break up their cabal, all Becker needed was for *one* paper supplier to blink—and the others would have to fall in line. Becker played chicken in a series of separate, but simultaneous, negotiations with the paper companies. It worked. "*Two* guys blinked—and we were home free," recalled Becker with understandable glee. Xerox sold 40% of all the paper used in the 914, and 100% of the papers used in the 2400 because Xerox paper never jammed.

Another problem was summer: The extra heat of summer shortened the useful life of the selenium-coated drum. Wilson decreed that unless the problem could be solved, the 813 would have to be withdrawn from the market. Jack Kinsella suggested it should be possible to increase drum life by adding arsenic to the selenium coating, but went on to explain that it would take as long as 18 months to determine the optimal concentration of arsenic. Hearing, "If it takes 18 months, the game is over!," Kinsella took a big chance—based on seasoned judgement—and tried an arsenic concentration of one-half of one percent. In just six weeks, it was proven effective and 813s were produced and placed in large volume.

The 813 cost only $800 to build and earned $5,000 a year in rentals because Xerox was so far ahead of its competition and so well protected by patents that it could price its product on the basis of value in use to the consumer, *not* on cost to produce *nor* relative to a competitor's price. Pricing policy was a continuously central part of Wilson's strategy to maximize the demand for copies. Pricing adjustments were made to adapt to specific demand characteristics. Learning that the average number of copies per original was only three in one market segment, Xerox introduced the 420, a modified version of the 914 with a new pricing scheme: 4¢ a copy for the first four copies, and then 2¢ for each additional copy. Over the next several years, further price reductions would be made almost regularly.

With a carefully accumulated inventory of 1,200 machines on hand, the 813 desktop copier was introduced in the fall of 1963. By the end of the year, 3,000 were installed.[2] In 1964, deliveries shot up, and 30,000 more machines were installed. The 813 won new customers for Xerox, and a significant percentage of these new customers traded up to a 914. A low monthly rental aimed at broadening the market as much as possible worked so well that both orders for new machines and copies per machine exceeded management expectations. Even at a production volume of 30,000 813s a year, a substantial back log of orders developed. In 1965, new placements peaked at 50,000 and then declined to 18,000 and then 13,000, but a "modular pricing" variant machine—the 330—sustained the growth of the 813 family.

The Webster assembly lines for the 914 had been humming by the time the 813 was put into production. The assembly line workers had established a "fair day's work" standard volume of output with the 914, and, since they regularly operated at a significantly higher pace, were consistently earning 15 to 20% bonuses. With the 813 going into production, the production supervisor wanted workers to transfer from the 914 line to the 813 line.

"Are you prepared to protect their present pay levels?" asked Bill Asher.

"Hell, no!"

Asher knew this attitude would be a major problem unless it was resolved quickly and before the workers or their union found out. The problem was taken to Joe Wilson who promptly called a workout meeting. Recognizing that the 914 production workers would never go over to the 813 line with new productivity standards just "for the greater glory of Xerox," Wilson gave the answer: "Keep 'em whole."

---

[2]The night before the introduction of the 813, some of the newer people were startled—but soon understood—when Joe Wilson stopped in at 2:00 AM to say "Thank you" to the busy workers. And when David Kearns, a native Rochestarian, joined Xerox from IBM, Wilson being Wilson, picked up the phone to call Kearns' parents to say how pleased he was.

Wilson was worried about the union trying to organize the engineers who serviced machines in customers' facilities, so he worked out a gentlemen's agreement with union leadership that these "Tech Reps" were part of *management*. As a symbol of this alignment, the field service engineers (Tech Reps) were required to dress as would be expected of "management"—in ties and jackets.

Wilson was increasingly achieving the "cooperative" labor relationship he had always wanted with the Amalgamated, but that didn't mean the union wasn't always pressing for more, such as a luncheon meeting initiated by the union's bearded Vice President, Jacob Potovsky. In his heavy accent, Potovsky asked Becker to have lunch with him in the company cafeteria. After they filled their trays and sat down at a table off to one side, Potovsky looked at Becker, paused and then asked, "Mister Becker, do you know what is the *most* important job of a union?"

Becker knew he must not to let himself get trapped and wasn't sure which way the next question might go, so he replied noncommittably: "No, Mr. Potovsky, I'm not sure what the most important job would be."

"Mr. Becker, the union's *most* important job is to make sure the company is *profitable!*"

"I thought that was *my* job. You didn't have to come over here just to tell me that."

"Mr. Becker, please, you haven't asked me the *second* job. Do you know the union's *next* most important job?"

"No. Please tell me, Mr. Potovsky."

"Make sure the workers get their *fair share*, Mr. Becker. You can't get blood from a stone, and it's no fun negotiating with a company that's not making good money!"

Discipline in labor negotiations meant, for Wilson and his company, a combination of long-term policies of candor about problems and rigorous documentation of the reasons behind all recommendations for changes. In the 1960 labor negotiations, Wilson had articulated Xerox's long-standing policy that the company would pay what it could and, to verify this, he reviewed the company's past record. Wilson directed the union negotiators' attention to the unhappy experience with Haloid's paper-sensitizing business, where profit margins were already very thin; foreign competition was preventing any price increases; and the company was experiencing more domestic competition, particularly from nonunion producers. A year later, Wilson gave the union more than six months' notice that the photographic business would be closed because the Air Force was cutting back, the movie business was gone, and the company had lost $300,000 due to price cuts it had made to sustain volume. Wilson planned to spend another $150,000 on job retraining to lessen the impact on union members, but he was careful to tell the Union that 102 people would be laid off, of which 69 had been hired in the past two years.

As negotiations began in 1962, Wilson told union representatives Chatman and Potovsky that Xerox would, as it had done consistently for the past 15 years, continue to the best of its ability to pay wages that were equal to, if not better than, the wages paid for comparable work in the Rochester area and in industries in which Xerox competed. In turn, Wilson said, the union must never ask the company to jeopardize its long-term ability to compete successfully by establishing unnecessarily high wages. Pointing to the wage and price guidelines put forward by President Kennedy and Labor Secretary Goldberg, Wilson showed that Xerox was paying wages somewhat above those in such comparable industries as photography, machinery, or office equipment and that the company's success was due to the contributions of many—not just to those in the bargaining unit—and that investors needed to see a good return on the massive capital they had been investing.

By 1963, union demands were clearly shifting to a demand for a larger slice of a rapidly growing Xerox profit pie—and would no longer be constrained by "comparables" at other companies. At the fifth negotiating session, Wilson protested in frustration that it was becoming clear to him that, by coming forward at the first meeting with what it thought was a fair settlement, the company was being "taken to the cleaners" and was "sure to lose no matter what it did." Wilson said he was particularly troubled by the union's suggestion that workers be empowered to switch their retirement security benefit into current cash compensation which would, he chided, defeat the whole purpose of the retirement program benefit. Wilson's insistence on disciplined negotiation strategies by the union was never confrontational, but always aimed at developing on both sides the habits of mind that could lead to "cooperative" labor management relationships.

Wilson's persistent drive for long-term cooperation in labor relations was characteristic of his long-term orientation in all areas of management, particularly corporate planning. After the wave of concentrated effort to launch the 914 and 813 crested, Wilson worked to re-establish the discipline of one- and five-year planning for each division. The need for good planing was accelerating as new machine concepts involved much larger capital commitments and incurred much larger marketing risks, and the appraisals from marketing and product development of major new products were often in conflict. With so many different projects, getting agreement would clearly be more difficult and, just as clearly, more important. Finally, with increasing cash flow, new acquisitions and new ventures—in education with University Microfilms and in technology with Electrical Optical Systems—would add to the planning challenges.

For the planning conference in 1962, Wilson again asked all 13 division heads to develop careful one-year and five-year plans that filled 3" books and served as the basis for serious discussions of the way forward. He requested particular focus on the choice between internal growth versus acquisitions, which led to establishing a long-range planning committee. Looking to the future, Wilson asked each division head to identify a potential successor, and made a similar selection. He chose Peter McColough as his likely successor and named him chair of the long-range planning committee, Vice

Chairman of the Operations Committee, overseer of acquisitions and an Executive Vice President.[3]

A s Xerox studied how and why customers used the 914, it realized that if copies could be made even faster, customers would increase the number of copies they made considerably, going from 20 to 50 copies, for example. The 720, a faster version of the 914, enabled Xerox to change the 914's flat-rate pricing so high-volume customers got a lower average cost per copy. For example, at 25 copies per original, the average cost per copy on a 720 was reduced to 4.1¢. A curved platen designed by John Rutkus allowed the lens and the light to remain in fixed position, while a narrow, lightweight mirror pivoted back and forth much more quickly than the prior shuttle process. This made much faster speeds possible. Wilson was aiming for an enormous new market, competing with 530,000 offset machines that produced 600 billion copies each year—50 times the volume of copies made by all copiers *and* growing. As a first step, the 2400, making 40 copies a minute, or 2400 an hour, was put into development before the 914 and 813 copiers achieved peak volume.

Wilson maintained that the 2400, introduced in 1965, was making a quantum jump forward by combining copying and duplication into a single process. (It had a small computer programmed to adjust the per copy price to the length of the run. Less than 10 copies would cost 5¢; 10 to 15 copies cost 75% as much; and more than 15 copies cost only 50% of the initial charge. (But some customers were too clever: They set the dial for 100 copies to get the low rate and changed originals after, say, 10 copies.) Wilson also made a significant change in marketing strategy by preannouncing the new product introduction. The investment in developing the 2400 was huge: $40 million. To capture its market, Wilson announced the 2400 a full year before it would be ready for delivery.[4]

[3]McKelvey VIII-26.
[4]In the subsequent FTC consent decree, such preannouncements were prohibited.

The 2400 copier-duplicator required important developments in several major components in order to offer a large reduction in cost per copy on large-volume runs. (Customers using the 2400 could opt for a new "by the hour used" pricing arrangement which could reduce per-copy charges to less than half a cent.) When the 2400 was having difficulties in manufacturing, many people wanted to slow down its introduction, but the product manager believed that from a marketing perspective Xerox should go ahead, so he went to Wilson and made his case. Wilson listened carefully, as always, and thought quietly for several minutes. Then he straightened up: "Let's announce!"

The 2400 came to market in 1965 and a 60-copy-a-minute upgrade—achieved by simply changing gears—was introduced in 1968 as the 3600. The 7000, which enabled users to copy-reduce large documents *or* double pages of books to 8½" × 11" formats, was a major success and provided Xerox with needed cash flow during the 1970s, as well as extending xerography into the offset market. But before the 7000 could be shipped, one more problem had to be solved: One vital part was missing. The camera lenses that were supposed to be coming from Bausch & Lomb didn't show up. Large numbers of 813s, without the essential lens, were soon piling up at the factory. Luckily, Horace Becker knew from his contacts with the Japanese that Fuji Photo could make very fine lenses. Anticipating that Fuji could meet the urgent need, Becker called and Fuji delivered: 10 lenses every day via air express. While getting off to an uncertain start, the 2400 became the most important and most profitable product in Xerox's history.[5]

From 1964 onward, Wilson was in a new and very unfamiliar position: Xerox was cash flow *positive*. After all those long years of

[5] The 2400 performed well as a *copier*, but ran into difficult resistance as a *duplicator*, its priority market, because customers' union workers' resisted the change in process and the threat to their employment. Also, placements of 2400s would have displaced equipment that prospective customers *owned* and had fully depreciated and therefore ran at very low costs.

mandatory cash-conserving disciplines, Xerox suddenly had more money than it needed, and the cash flow surpluses were guaranteed to get larger and larger every year. Investing that huge cash flow would become the major strategic challenge facing Wilson's company.

At the same time, another major social issue was about to rock Joe Wilson's community.

25

MINISTER FLORENCE

"I t was night. Late. And here was Joe Wilson on Prospect Street—alone in his car with the windows rolled down—looking for the *leaders*—for the leaders of the black community," remembered Minister Franklin Delano Roosevelt Florence, an aggressive, young, charismatic African-American leader of the 1960s.[1] "There was Joe Wilson, coming onto our turf, coming to where the riots had been—and the fires and the glass. And the angry people, burning and shouting, we weren't *rioting*. We were in *rebellion*. Black Power was coming on *strong*."

The acceleration of events commanding national attention began with the Supreme Court's 1954 desegregation decision of *Brown v. Board of Education* and continued with Rosa Park's arrest in

[1] The Wilsons had been enjoying a long and relaxed family vacation in Europe—with extended time, particularly in Italy in the summer of 1964—when on July 25 the news came that an inner-city riot had erupted in Rochester. Wilson spent a day on the telephone, trying to decide whether he should fly back immediately to help restore order, but was persuaded to stay a few more days on the trip. On arrival in New York City, the Wilsons were surprised by a command invitation to dinner at the White House. They scrambled to repack bags and get to the Capitol just in time for the dinner (One personal highlight was when LBJ asked Peggy for the evening's first dance.) Late that night, they flew home to Rochester. It had been a long day.

Birmingham in 1955, Central High School in Little Rock in September 1959, the 1963 March on Washington, John F. Kennedy's Civil Rights Bill, the assassination of NAACP leader Medgar Evers, the dynamite blast at the 16th Street Baptist Church that killed four girls, the assassination of President Kennedy, racial violence in St. Augustine, Florida, in 1964, Martin Luther King Jr.'s *Why We Can't Wait*, the Civil Rights Act of 1964, and the killing of civil rights workers in the Mississippi Delta.

Three days of rioting and racial disturbances shook Rochester from July 24 to 26, 1964. It began with an arrest after a chaperone at a street dance sponsored by the North Mothers Improvement Association complained about an African-American, who was apparently drunk and disorderly. It ended with four deaths, 350 injuries, $1 million of property damage, and 800 arrests. (The Watts riots would come the following summer.)

"Joe Wilson broke the mold," said Minister Florence. He made contact. He came to *us* that night; came to us as human beings. Where others would *look* down, he *came* down. He came down here by himself, got out of his car, came into the headquarters and asked to see *me*. And I said, 'OK, what does he want down here at 9:00 at night—all by himself?'"

Passing through the milling throng, and into the two-story wooden building, Wilson went up the narrow, dark staircase and sat at the small table in Minister Franklin Florence's crowded office on the second floor. Florence remembers: "He was not afraid. He walked in and sat at the table. You could tell he was comfortable with himself."

Wilson spoke quietly: "I'm Joe Wilson. You may not believe this, but anybody in this community who knows me, knows that I'm a man of my word. I want to help. I don't know just what to do, but I know we need to do something to pull this community together. I want to work with you and your organization.

"I've come here to see if we can work together—to do something constructive for the community. I want to help and be a part of it. I hear you are interested in jobs. Well, we need workers at Xerox. Can you supply us with workers to help us do what we need done?"

Minister Florence was surprised. This Wilson was different, very different: "He was interested—really *interested*—in hearing and understanding the views of our people. And he listened when we talked about wanting jobs and wanting education for our people. Joe Wilson had *authenticity*. That man had many peers, but few equals. He didn't say much. Didn't use a lot of words. But you knew, you just *knew*, he was sincere. He had empathy. He was so different from all the others. The big corporations had all the real power in Rochester—from birth to grave—and they were entirely separated from the African-American community. They saw no reason to get involved with us: to be in contact; to be in communication. As far as they were concerned, we did not *exist* as individual human beings."

Today with the benefit of 20/20 hindsight, the intolerable pressure caused by the continued separation and denial of opportunity is obvious. But we can only see what we are ready to see, and in the 1960s, leaders of the northern cities did not see the problem, at least in part because they weren't looking and in part because they did not want to see or understand—and partly because the problem came on so fast. In the 1950s, Rochester's African American population tripled from 7,700 to 24,500. By 1964, it had increased to 34,000, up 40% in just four years and more than 400% in 14 years.

Rochester had an established social and political system that had always "worked." It was conservative, stable, Republican, and white. A nice place to raise families, Rochester had the sort of self-satisfied local pride in the strengths of the city that outsiders found hard to penetrate. Rochester was the sort of safely established community where nobody wanted to be "different."

Then came an increasingly large number of *very* different people: different race, different education, different social ways and customs and life experiences. And they were not only getting more numerous, they were getting angry because they had come north to get work and earn the big money they'd heard so much about, but Rochester did not accept the new arrivals: Even as more African-Americans moved into the city, they were excluded and ignored.

The movement of African-Americans into Rochester was, in many ways, typical of the northward migration of millions of people in the years after World War II following the introduction of cotton-picking machines in the South. Poorly educated people moved out of the agricultural South, looking for work in Northern cities. But they didn't find work; they found walls. Race was a wall. Education was a wall—one of the strongest walls—because major employers like Eastman Kodak, Bausch & Lomb, and Xerox all required at least a high school diploma—to be sure their new hires would be ready for training in job-specific skills. But most of the new arrivals coming up from the rural South were farm workers who never went to high school and most of those who did go never graduated.

The walls of cultural separation between rural blacks and urban whites were high and strong.

The established white leadership and newly arrived African-Americans were not in communication. The African-American community was organized around the one institution they had: church. In addition to an established social network, the white community was organized around many different institutions: churches, social clubs, municipal government, country clubs, and corporations. And each area was separate: Corporations didn't discuss religion and churches didn't discuss jobs.

Eastman Kodak was Rochester's leading corporation and, for conservative Rochester, one of the more progressive employers. But to African-Americans without high school diplomas, it was closed, which was not much different from the other companies in Rochester. Eastman Kodak, with 54,000 employees and only 4% annual turnover, traditionally celebrated the very large proportion of its employees who had always worked for Kodak, as their fathers had before them. Kodak also celebrated its profit-sharing annual bonus *and* the fact that it had no labor union coming between the corporation and its work-ers. More than most U.S. companies, Kodak was conservative—just like Rochester—and self-sufficient. Kodak made its own film, photo-graphic paper, plastic reels, and even the mail-in envelopes for cus-tomers who wanted Kodak to do the processing. This self-sufficiency always made Kodak's famous proposition possible: "You press the but-ton and we do the rest!"

Kodak's non-responsive response to the African-American lead-ers who were saying, "We want meaningful *jobs!*" was simple: "Come to the Employment Office and fill out the required forms. If you are qualified, you'll get jobs." But "qualified" meant having at least a high school diploma so "come on down" meant absolutely nothing to those moving up from the South. Job applicants found doors closed tight: "Do you have a high school diploma? You don't? Sorry, you *must* have your diploma to work here." No diploma, no jobs. Under-standable up North, but in the rural agricultural South with segre-gated schools, most blue-collar workers left school to work long before graduation and a high school diploma.

A decade or two earlier, there would have been work in semi-skilled jobs. Rochester had been a major producer of men's suits. But the companies in the garment trade, whose entry-level jobs did not require high school graduation and might have provided the needed start, were already leaving Rochester and heading South. So there were no jobs for the new arrivals—and no hope—in Rochester, "Smug Town, USA." It was quite unable to care about uneducated, rural African-Americans with all of their cultural differences. So, for many years, Rochester did not respond to the major inward migra-tion of African-Americans moving up from the South, while the problems accumulated steadily, got bigger and worse.

Minister Franklin Florence, the charismatic and inspiring young preacher with a talent for organizing and a deep sense of mission to serve his people, was searching for ways to communicate and connect with the corporate community. He focused on Eastman Kodak, the largest employer and the recognized business leader in Rochester. But

Florence was getting nowhere with Kodak when a dreadful blunder was made. Kodak's assistant vice president for community relations, John G. Mulder, entered into quiet negotiations, hoping to find a constructive resolution. Thinking he had found one, Mulder agreed to an accommodation with Minister Florence. Florence took this agreement back to his community organization as a major victory to ratify and celebrate—only to have Kodak's Board of Directors refuse to honor the deal and fire Mulder for exceeding his authority.

Minister Florence was clearly, decisively, and publicly embarrassed. (Kodak's action created a new word for a public double-cross: being "mulderized.") Florence still felt the anguish many years later: "Kodak's top man was on TV, asking, 'What do they *want?*' and pointing out that Kodak had just built new facilities. What did we *want?* Good Jobs!! That's what we wanted: *Jobs!* And we weren't getting jobs at Kodak or Bausch & Lomb. We had finally come to recognize that we were never going to get jobs—unless we took *action.*"

This was no ordinary time. Malcolm X's home had been firebombed the weekend before he arrived in Rochester on one of several trips to speak at meetings organized by the African-American community leaders. The shirt he wore during his visit to Rochester was scorched and still smelled of smoke.

Sol Alinsky, the political protest organizer, was particularly significant to Minister Florence in his role as a young leader of his community. Alinsky was paid $100,000 to come to Rochester and work with Florence and his organization. As Florence described it: "In our organization, with over 3,000 members, we elected committees for each area of our interest—education, police, health and so on—and we had weekly meetings of the cabinet and monthly meetings of the delegates with all our decisions made by vote. We were *together* as a people, and we were *strong*.

"Alinsky had the best mind for organizing people of anyone. He was *so* effective. He just *knew.* He *knew* that I was somehow intimidated about speaking directly to people like Governor Rockefeller. So he said, 'You were *scared;* scared to talk to him. You need to *learn.*

Learn what will help us free your people. Go learn how—and then use it. You need to understand white people.'"

The Black Muslims had a Mosque in downtown Rochester and one rule was strict: No white person was allowed inside—*ever*. According to Florence, "But Rochester police—*white* police—raided the Mosque like Nazi storm troopers. They violated Malcolm's trust, so he gave an ultimatum to the black church: 'Resist this intrusion and stand with your brothers.' One week later, a white cop went into a black Methodist church during the 11:00 service—with dogs and a gun."

That act of police hostility broke the dam and all the bottled up rage burst out. Rochestarians were startled and scared when the race riot exploded in their safe, quiet, reliable Rochester.

Some years before, Joe Wilson had asked Bill Asher how many African-Americans Haloid employed. Both knew there weren't many. Asher checked around and informed Wilson: "Two, Joe." "That not acceptable, Bill. See what you can do to achieve a real increase." Wilson clearly expected Asher to go looking, and to *find* minority workers. But skilled African-American workers could not be found, so only semiskilled men could be hired. The first men hired were assigned to work with photographic chemicals in the darkrooms. White women protested having to work with black men in a room without lights and they threatened to file grievances.

The union business agent stepped in promptly to abort the problem before it spread or magnified: He refused to accept a grievance. Then he sternly asked each of the women: "Are you ready to go back to work now?" If the answer was yes, no matter how reluctantly it was said, things were okay. But if the answer was no, that worker's resignation was "accepted" immediately. The dispute was quickly over. But it indicates how far from ready Rochester was half a century ago.

When race riots began to burst out in America's center cities, the conventional reaction of senior corporate executives was to call the police or, if the riot were very serious, call out the National Guard and get tough with rioters and looters. Instead, Joe Wilson called Asher, "Bill, how many black workers do we *now* have?"

"Six."

"*Still* only six? What do we need to do to hire these people in decent numbers?"

"Joe, we'd have to relax our long-standing rule requiring a high school diploma."

"Let's find a way, Bill."

Like all the other large companies in Rochester, Haloid had only hired high school graduates. Because of his personality and his long record of cooperation, Wilson had an excellent relationship with union leader Abe Chatman, so he could say to Asher, "We've got to get out ahead of Minister Florence or he'll be at *our* door. Go back to Webster and come up with a plan."

For a while, Minister Florence was deeply suspicious: "We thought he was coming through the back door for the police. But he allayed those fears. He said, 'I'm not doing it for any one individual. We need people and if you can supply us with people who need jobs, that's all we want.' "

Out of this grew a job-training plan called Operation Step Up which brought minority workers to Xerox.[2]

Asher in Labor Relations and Chatman of the Amalgamated jointly developed Operation Step Up to advance minority workers by providing special training to prepare them for the high-paying jobs in the Xerox plant. As he had requested, the program was brought to Wilson as soon as it could be roughed out. It was as fresh and original as he had hoped. The new arrangement would be very different: People without a high school diploma would spend half the day in school and half the day at work.

[2]In Chicago, Sol Alinsky's hometown, Xerox worked with TWO (The Woodlawn Organization), the militant group on the tough South Side. Xerox actually was a subcontractor to TWO on its contract with the Office of Economic Opportunity working through the leaders of two gangs—the Blackstone Rangers and the East Side Disciples.

Wilson was pleased: "Sounds like a great idea." Then, looking almost instinctively for a partner to help defray costs, he added: "Let's see if the U.S. Labor Department will grant funds for the high school part of our plan."

Classrooms were built at Webster and teachers were hired to teach high school equivalency courses until participants, who were mostly 18 to 25 years of age, were ready to switch over to regular work in the factory. The program began in 1966 with another wave in 1967. Minister Florence carefully selected the 25 young men for the first classes. (Florence was also responsible for removing anyone who was not "up to expectations.") In time, six classes of 20 to 25 participants went through the program and into jobs at Xerox. Union seniority was negotiated to begin on their first day in classes, but they would not be union members until graduation.

"The union leaders bought into the program," said Asher, "because they trusted Joe Wilson."

"Florence was the absolute leader at the time of the riots," explained Becker. "He knew how to lead *and* how to confront. Florence really stacked the deck with winners, particularly in that first group of 25 men to go into training. The men Florence selected were all potential winners. And they *all* had tough moms at home—watching."

Minister Florence made them all role-play various situations like being called 'Boy!' and all the other things that could provoke a young guy to anger. This training was needed because many foremen on the assembly line were pretty new to their jobs, and the only way they knew to make production targets was to use rough language. The Xerox production line foremen needed special training as well—to learn how to stop talking down to the new workers.

Wilson set the tone from the very start: "These people will be treated with respect," and supervisors followed Wilson's clear guideline.

"An assembly line *requires* everyone to show up on time," continued Becker. "So we called guys if they were late. And for some, we went into their homes and pulled them right out of their beds. We helped the guys with their personal expenses. We had to give them cash in advance because their paychecks came every other week and most started with no money. We hired a nun and a priest to run the classrooms. (They're married now. She runs a home for battered women.)"

Looking back on the experience, Florence recalled: "Both of us—and we knew it—were on very thin ice. We were in the position of mutual *dependence*, his success and mine. We depended on each other. He depended on my ability to speak to my people and I depended on him to speak to his people. Joe Wilson saw himself as a trustee, a steward of the Rochester community."

In the summer of 1968, a "people's" manufacturing plant, planned for 100 workers, began producing metal stampings and electrical transformers and later converted to manufacturing small appliances like hand-held vacuum cleaners for Xerox machines. The operation was cosponsored by Xerox and Florence's organization, which was called FIGHT (Freedom, Integration, God, Honor, Today). It later became Fight On, the first attempt by the U.S. government and private industry to start a business wholly owned by African-Americans.

Minister Florence called it "a first for the nation—and more radical and militant than all the riots put together." Fight On was supported by a $445,000 training grant from the Department of Labor and a $500,000 guarantee by Xerox to purchase that much output in each of the first two years.[3] (Kodak offered to set up a wooden pallet maker too as an African-American-owned business, but that was obviously low-grade work with no prospects for improvement, so Florence rejected that idea as "no better than picking cotton." He insisted on Class A jobs.)

Wilson was directly involved on a daily basis with Fight On. When obtaining a federal grant first became possible, Minister

---

[3]The Department of Labor grant was increased from a smaller amount by Labor Secretary Willard M. Wirtz. *New York Times*, June 21, 1968.

Florence was flown to Washington on a Xerox corporate plane to meet Labor Secretary Willard Wirtz. Recognizing that the Xerox people assigned to Operation Step Up might be uncomfortable being paid by Fight On, Wilson arranged to have them paid by Xerox.

"He was always a very strong *passive* force," remembered Florence. "He had no apprehensiveness about moving with you. He was not one of those leaders that are afraid to talk to our people. In his quiet way, he was strong as steel."

Wilson was not easy in negotiations with Florence any more than he was easy in labor negotiations. When Florence asked for an exclusive on making job referrals to Xerox for minority workers, he was told "No, we also have an important, long-term relationship with the Urban League."[4]

At the next Xerox annual meeting, Reverend Herbert C. Shankle rose and, speaking for Minister Florence and his organization, said how admirable and useful Xerox had been, and praised Joe Wilson's personal leadership: "Your willingness to shoulder the community and social responsibility of tackling the hard core unemployment problems speaks well for the American free enterprise system. As we have said time and again, the melting pot theory as a solution is fine. The problem is not whether we can melt, but whether we can ever get into the pot *to* melt. We are encouraging religious organizations and institutions throughout the country and our friends to buy Xerox products. Let me say, 'Thank you.'"

As the shareholders' applause quieted, Wilson expressed his

---

[4]On the same page of the *New York Times* that reported about Fight On were articles on the Secretary of Defense acting to prevent racial discrimination in renting housing to servicemen; a picture of demonstrators scattering at Resurrection City after police threw tear gas canisters; and how Mt. Vernon's school board protested an order by James Allen, New York State Commissioner of Education, that it integrate its 11 elementary schools by busing 3,000 children and installing 10 lunchrooms.

thanks and acknowledged that Xerox had been working with Fight On and Step Up—and also with the Urban League—to find ways to employ those who were not qualified by traditional standards.

Then, with obvious distress about the unfavorable judgment of Kodak that Shankle included in his statement, Wilson continued to speak, his voice filled with conviction as he described Kodak as "one of the most enlightened" corporations in the area of industrial relations. "They were one of the pioneers in profit sharing, beginning in 1911 and 1912, and one of the first companies in the country to have a retirement program. Many of us who have lived all of our lives in Rochester probably have a philosophy that is an imitation of their philosophy." Wilson went on to express appreciation for what Kodak was doing with African-American and Puerto Rican workers and noted that Kodak's relationship with FIGHT had significant differences and that there were clearly two sides to the issue. He concluded with a strong statement that Kodak with "75 years of enlightened policy deserves more credit than it was just given."

As usual, Wilson had a balanced view and was gracious toward others. But he was determined to effect real change. When many African-Americans may have felt they were going to have to accept the "facts of life," Joe Wilson was one of the first to see the problem for what it really was; urge real response; and find pragmatic ways to make progress. He believed that racism was the most serious problem in the United States.

26

LIFE

In the 1960s, *LIFE* magazine was the single most powerful communications medium in America. Television was rapidly growing in both reach and impact and would soon become dominant, but in the summer of 1966, *LIFE* was still America's favorite family magazine. An important series of articles helped unify the nation's will to end racial segregation and helped launch John F. Kennedy's presidential campaign. Other articles told the inspiring stories of America's successes in space, science, and education. *LIFE* was the magazine people like Joe and Peggy Wilson enjoyed reading every week.

In the early summer of 1966, Peggy Wilson was particularly keen to see the July 1 issue of *LIFE* because it was expected to have a feature article about Joe Wilson's Xerox. (*LIFE* was distributed to subscribers nearly one week ahead of the publication date, so the July 1 issue actually arrived at the Wilson's home in late June.) Photographers had taken many pictures and senior editor Jane Howard had spent a whole day in Rochester interviewing Joe and his colleagues. She then followed up with several telephone interviews to be sure her facts were correct on the xerographic process, the introduction of the 914 and the 813, and tales of the old Haloid. Naturally, Peggy Wilson was eagerly looking forward to a pleasant time reading *LIFE*'s article on Xerox and her husband's remarkable achievements.

Peggy knew all the details of how long and hard Joe had worked; how intently he had focused all his time and energies on bringing xerography to fruition; how much he had given up in vacations, travel, and recreation to concentrate on his job at the company; and how much he had risked financially through all those long, stressful years of struggle. Honors were coming to Joe now, including invitations to White House dinners, honorary degrees, and Joe's picture on the covers of important business magazines such as *Business Week, Forbes* and *Newsweek*. Now, a major story in *LIFE* would be the ultimate accolade for Joe Wilson's exemplary career.

The initiative for the *LIFE* article had originated with Sol Linowitz, who was increasingly active in Washington circles, both as a representative for Xerox, particularly on government contracts, and as a citizen with interests in public service. He had arranged for Jane Howard to visit Rochester and interview Wilson, McColough, and himself for the feature article. The luncheon interview went well and photographers took lots of pictures. Linowitz offered to stay in contact with Howard to help with the story and arranged to spend an extra day with her and a photographer.

Nearly a year before, in September, 1965, many Xerox people had been quite upset to see a feature article in the Sunday *New York Times Magazine* entitled "The Man from Xerox Multiplies His Roles."[1] Surprisingly, that article was *not* about Joe Wilson. Instead, it was all about Sol Linowitz. People at Xerox were upset to see Linowitz positioned as Xerox's real leader, the one who had pulled off the Xerox triumph—with Joe Wilson described only as "the other Mr. Xerox." And they were also upset by the demeaning inclusion of just one photograph of Wilson "doing nothing more important than gazing into an open lunch box," according to Bill Asher. Linowitz had described the article's representation as only "unfortunate" journalism. Xerox people couldn't understand Linowitz's appearing not to appreciate the magnitude of the mistake, and they wondered aloud exactly how much of the coverage Linowitz had orchestrated

[1]Written by Martin Mayer who later was ghostwriter for Linowitz's autobiography, *The Making of a Public Man*.

himself as a skilled and experienced practitioner of the arts of press relations.

Hearing the complaining, Joe Wilson would have none of it. Rising to his feet at a regular management meeting, Wilson spoke bluntly: "Sol is my best friend. So far as I'm concerned, any attack on Sol is an attack on me." Wilson's strong defense of Linowitz silenced the complainers, but the consensus at Xerox was clear that Linowitz was a very ambitious, self-promotional man.

Linowitz loved making connections and being in the limelight in Washington. He was skillful in adjusting and adapting his position in order to advance. That's why he and Toni had decided together that Sol should stop telling the Yiddish jokes he had learned while working as a busboy and waiter in the Catskills, even though he told them very well and they had been helpful to his early career advancement. Such levities were put behind him now; his future called for greater gravitas. A Democrat, he once thought of running for Congress; later he hoped to be a senator. But when Robert F. Kennedy was building a power base in New York and courted Linowitz, he assured him that extensive private polls showed he could win and urged him to accept the Democratic nomination and run for the governor's office. However, Linowitz cautiously declined. Running without the advantages of incumbency would be too risky for him and would leave Linowitz too exposed. He wouldn't want to be open to people taking shots at him, admitting in his charming, slightly self-depreciating way, "My skin is just not thick enough." He wanted a surer, safer pathway: He hoped, for example, to get appointed to complete an unfinished senatorial term, and *then* run as an incumbent. Linowitz knew he was rising in prominence in Washington. President Lyndon Johnson was reaching out to him; he was becoming friendly with Jackie Kennedy; and he knew important people and was becoming a known person himself.

Now, nine months after the *New York Times Magazine* article, Peggy was opening the July issue of *LIFE* to the table of contents to see if the article on Xerox and Joe's triumph would be in this issue. It was—in a major six-page feature article aptly titled, "The Busiest Copycat of Them All." She turned eagerly to page 69.

The Busiest Copycat of Them All

By JANE HOWARD

CLOSE-UP / AMONG OTHER THINGS
SOL LINOWITZ RUNS XEROX

Sol Myron Linowitz. As a matter of fact, Sol Myron Linowitz of Xerox. The name, including as it does all those rarely used letters of the alphabet, sounds more like a Scrabble player's wistful fantasy than something out of the Rochester, N.Y. telephone directory. It is right there, though—there and a lot of other places. As much as any man in any American phone book, Sol Linowitz, who is 52, gets around.

Last month, after five years as general counsel, executive committee chairman and chairman of the board of Xerox Corporation,

he dropped the latter title and took on a new and to him more exciting one, as chief executive officer of a new offshoot called Xerox International. The week before he turned down a major federal appointment but accepted the post of chairman of the American Jewish Committee. The week before that Linowitz received in the mail a set of cufflinks from the vice-president of the United States. One said "HHH," the other "SML," and they came, Linowitz said, "because I was able to be helpful to him." What a good many people now hope—Senator Robert F.

On a lunch-hour visit to Xerox's main factory, Linowitz stops for a chat with one of the firm's 8,000 Rochester employees.

"Wherever I go the thing I enjoy most and find most enlightening, is reaching out to other people to see what's on their minds. The man here ended up telling me how his former work as a cabinetmaker had given him a lot more satisfaction than his job for us does. I could easily see his point. We in business must grope constantly for new ways to give human beings like this man a feeling of personal accomplishment when they go home from a day's work."

Kennedy among them—is that Linowitz will decide he would like to try to be helpful to the Democrats as candidate for governor of New York.

The reasoning, widely echoed, goes like this: Somebody, after all, has to be nominated in September to run against Nelson Rockefeller in November. The likeliest candidates thus far— Franklin D. Roosevelt Jr., Eugene Nickerson, Frank O'Connor and Howard Samuels—all have political shortcomings. What could be wrong with a brand new face from upstate, unblemished by the bitter party skirmishes of New York City but by no means naive, with a record as blameless and shining as that of, say, Sol Linowitz?

Everybody who's anybody knows Sol

(Photp by: Henry Grossman)

WITH SENATOR ROBERT KENNEDY

(Photo by: Louis Ouzer)

WITH VICE PRESIDENT HUMPHREY

(Photp by: Henry Grossman)

WITH U THANT

WITH DAVID ROCKEFELLER

His myriad activities have brought Linowitz close to government, financial and cultural leaders all over.

"The people I meet offer constant surprises. For instance, I never suspected before I knew him that Senator Kennedy is in reality a very shy person—much quieter and deeper than is commonly thought. People assume that U Thant is a totally impassive, serene Buddhist as he presides over the problems of the world, but he is also a man of humor and emotion. He's talked for hours with my wife about the problems of children."

WITH MRS. JOHN F. KENNEDY

307

Peggy was stunned.

The *LIFE* story was *not* about Joe Wilson. It was all about Sol Linowitz: Sol with Lyndon Johnson, Sol with Jackie Kennedy, Sol with Bobby Kennedy, Sol with Hubert Humphrey, Sol smiling, Sol serious. And Sol as the man who ran Xerox. The title of the article rubbed it in: "Among Other Things, Sol Linowitz Runs Xerox." There was not even one mention of Joe Wilson.

Peggy was horrified—and very, very angry. She knew that Sol craved recognition and was always attentive to appearances, particularly appearances in the press. He would, of course, be most particularly attentive to a major feature article in a widely read, national magazine like *LIFE*. Now—while always presenting himself as Joe's best friend—here he was orchestrating the press coverage so he got all the recognition and all the credit in *LIFE* for what Joe had so clearly done over all those years.

While Joe had been generous and warm to him, Peggy had never really liked nor completely trusted Sol Linowitz. After what he had just done, she quietly decided that she would have nothing to do with that man ever again—*ever*.[2]

What Peggy Wilson didn't know was that, a few years before the *LIFE* article, Linowitz had complained to Jack Hartnett about Joe "getting all the national publicity," asserting that Joe should have

---

[2]When Rochester's historian Blake McKelvey interviewed her about a biography he planned to write about Joe Wilson, she made one request, "Please be sure you don't mention Sol Linowitz in your book."

At Joe Wilson's funeral reception at Clover Street, Peggy was determined to get through the strain in the calm, steady way she and Joe both practiced in public situations. Having Sol Linowitz there would have been more than she could bear, so when she saw him coming up the pathway to her home glad-handing everyone—she told her brother to be sure he was told to leave her house immediately. Dave Curtin got the word and intercepted him and said, "It's my sad duty to tell you, you're not welcome in this home."

Linowitz brushed Curtin off, saying, "Oh come on, Dave." and walked right past him and into the house.

But after a few minutes, he realized that the message was absolutely real. He said nothing and made no protest. Just put on his hat and coat, went back down the path, got into a limo and rode away.

shared the honors more with others. Hartnett took that complaint to mean only one thing: Share more honors with me, Sol Linowitz. (Hartnett did not reveal his own view that if Joe had erred, it was in sharing too much of the credit for what Joe had done unusually well himself.) Nor did Peggy know that Linowitz's political friends had recently been working to build up his public image and recognition. Some even said that Lyndon Johnson—notoriously skillful at manipulating the press—engineered the *LIFE* article to position Sol as the CEO of Xerox in order to raise his public stature before appointing him to high public office.

Joe Wilson did not react. At least nobody at Xerox ever saw him react. Always inner-directed, he buried any personal feelings and gave almost no indication that he'd even seen the article in *LIFE*. But others at Xerox were very distressed. Dave Curtin was as surprised and upset as Peggy Wilson. In addition to his personal affection for Joe Wilson, public relations was his job and he had worked out all the details of Jane Howard's visit, the picture-taking, and the follow-up, including additional pictures and interviews with Linowitz after the day in Rochester. But Curtin had no idea that the results would be anything like this. Much later, he would say ruefully, "Sol could tie knots a sailor never knew."

Taking a few days' vacation after visiting various Rank-Xerox facilities in Europe, Linowitz was in Italy when *LIFE* came out. Curtin reached him by telephone: "Sol, the article is all about *you*. Joe's not mentioned even once. It says *you* run Xerox."

"No!"

"Oh yes, Sol. That's exactly the way it's printed. It's all about you, Sol. The article makes it look as though you—and you alone—are the leader of Xerox!"

"Oh, God, that's awful!" replied Linowitz. And he immediately focused on what had always been his first priority: "How does Joe feel?"

"Joe hasn't said a word. But everyone else at Xerox is really upset. Really upset."

"What should we do?"

"You cannot let this stand, Sol. We need to demand a correction right away."

"Absolutely, David. I agree."

Linowitz had said he fully understood, but there was no call or cable from him the next day. Nor the next. With nothing coming in from Linowitz and knowing that a quick correction was essential, Curtin called Italy again. When he finally reached him, Curtin was dismayed by the way Linowitz's mind had been working—and his concluding proposition: "David, I've given this matter a lot of serious thought. Bringing it up again with a letter to the editor will just call more attention to this unfortunate episode and just keep it going. Why not just let the matter die?"

"Sol, we can't 'just let it die.' *It won't die.*"

"Well, David, let's get together and talk about it when I get back to the States."

That would mean another week would pass before a correction could be made. By then, the *LIFE* editors would see it as old news and would be very unlikely to print a letter or correction on this simple theory: If it took so long to demand a correction, it must not be very important to Xerox, Wilson, or Linowitz. As Curtin recalls, "I really had to put the pressure on Sol—and insist that he send a telegram demanding a correction."

After his return from Italy, Linowitz wrote the following telegram to the editor, which could easily be skipped over by readers skimming through the letters to the editor: "I am flattered by the generous close-up by Jane Howard, but it would be wrong to leave readers with an incorrect impression of my role at Xerox created by a headline." After that bland introduction, the letter turned to substance: "I do not run and have not run the company. Joseph C. Wilson has been and is chief executive officer of Xerox. He and I have worked together closely over the years, but there has never been any question as to his top responsibility. Peter McColough is now president of the company. My own responsibilities . . . have been and remain primarily legal and international. . . ." This demurral was gentle and tangential compared to the direct and forceful impact of *LIFE's* feature article, particularly in Washington, DC, where politicians are at least as unsophisticated about corporations and business as businessmen are about politics and politicians.[3]

Reactions around Xerox were close to Peggy Wilson's—and appraisals of Linowitz were both blunt and negative.

Wilson was unwilling to hear any part of this and brushed aside all expressions of concern. He told Curtin to calm down and that it wasn't that big a deal. After receiving several *LIFE* clippings tucked into letters, he said he was sick and tired of receiving them, and to make his views clear, had printed and circulated to all executives and managers copies of Linowitz's telegram to the editor of *LIFE* with a cover note saying: "The story in the current issue of *LIFE* magazine has many unfortunate inaccuracies through no fault of his own. Will you please convey immediately his statements to all your people."

In Washington—where Linowitz was headed—the *LIFE* article was clear and powerful: Sol Linowitz ran Xerox and was a big-time corporate leader. Even more important, in the nation's capital Linowitz had many important political connections—at the very top.

Time after time—particularly after his move to Washington—Linowitz would allow people to describe him as the real leader and CEO of Xerox. He would not, or could not, correct them. John Brooks, writing for *The New Yorker*, later observed, "Since Xerox became famous, the general public has tended to think of Linowitz as . . . the company's chief executive. Xerox officials are aware of this misconception and are mystified by it." Linowitz's accepting credit for the success of Xerox and allowing and even welcoming others to give him credit may have been unconscious or just instinctive in his nature. Wilson didn't or couldn't believe that it was deliberate. But the consensus among Xerox executives who knew Linowitz well was that it was a calculated way to enhance Sol's own stature.

[3]Andrew Heiskel, CEO of Time, Inc., later sent a telegram to Joe Wilson expressing regret about the *LIFE* "misunderstanding."

In frustration, Peter McColough took Linowitz aside and reviewed the numerous times Linowitz had allowed others to repeat the error of introducing him as the leader of Xerox and insisted it must be stopped.

"Sol never denied or demurred when other people were crediting him with being the real head of Xerox," recalled McColough. "And his getting credit and taking credit for being the leader of Xerox was becoming a real problem for the company. Joe wouldn't talk about it—so I did."

McColough collected together all the introductions that various public figures had used in presenting Linowitz and, in a face-to-face meeting, confronted Linowitz with the long, factual record. "Sol sat there looking meekly back at me, as tears filled his eyes and rolled down his cheeks. Not that he ever actually *claimed* he was the head of Xerox. It was not that simple. It's not what Sol said; it's what he didn't say that hurt. Linowitz never stopped anyone who was introducing him or saluting him as the leader of Xerox to say: 'No, it was not me. The real leader of Xerox has always been Joe Wilson!'" McColough continued, "But he did not—would not or could not—stop the adulation coming from others who gave him what we all knew was way too much credit."

In the spring of 1971, McColough had had enough and sent a memo to Wilson, saying, "I'm utterly disgusted to see that Sol has not, despite the very forthright talk I had with him a couple of years ago, in any way changed his stripes." New York's Mayor John Lindsay had recently introduced Linowitz as "the former CEO of Xerox Corporation" on television that week, and McColough was disturbed that Linowitz had not disclaimed the title long held Joe Wilson.

A few days later, Wilson replied: "I don't blame you for sizzling at the transcript of the Lindsay-Linowitz discussion. I do note one parenthetical phrase 'Linowitz tries to interrupt,' but he doesn't make any correction in the next paragraph, so the effort must have been a pretty weak one. You do whatever you like. I see no great harm in letting him know somehow that this continued tendency to allow misconceptions to go uncorrected is not going unnoticed by us. On the other hand, if, when you have cooled off, it doesn't seem worthwhile to do it, let it go."[4] Joe Wilson was concentrating on preparing the company for a change in leadership and passing the CEO's baton. As usual, he concentrated on substance.

A few weeks after the article in *LIFE*, Bill Asher got a call, "Would your CEO come to Washington to accept the Presidential Medal of Freedom?" The caller was Al Barker from the political action committee of the AFL-CIO, and he was checking in with Xerox's head of labor relations. "Could you check for me please to be sure it's OK with Mr. Linowitz?"

"Al," intercepted Asher, "Sol Linowitz is *not* our CEO! Our CEO is Joe Wilson."

"Well, Sol Linowitz is the name we got straight from President Johnson."

"You better check. That award has certainly been earned by our CEO. And just as certainly, our CEO is *not* Sol Linowitz. It's Joe Wilson."

"OK, I'll check it out."

Nothing was ever said again about the Presidential Medal of Freedom, but more than three decades later, the Presidential Medal was awarded to Sol M. Linowitz by President William Jefferson Clinton.

[4]Interoffice memorandum, May 10, 1971.

27

PUBLIC SERVICE

Joe Wilson always thought seriously about the future—often looking 20 years ahead and characteristically saying: "We *overestimate* what we can do in the short run—and *underestimate* what we can do in the long run." Wilson consistently took a broad view of responsible, reciprocal leadership, seeing how a better community—local, national, and international—could enrich the environment for his company *and* how his company could act to enhance on community. Wilson embraced a broad view of corporate responsibilities. "If we are to play a useful part and accept the benefits, we must shoulder some of the obligations of the community, the nation, and man. We must, we think, commit to solving the great issues that plague the West, such as poverty abroad and education at home."

Wilson's strong commitment to social enterprise was never "for show," and he always encouraged others to join in. Within Xerox, Wilson created an atmosphere that strongly encouraged community involvement. For Wilson, it was not simply good to give; it was *wise* to give. "A community needs institutions that work. Doing good works is pragmatic: It works. It's *not* charity; it's how we build a strong community—together. It's in our own self-interest because it attracts bright, caring people, particularly scientists and technicians who want more out of life than a paycheck. If we don't build, they won't come."

With Wilson's leadership and steady encouragement, Xerox executives became unusually deeply involved in leading the many organizations that made Rochester special.

Wilson became active and committed to socially responsible action early—when Haloid was small and Wilson was young—and he never let up. Wilson's specific public commitments were remarkably numerous, varied, and sustained over many years—partly because he was known and admired as an articulate and effective leader and partly because he wanted to see real progress made on the nation's problems. Wilson was often asked to serve as a leader— often as *the* leader—of social service organizations. As a consequence, he was over-committed for most of his life and the extent of his over-commitment increased as the years went by.

Starting in 1950, he was a member of the board of directors of the Community Chest of Rochester and Monroe County. In 1951, he served as general chairman for a fund-raising campaign for the United Negro College Fund; and in 1952, as president of the Rochester Chamber of Commerce. Also in 1952, at Wilson's initiative, the company established the Haloid Fund for local good works, and he got involved at the start of the Human Relations Commission in Rochester and, as "the logical man to guide the destinies" of the Citizens Council for a Better Rochester, organized a long list of projects necessary for a more progressive Rochester: public library branches, slum rehabilitation, and river beautification. His long involvement in the Community Chest led to his chairing what Chest sources called "the most innovative committee we ever had," which implemented sweeping reforms.[1]

Wilson's imaginative approach to dealing with major problems and his belief in research as the key to innovation were illustrated by an idea he was incubating at the university in the early 1950s: a

---

[1]*Rochester Times-Union*, November 23, 1971.

think tank or research institute focused on economic issues, social problems like affordable housing and healthcare, and other problems on the national agenda.[2]

Unfortunately, the initiative was sidetracked by Wilson's heart attack, which required him to limit his activities just as the company's drive toward a copier was picking up steam and required all his time. As the University of Rochester's development director later observed, "Anyone who knew Joe Wilson would surely have felt that his research institution would have brought new vision and new ideas to the often arcane world of charitable foundations."

In 1962, when Wilson was made a member of the Committee for Economic Development (CED), he wrote with delight to Marion Folsom, "I think you knew that for years and years no other organization of businessmen would really attract me."

Two years later, although trying to reduce outside commitments, he accepted election to the CED's board of trustees. He was a trustee of the Alfred P. Sloan Foundation, a fellow of the American Academy of Arts and Sciences, founding member of the Business Committee for the Arts, and a director of the Council for Financial Aid to Education. In 1966, he was made the chairman of the United Nations Association of the United States, with Dwight Eisenhower and Harry Truman serving as honorary chairmen.

In 1967, Wilson was chairman of Rochester's Metropolitan Housing Committee to study the shortage of low and moderate-income housing. When city and county funding ran out, he personally contributed $20,000 to cover the cost of completing the five-volume study that was released in 1970 and led to the creation of the Housing Council of Monroe County. He was appointed head of the Presidential Committee on Health Education and served on many other governmental committees, including the National Advisory Committee on Health Manpower, and the Governor's Steering Committee on Social Problems. He served two years as national

[2]Andrew D. Wolfe in the *Brighton-Pittsford Post*, February 7, 1996, page 19.

chairman of the National Council of Christians and Jews. As a corporate director, he served several companies, including First National City Bank (now Citigroup) and Massachusetts Mutual Life.

Wilson engaged more and more actively in an ever-widening range of societal commitments. By the 1960s, he was one of the most visibly committed business leaders in a remarkably wide range of *pro bono* responsibilities in Rochester, in New York State, and in the nation. When asked by his daughter why he didn't run for high public office so he could accomplish his societal goals, Wilson replied, "Because I can accomplish so much more by speaking out as a corporate executive."

In the 1960s, Wilson's service commitments expanded and he worked on several presidential commissions and for many national organizations. Wilson learned management techniques in business that he applied to his work in public service, and learned lessons in public service that he applied to his work at Xerox. He dealt with each major commitment in social service in the same thorough ways: making direct, personal contact; learning what others had done that worked; designing an orderly strategy; preparing fully and well in advance; organizing an effective team to achieve the objective; personally making a visible "leadership" financial contribution; and making key calls himself.

When asked to head a committee to develop a fund-raising strategy for Rochester's hospitals, he agreed with his typical condition that several "big angels" would be on his committee. Then Wilson and two committee members went to Columbus to learn about getting both public and private funding. In Rochester, he had a list compiled of the names and addresses of all past donors to all hospital drives. Then, he arranged for Xerox to adopt a plan developed at Kodak and make a three-year pledge of $150,000, or $70 per employee *and* extend the challenge that every employer in Rochester do the same.

Imaginative and inspiring as he often was, Wilson was always pragmatic and his ideas well grounded. He had no patience with "nice concepts" that were unrealistic. He rejected as unrealistic and naïve the idea that all or most of Rochester's major companies should simultaneously agree to rebuild the downtown area together. Wilson knew it would be impossible, citing the obvious reality that they each had their own headquarters already; all were accustomed to being located right where they were. In addition, the problems of downtown Rochester were too great and too obvious for a dozen corporations to agree simultaneously to move their headquarters into the center city. But that didn't mean Xerox could not act alone. Several years later, as Wilson studied the drawings for Xerox's new headquarters office building planned for Webster, he changed the plans decisively: "We made a terrible mistake a few years ago. We cut Rochester out of all the business it might get from Xerox. We can't do that. This is our city. We cannot abandon downtown. We've gotta go downtown!"—and initiated Xerox Square, a strikingly handsome, modern building with the nation's first internal shopping mall.

Wilson believed that a corporation was always within and part of society and that a company's responsibility for service to society went far beyond earning good profits. This is why he conceptualized the social services program at Xerox, in which a group of selected Xerox employees, still on the company payroll, worked full-time for charitable and service organizations. After all, if a corporation is part of a society, why wouldn't investing the time of talented *people* be as productive a contribution as investing *money*.[3]

[3]On its 20th anniversary in 1982, Tony Kobayashi decided Fuji-Xerox should do as Xerox had done for nearly 20 years: endorse and support with full pay employees working voluntarily in social service in Japan. "Despite our noble intentions, we ran into real resistance—particularly at the organizations we hoped to serve. They could not believe that a serious corporation would send serious people to work for them *unless* we had a second agenda—such as uncovering from within their organization some new ways to obtain more sales for Fuji-Xerox. So we had to withdraw and wait five more years before our offer of employees for social services could become a reality. Then our program was accepted—and became important news. Now, a dozen or so other companies have followed our example."

In a 1967 *New Yorker* interview, Wilson explained his concepts of corporate social activism, saying, "It's a matter of balance. You can't just be bland, or you throw away your influence. But you can't take a stand on every major issue, either. Issues like university education, civil rights, and Negro employment clearly *are* our business. I'd hope that we would have the courage to stand up for a point of view that was unpopular if we thought it was appropriate to do so. So far, we haven't faced that situation—we haven't found a conflict between what we consider our civic responsibility and good business. But the time may come. We may have to stand on the firing line yet."[4]

More and more people felt frustrated in the late 1960s, with the intractable problems of poverty and welfare and the prospect of the nation unintentionally producing a permanent underclass. Wilson was an ideal choice to lead a public examination of these issues at a conference called by New York Governor Nelson Rockefeller to be held at Arden House, the former estate of E.H. Harriman. The *New York Times* described the Arden House Conference on Welfare Reform as "a landmark meeting at which a group of top corporate executives from across the nation decided that income maintenance, rather than the welfare check, was a desirable goal, propelling this social scientists' dream into the forefront of active, political consideration."

As he opened the Arden House Conference, Wilson quoted Bernard Baruch, "Private property and community interest are interdependent in a free society."[5] Then quoting Franklin D. Roosevelt, Wilson continued: "The test of our progress is not whether we add more to the abundance of those who have much; it is whether we do enough for those who have little."

The Arden House Conference centered on identifying new ideas, new policies, and new programs to combat poverty in the United States and on answering the question: "If the problem of

---

[4]Interview by author John Brooks.
[5]The conference consisted of 55 business leaders: 7 from labor, 13 from foundations, 10 from communications, 12 from education, and 10 from government.

public welfare were given to you, what would you recommend as sound public policy?"

Governor Rockefeller later stated that 80 to 85% of the recommendations made in the Arden House Conference on Public Welfare were incorporated in specific legislative initiatives."[6] As the *New York Times* reported, "instead of the conventional attacks on welfare costs, the participants attacked the paucity of programs for building hope and opportunity for those on the relief roles."

Wilsonian organization was evident: Each business, labor, and academic leader participating in the conference received, months in advance, three thoughtfully creative briefing papers by Daniel Patrick Moynihan, Arthur Burns, and Leland Hazard. Each delegate was asked to study the materials and respond in writing. Responses were collated and distributed to all delegates to assure an exchange of views prior to the meetings.[7] Workshop discussions were led by three university presidents, with distinguished journalists recording the substance of each session. Senators Jacob Javits and Edward Kennedy both spoke. In appreciation of his genial leadership that combined thoughtfulness with enlightened concepts of social responsibility, firmness in making decisions, and unrelenting persistence in following through to see that they became effective, the Arden House staff nicknamed Wilson "The Gentle Giant."[8]

Wilson urged the conferees to agree that their goal was not to make decisions or advocate specific actions, but to concentrate on awareness and understanding of the nature of the problem and the possibilities for progress and eventual solution. Toward the end of the conference, participants agreed on the critical need to "break the cycle of dependency" and that industry needed to take the lead on developing job training and job opportunities for the hitherto "untrainable." This outcome fit with Wilson's philosophy of business

[6]*New York Times*, November 9, 1969.
[7]November 2–3, 1967.
[8]*New York Times*, November 23, 1971.

responsibility and his conception of industrial statesmanship, so he accepted Governor Rockefeller's request that he chair the ad hoc committee that would follow up on the numerous ideas and proposals coming out of the conference. (Governor Rockefeller later asked Wilson to gather data and convene another conference of 100 national leaders to focus on the cost, distribution, and quality of medical care. Wilson again agreed to chair the conference with Victor Weingarten directing the staff.)

The core of Wilson's Arden House report was remarkably advanced:

> The present system of public assistance does not work well. It covers only 8 million of the 30 million Americans living in poverty. It is demeaning, inefficient, inadequate, and has so many disincentives built into it that it encourages continued dependency. It should be replaced with an income maintenance system, possibly a negative income tax, which would bring all Americans up to a least the official Federal poverty line. Such a system should contain strong incentives to work, try to contain regional cost of living differentials, and be administered by the Internal Revenue Service to provide greater administrative efficiency and effectiveness than now exists.
>
> Solid research is virtually unknown in public welfare. Less than $\frac{1}{10}$ of 1% of welfare funds are spent for that purpose. Rarely has so costly a program operated with so little knowledge. More research is urged in all aspects of the public assistance and public welfare programs. Until a new system of income maintenance, after thorough study, is adopted, the present welfare system needs drastic and immediate reform.

Recognizing that the direct cost of welfare is usually thought of as "only 1%" of GNP, Wilson wrote in a guest editorial in *Saturday Review* that the real cost was closer to 7%—not $10 billion, but $70 billion—when the higher costs of fire, police, and health services in poor areas are included:

> If every eligible family in the nation were to avail itself of the full income subsidy and food stamp provision in the proposed legislation, the numbers of Americans living below the official poverty line would be reduced by almost 60%—from the present twenty-five million to approximately ten million. Instead of 13% of our population being in want, only 5% would be in dire need.
>
> Many of us believe that our country is at a stage in its history where it cannot afford to tolerate a situation in which twenty-five million Americans—fifteen million of whom are in families with full- or part-time wage earners—do not earn enough to support a family at a poverty level. Of the remaining ten million, most of whom have been receiving assistance through welfare grants, more than 80% are too old, too young, too sick, too disabled, or too blind to work. Of those left, an additional one and one-half million are mothers of young children, most of whom want to work and become self-supporting, but are denied the opportunity because of inadequate or, in many parts of the country, non-existent child-care facilities. Fewer than 3% of those who have been receiving public assistance are able-bodied, and able to work. Their average stay on welfare is less than eighteen months. From a humanitarian point of view, therefore, most of those who depend upon public assistance are helpless victims of a system that is outworn, expensive, inefficient, and wasteful—and has not done the job.
>
> The most serious threat to the world today is the potentiality of racial strife in the urban north of the United States.

After reminding the conferees of the recent demonstrations, he concluded soberly, "All of us in this audience know that the problem of welfare is related to this problem of race. Therefore, we are here to deal, it seems to me, with perhaps the most important problem of our time."[9]

Amid the euphoria over the success of the conference, Wilson's friend, Buck Lanham, expressed real concern: "You looked plain country tired. Even your eyes looked tired. This is no damned good, Joe. You are doing too much and it is beginning to show." Lanham was right, but Wilson kept up the pace.

[9]Francis Keppel, whom Wilson had once interviewed as a presidential candidate for the University of Rochester, was impressed and invited Wilson to an Oyster Bay meeting of industrialists to discuss ways business could help in education. Keppel later selected Wilson to report the group's conclusions to President Johnson, who agreed with their recommendation that "business, labor and government leaders be brought into close collaboration." A few months later, Nixon appointed Wilson to chair the National Advisory Committee on Health Manpower.

28

WINDING DOWN

In early 1966, Wilson again restructured the senior management organization of Xerox, this time moving away from the traditional functional divisions, such as marketing and manufacturing, and into four business-centered divisions. Rutledge was assigned to business products; Pallicheck to information systems; Telischaks to corporate administration; and McColough to educational services. Significantly, McColough, as Executive Vice President, would supervise the other operating divisions as well as departments such as Advertising, Finance, and Control. Corporate Planning and Business Development would report directly to Wilson as would Linowitz and Dessauer.

The most important parts of this major restructuring were not announced or made explicit, but they were obvious to everyone at Xerox: Joe Wilson would be winding down and Jack Rutledge was no longer a candidate to succeed Wilson as CEO. It would be Peter McColough. McColough had great personality and was particularly good with people. For Xerox, he had helped build and then managed one of the world's best and largest sales and servicing organizations. Gregarious and upbeat, he was fun to be with and projected great self-assurance. With both a law degree and an MBA, he had

had military command and showed all the drive and energy of the young man he was at 43.

When Abe Chatman heard that McColough was to be Wilson's heir apparent, he whispered to Bill Asher, "Tell Joe it's a mistake!"

Because they have to make judgments about people without knowing all the inside information, labor leaders often develop a keen intuition about people, including senior corporate executives. But Wilson had been affronted when Asher relayed Chatman's view, and said, "You tell Abe Chatman I will pick my own successor—*not* the union!"

Asher advised Chatman: "Resign yourself."

Wilson would soon have reason to have paid greater heed to Abe Chatman's concerns.

In 1966, Wilson was gaining increasing recognition even as he was coming to the end of his career with Xerox. After more than 30 years of extraordinarily successful leadership, he was clearly in a transitional role. While eager to share and even delegate responsibility, he was not yet willing to relinquish the CEO's authority, especially in setting strategic objectives. Personally contemplating retirement, he looked forward to having time for some of the many trips and adventures he and Peggy had long ago agreed to subordinate to his commitment to transforming Haloid into Xerox. As he put it: "It's been a long run. I feel some strain and it's good to have people in their 40s running with the ball."

A few weeks later, Wilson and Linowitz were at the Mauna-Kea Hotel in Hawaii before flying on to Tokyo for a Fuji-Xerox board meeting. Wilson reminded Linowitz of his intention to make McColough President, explaining that he felt he really had no choice because he believed he had to select someone from within Xerox, and there were now no alternatives to McColough. Then 58, Wilson felt he should continue as CEO and become Chairman, changing that position from "just parsley on the potatoes" to one of real power, and suggested Linowitz become Honorary Chairman while retaining his position as General Counsel and Chairman of the Executive Committee.

Linowitz laughed that Honorary Chairman sounded older than he felt and that the honorary halo seemed premature. So he suggested his title be chairman of something like Xerox International, with a mandate to pull together all the international operations. Wilson recognized this would also give Linowitz an impressive title to use in his extracurricular activities, particularly in Washington.

How useful this would be to Linowitz was soon made very clear. In November, Linowitz made a surprising announcement: He was leaving Xerox. Linowitz had agreed to become U.S. Ambassador to the Organization of American States and U.S. Representative of the Inter-American Committee of the Alliance for Progress. Of the three great motivators—love, power, and money—Linowitz did not particularly care about love or money. He had made himself emotionally independent long ago, and he had become financially independent through Xerox stock options. Influence and power fit with his strong ambitions, and he was drawn to Washington, the center of power, where he was recognized as an outstanding legal technician and counselor.

For Linowitz, his relationship with Joe Wilson had become a "step along the way." He had, as he apparently saw it, grown up to and then grown beyond Joe Wilson. For Sol Linowitz, there was no comparison between Wilson's center of gravity—Xerox in upstate Rochester—and the White House in the nation's capital.

Linowitz's sudden resignation—he was one of the first executives ever to leave Xerox—came as a real surprise. Despite general discussions of the abstract idea of his going into public service some day, his abrupt departure was a personal blow to Joe Wilson. This was a kind of decision that Wilson did not understand and could not have made when there was so much work to do at Xerox. (Linowitz also resigned from the University of Rochester board of trustees, which Wilson had arranged for him. At first, this seemed understandable when Linowitz pleaded that he needed to cut back because of his increasingly demanding schedule in national service.

However, Wilson later learned from others that Linowitz had *not* resigned as a trustee of either Hamilton College or Cornell.)

True to his self-discipline, when announcing the appointment, Wilson emphasized the honor it conferred on the company—but the familiar warmth and enthusiasm with which he had so often spoken of Linowitz was clearly missing. Wilson presided at a Country Club dinner on January 28 at which the Rochester community gathered to honor the new ambassador. But earlier, when invited to the swearing-in ceremonies in Washington on November 9, Wilson wired his regrets, saying he had London guests arriving that day, so he would not be able to make it to the capital.[1]

Repetitive mentions of Linowitz as "the former head of Xerox" in press coverage of the OAS appointment and his subsequent activities, aggravated many of his former associates, but Wilson brushed them

---

[1]Many years later, Joe Wilson's daughter, Chris, put the question directly to Linowitz: "Something happened between you and Dad that created distance. What was it?" But even with the passage of decades, Linowitz dissembled.

"I had that feeling too. I didn't do very well at probing: Why? I must tell you honestly that even though your father was very encouraging and supportive about my leaving the company and going to OAS—and this is something I didn't think of until I tried to answer the same question—he was not pleased at my leaving. There was a bristling—even though publicly, he was saying, 'We're proud of this.' "

Then, Linowitz shifted the focus away from himself with a tone of confidentiality: "Others have tried to come between Joe and me. Dave Curtin was one of these back stabbers." Then, changing to another tack, he was sure that "If Joe and I sat down together today, we could recreate most of what we had nearly 40 years ago." Then, Linowitz suggested: "We tried to get together as couples—Toni and I with Joe and Peggy—six different times, but each time, Joe had to cancel." He did not recognize how hard it would be for his listener to believe that after all those years with her father, Linowitz wouldn't realize that something important was seriously amiss and required his personal attention, *or* that Chris's mother would even consider getting together, *or* that her father, knowing her mother's views, would ever have made such a commitment.

Somehow not seeing the combined impact of his leaving and the *LIFE* article, Linowitz went on: "Something happened that destroyed that feeling we'd always had that there were just the two of us—and then there was the rest of the world. Somewhere in my files are letters I wrote to him. I never got a reciprocal sort of

aside. He finally confessed to Buck Lanaman, who had sent him such a clipping, that he was tired of receiving them. Still, close associates sensed that Wilson's communications with Linowitz were more formal, and lacked the warmth that had always characterized them before.

As usual, Wilson disciplined himself to focus on his tasks and the responsibilities that lay ahead and the role he believed he should perform as new priorities arose. As he now had more time, the second half of the 1960s opened up intriguing opportunities in public service. These years brought Wilson considerable public recognition, as he was increasingly honored and celebrated as an exemplary business leader.

In that year, *Saturday Review*, a widely read and highly respected journal of opinion and news analysis, cited Wilson as Businessman of the Year, saying:

With more than 90 percent of the scientists in the entire history of the world now alive, and with the great bulk of mankind's entire scientific literature having been published

---

tone [in the letters of reply]." He then added: "And they were typewritten, not in that horrible handwriting of Joe's."

"In those five years [before Joe's death] I was very conscious something was wrong, but I didn't presume to think that I was part of it, that I was the cause of it." Then, saying that he felt he had done all that was responsible, Linowitz mused quietly, "I don't know if I could have done something that I didn't do."

When Chris Wilson had asked her father why Linowitz was no longer welcome at the Wilson's home and suggested he must be angry, Wilson's quiet response was: "No, Chris." And then more quietly and to no person in particular, he added, "I can do better than that."

After a few years in Washington, Ambassador Linowitz was invited to give a speech in Rochester. At the podium with tiered tables to his left and right, he spoke with great pleasure, and was obviously emotional as he said how proud he was to return to Rochester where so many wonderful people had been so helpful and meant so much to him and that he had been moved by the flag-waving crowds lining the route of his cavalcade in from the airport. As he described the scene— an impressive homecoming for a beloved public servant—his daughter mused aloud to a friend, "I wonder why Dad says all that stuff. There were no crowds. There were no flags. Nobody waved."

in the past ten years, the techniques and facilities for capturing, managing, retrieving, transmitting, and presenting information for society's use have become central to the management of the human community around the globe.

One man who sees this challenge with impressive clarity is Joseph Chamberlain Wilson, president of the Xerox Corporation. He is both an idealist who is the chief architect of one of the great corporate successes of American business and a hard-headed realist who believes profoundly that public service is essential to the health of private enterprise. Mr. Wilson, who was fifty-six years old last month, personifies *Saturday Review's* conviction that in our complex socioeconomic system, the modern executive must embody a personal commitment to the good society as well as to a sound economy in order to make that system work.

Notre Dame awarded Wilson an honorary degree as doctor of laws and in 1967, Boston University awarded Wilson his fifth honorary degree: doctor of humane letters. Both were eclipsed later that spring when he received an honorary doctor of laws at Harvard. (Other honorands that day included musician Leonard Bernstein, artist Ben Shahn, and scientist Lord Florey for his work on penicillin.) It was an exhilarating experience as president Nathan Pusey read the citation, which included: "An eminent industrial leader and exemplary benefactor of education and public causes; would that we could multicopy his kind throughout the land."[2]

Delighted by this high honor, Wilson proudly bought enough copies of each of the Boston newspapers to give a full set to each of his children.

Asked how his commitment to social consciousness related to Xerox as a business corporation, Wilson replied in his typically high-

[2]A year later Wilson would become a member of the Overseers' Committee to Visit the Harvard Business School.

minded and reflective way: "Of course, you have to believe [in the concept of] duty to society to have it make any sense at all. We think that the evidence is clear throughout the world that unless a business institution demonstrates that it's concerned about racial problems . . . that it's concerned about war and peace . . . that it's concerned about urban renewal and pollution of the atmosphere and waters, etc.—then the whole system of free institutions, which we happen to believe in, ultimately will be circumscripted and government or other political beliefs will take its place or completely erode its position.

"So there's a pragmatic element in this which happens to coincide with our beliefs. I see no dichotomy in this situation. Any band of people who are working for something can't ignore the things around them. This applies to a church, a university, a business or a municipal government or any other institution. We don't see any particular distinction except, of course, that a business has to operate as a successful business. It must be a profit-making enterprise. This rarely causes business to take an antisocial position and we think there are many, many opportunities for business to be positive in its sense of social responsibility and its social activity. Happily, the people around here—I suppose there are exceptions—believe this."[3]

Wilson was not usually so free from immediate concerns to be so philosophical. More typically engaged in implementing his long-term policies, in the 1966 labor negotiations Wilson told union negotiators that he found the current negotiations very upsetting because the union was getting away from the past practice of always working toward wage agreements using three well-developed guidelines:

- Agreeing on wage rates which were "competitive with the best competitors"

---

[3]Interview with Allan Fenton, managing editor of *Executive Magazine* on June 8, 1966, in Rochester.

- Establishing benefits that were "generous but would keep the company competitive"
- Keeping Eastman Kodak as "a sort of benchmark company"

Following the sit-down strike of 1936, it had taken more than a decade to overcome the bitterness the union and workers had felt toward the former management. Since then, relations had developed so well that frank and open negotiations had produced a series of reasoned settlements. But now, all the gains from three decades of disciplined cooperation appeared to Wilson to be at risk. Significantly, the union's only justification for its new wage demands was that Xerox could afford them.

Turning to specific causes for concern, Wilson cited a small minority of workers who seemed determined to hurt the union-company relationship through production slowdowns, despite a solemn union promise that such things would not occur. He cited an anonymous letter that said in part: "Now is the time to get as much as we can" and "It is just plain common sense, you ask for it while it is there." Then, Wilson said how sorry he felt to be forced to come "within an ace" of withdrawing the company's present wage increase offer after years and years of working on the basis of fair facts with the union's leaders. He continued: "If a small fringe group of union workers wanted to pressure the Company in an unreasonable way" through wildcat strikes or the like, the "Company would respond accordingly and its attitude would never be the same again."[4]

Wilson reminded the union representatives that if they began with inflated demands, they would create their own political problem because "the final settlement would look like peanuts in the eyes of the employees." Then, sharing an internal document on corporate objectives, which included a commitment to continue achieving strong growth in earnings, Wilson directed the union leaders' attention to the balanced commitment to serve three main constituencies: customers,

[4]Interoffice memorandum by J.R. O'Malley on March 16, 1966.

investors, and employees: "Through developing, making, selling and servicing reliable products and services of high quality; to render worthwhile values to our customers; through the attainment of these financial objectives, to make Xerox Corporation a rewarding investment for present and future shareholders and creditors; and through sound, progressive employment practices and policies, to make Xerox Corporation a superior place of employment for its people [with a specific commitment] to continue an industrial relations policy which is concerned with the welfare of each individual in the organization, and at the same time inspire the people as a whole to dedicated effort."[5]

Keeping with his long-standing practice of using data and logic to develop, explain, and support his views, Wilson presented more than a dozen charts documenting a series of external year-by-year benchmarks at companies in the region or in comparable industries—particularly, Eastman Kodak. He again offered a 3.5% increase—far below the union's proposal of 10%—and asked the union for logic and data to support its numbers *or* to agree to 3.5%. Over a few days, the union's 10% went to 7% and then to 6%. Wilson persisted in asking *why* the company should pay anything above the going rate. At each and every round, Wilson used facts and logic to support his proposals and asked as much of the union negotiations, but the union did not have the necessary facts, made errors in calculations, and seldom had relevant information to support or justify its proposal. Wilson also insisted on getting unanimous assurance from the union leadership that poor attitudes and behavior by workers would not be tolerated before he would condone a wage settlement. In the end, the union and the company agreed on 4%. Wilson's persistent discipline had again proven effective, but after 30 years, that year's negotiations would be his personal "swan song."

Change or transition was coming in the marketplace, too. The business of Xerox was maturing. In the mid-1960s, the U.S.

---

[5] Interoffice memorandum by R.J. Landsman on January 26, 1967.

government, striving to reduce costs, made Xerox machines a specific target. This was important because the government accounted for 10% of Xerox revenues and its defense contractors represented another 8%. In response, Xerox introduced copiers that adjusted charges to copy volume and initiated a special pricing structure for the government. And, given increasing competition, the price of toner was cut 35%. Changes also included increasing copier competition from other suppliers. (IBM announced the IBM 9370 Document Processor at $13,000 to $15,000: it would make 25,000 copies an hour on roll paper from offset masters. Litton entered the copier field in 1965, and Polaroid was reported to be interested.)

For an executive as disciplined about long-range forward planning as he always was, Wilson must have been concerned about his ability to select the next generation of leadership for Xerox as the freedom of time and the choice of alternatives he once had were collapsing in on him. Just five years before, he could have expected that he would continue as CEO until he was 60 years old, and then serve at least another five years as chairman, during which time he could surely develop an outstanding board of directors. Linowitz, being younger, would have been expected to continue serving as a wise, engaged counselor for at least ten years. And Wilson would have had ample time to knit together as one executive team the talented individuals he had so successfully recruited over the years, even adding a few more top executives to the group if extra skills were desired. (He had even thought of personally relocating to London as a way of both making room for his successor to get established in Rochester and giving special emphasis to international operations. Besides, on a personal basis, he and Peggy always enjoyed London and the British people.) But that was before Jack Rutledge and Don Clark took themselves out of the running and, of course, before Sol Linowitz left. The Doppler effect of foreshortened time, with specific events crowding faster and faster into "future shock" was seriously limiting Wilson's choices.

Successfully transferring leadership from a long-serving, highly successful, and much admired organization-builder to a selected successor is notoriously difficult. For Xerox, the challenge was unusually great because Joe Wilson had served so many years with such extraordinary success and was uniformly so very greatly admired. For all his modesty and all his deliberate celebration of the contributions of others, almost everyone knew that Xerox was really Joe Wilson's company and its successes were really his successes. Still, succession was inevitable and the formidable challenges of company leadership were rapidly increasing.

Xerox was already a large company *and* growing fast. Each year, more new people and new sales were added than the *total* workforce of just five years before. And Xerox was a truly global business with all of its formidable challenges. Dozens of competitors were striving to find technological breakthroughs. Copying and computing were sure to converge. And IBM, with all its strengths, was sure to be a leading challenger. Another challenge was the obvious reality that Xerox produced an increasingly torrential cash flow that had to be invested profitably. And the high price-earnings multiple of Xerox stock—on which all key employees had stock options—showed that investors had high expectations for continuing rapid growth in earnings.[6]

Wilson had good reason to believe McColough understood and fully agreed with all the strategies and policies he had so carefully and rigorously worked out over many years. He had always engaged

---

[6]Joe Wilson's thoughtful attention to individuals—even as successes were flooding his way—is illustrated by a minor story. In the late 1960s, two Xerox scientists and their wives, who kept Kosher diets, were coming to Rochester on a Monday. Fox's delicatessen would be closed that day, but Mr. Fox himself agreed to prepare Kosher box lunches. (To provide a table for the meal, Xerox reserved a table at a nearby diner—for $10—which was more than the $9.20 cost of Fox's box lunches for four.) A few weeks later, Wilson made a point of going to Fox's delicatessen for dinner. "People mean a lot to us," said Wilson, who went on to say how much he appreciated Mr. Fox for making the box lunches even though his delicatessen was closed. Wilson said he hoped to help Fox's business, and indeed he did. Over the next ten years, Fox's provided Kosher lunches at the three shareholder's meetings held at Webster. The last one involved 235 meals for more than $2,000. (Peter B. Taub, Rochester, NY, June 5, 1980.)

McColough and the others in the process and always explained how decisions fit within Xerox's core values. If McColough had not mastered all the technology, that was understandable since he was not personally as fascinated by the puzzle-solving process. His strengths were obvious: He was very likeable, took a balanced view of major issues, and was a committed internationalist. Besides, he was young and, as a quick study, would keep learning. So Wilson made his choice. And, as was his practice and philosophy, he generously gave what McColough most needed from Wilson—visible, consistent support both for him as a young new CEO *and* for his decisions. That strong support was and always would be Wilson's way, whether it was with subordinates at Xerox, with presidents at the university, or with heads of the social service organizations.

At the May 1968 annual meeting, Wilson said, "I have a brief prediction to make. At our Board meeting this afternoon, we will be adopting an important modification in the executive structure to Xerox. It is something that I am deeply happy to report to you because it represents the realization of an objective that I and my colleagues have planned for over five years." That afternoon Joe Wilson announced his successor. As expected, it was Peter McColough.

The gracious way of passing the CEO's baton was so characteristic of Joe Wilson and so carefully planned and prepared for that neither Wilson nor any of his colleagues would see what Abe Chatman had somehow seen years before: For all of his talent, charm, and energy, Peter McColough would not be successful as CEO. In addition to adding more and more operating divisions to McColough's portfolio of responsibilities, Wilson had put him in charge of acquisitions to give him experience in corporate strategy. Ironically, acquisitions would become the area of McColough's most dramatic mistakes.

29

NO LONGER CEO

Change is hard. Changing leaders of very successful organizations is very hard, particularly for the two individuals most directly involved and with the most at stake: the outgoing and the incoming CEOs. The risk of disappointment and even failure lurks over every leadership transition.

For Joe Wilson, whose career enjoyed so very many successes and who excelled at the creative discipline of strategic planning and effective execution, his confidence in his chosen successor took on the characteristics of Greek tragedy.

Basic Systems, a small company specializing in programmed learning at every level from preschool to adult on-the-job training, was one of Peter McColough's first acquisitions in the field of education. With sales of just $1 million, it had made no profits. A few months after becoming CEO, McColough observed sardonically why his small acquisition was not working out: The operation was "run by bright, fast-talking people who failed in only two things: running the company and developing a workable marketing strategy."

Wilson may well have wondered why, with such clearly visible problems, Basic Systems had been acquired without enough due diligence to anticipate troubles, and why, if marketing strategy and operations were weaknesses, McColough, who was supposed to be strong in both, had been unable to find a way to develop the necessary strengths. If he wondered about these things, Wilson kept his concerns to himself. If he wasn't concerned, he should have been.

McColough then compounded the problem at Basic Systems when he decided to hire an executive from the industrial chemicals and plastics division of a major oil company to lead the expansion into education.[1] Apparently McColough assumed that the new executive must know about education because he had a doctorate and had taught briefly at Harvard Business School. With all his experience at the university, Wilson would have known that faculty members are notorious for not understanding what it takes to lead and manage an educational institution. Besides, education runs the gamut from preschools to universities, so if education were to provide the strategic growth opportunity that Xerox intended, its lead manager would need great expertise in many aspects of education *and* would need to understand how a new entrant like Xerox could "outsmart the problems." In several ways, McColough's first acquisition was a failure. It was not his last.

In his first year as CEO, McColough acquired Ginn & Co., a New England textbook publisher. The price of $127 million was extraordinarily high relative to earnings of $2.7 million: 46 *times* earnings. Worse, Ginn had lost momentum during the 1950s and never regained its past strength. Even without Ginn's internal problems, Wilson must have wondered at the very high price McColough paid, but as always, he believed in supporting the decision-maker and said he believed "Peter was learning." McColough laconically observed one of the truths of acquisitions: "One of the things I learned from problems with some of our education acquisitions was that we have to make acquired companies feel right away that they are an important part of Xerox."

More lessons were to be learned. Fortunately, the next—but only the next—lesson was on a small scale. R.D. Dowler Co., a 66-year-old

---

[1]Dr. Robert Hugh.

publisher of *Publisher's Weekly*, *Library Journal*, and *Books in Print*, made $1 million pretax on $10 million in sales when it was acquired. The idea was to modernize Dowler's processes, but it didn't work out as hoped. Trying to computerize *Books in Print* produced 17,000 errors. Dowler's president quit when Xerox management stepped in to "help." The company would lose money in both 1969 and 1970.

In September 1968, McColough, apparently determined to make his major mark as CEO, dramatically agreed to merge Xerox with CIT Financial in what would have been one of the largest corporate mergers in history. CIT had been making acquisitions for several years, but was having increasing difficulty attracting other companies to the merger alter because its earnings record was poor and management at all levels was considered "sclerosic." After six years of experience advising CIT on possible acquisitions, an investment banker sensed that CIT might instead be willing to *be* acquired.[2] He arranged a meeting between CIT chairman L. Walter Lundell and Peter McColough on September 20, 1968. Just two meetings and only seven days later, the two CEOs announced their giant merger.

Wall Street was shocked. The two companies' businesses were almost completely unrelated, and the stock-for-stock exchange valued CIT at such a high price   McColough offered to pay a 55% premium—that institutional investors were up in arms. McColough apparently believed the 55% premium would satisfy the CIT investors who were giving up the rich dividends that had been their main attraction for buying CIT stock *and* that Xerox shareholders wouldn't mind the big premium because the impact on current earnings per share would be "small."

When he learned of it, Wilson must have been chagrined. For so many years, he had always insisted that every acquisition must fit in with Xerox's core strategy, and he had always done very careful

---

[2] Jonathan de Sola Mendes, with assistance from John Loeb of Loeb, Rhoades & Co.

homework. In contrast, McColough and Lundell—whose very first question was "Why are you interested?"—announced their agreement without adequate time for due diligence and without any consideration by their boards of directors. As *Time* magazine reported, "Both executives were a bit vague when it came to discussing what their multi-million dollar handshake would produce."[3]

This rush to action was hard to justify on either the basic idea or the price. McColough gave a curious explanation: To expand strongly in education, health, and computer peripherals, he said Xerox would need capital. But as any financial analyst knew, if CIT could provide capital, so could Xerox with its surging cash flow. What McColough really did with his merger proposal, as professional investors soon recognized, was declare publicly that Xerox stock was way overpriced.

Not surprisingly, the CIT deal did *not* go through. After a whirlwind courtship, the two CEOs had a sudden falling out and CIT's CEO stalked out of the meeting room: The deal was off. But it was not the last big acquisition surprise. Another deal was soon announced.

McColough had come to the understandable conclusion that Xerox had a long-term strategic need for major strength in computers. Xerox's capabilities in graphics were very good, but it needed comparable digital capabilities, which would take too long to develop internally. McColough asked Wilson to join him in visiting with Georges Doriot, the visionary Harvard Business School professor and head of American Research & Development. This firm was one of the original venture capital funds and had a major stake in Digital Equipment Corp. His purpose was to enquire into the possibility of Xerox acquiring Digital. Doriot was interested, but Digital CEO Ken Olsen refused even to consider the idea.

Still, McColough was determined to acquire a computer company to make Xerox "digital" and make his own major mark on

[3]*Time*, October 4, 1969, page 95.

Xerox. Abe Zarem, the brilliant and well-connected technologist who came in with the acquisition of EOS, suggested two different computer companies as possible acquisition candidates. Both were financially feasible, but both were rejected out of hand. As one of the Xerox executives of that era explained, "Peter *never* could learn to listen. And he lacked the mental grace to keep the good ideas and discard the bad—a most significant human failure."

McColough believed that "speed to scale" in data processing was strategically essential and that a major acquisition was the only way. However, well-known antitrust guidelines from the Justice Department meant that all the large business equipment companies were off limits to Xerox. So when Scientific Data Systems first came up as an acquisition possibility, it looked to McColough like his one big chance, and he went for it. He called Arthur Rock, a successful investment banker who had become a leading venture capitalist and, with Max Palevsky, had organized SDS as a scientific computer company just a few years before. Taking their new company public, where it rapidly rose to a high price-earnings multiple, Rock and Palevsky were privately hoping to be acquired so they could get out at a superb profit.

With SDS, *not* listening would be a major problem. McColough never asked Jack Goldman, his Executive Vice President for Technology, nor Abe Zarem what they thought of an SDS acquisition. If he had asked, he'd have learned that everyone at Xerox who knew computers was strongly opposed. Already a high flyer without a proven product line, Scientific Data Systems was "in a different movie" and clearly did not fit with Xerox's business. SDS software was designed for large-scale number crunching in scientific work and time-sharing, *not* repetitive, routine calculations on large volumes of data in business applications like accounting, inventories, or billing that might be important to Xerox customers. But they did not need and could not use SDS's capacity to do complex calculations on relatively small bodies of date. For SDS, 75% of its output was scientific and 15% was time-sharing—which left only 10% in business applications. There was virtually no strategic fit with Xerox.

While the benefit of this acquisition was microscopic, the price McColough offered was astronomical: nearly 10 million shares of Xerox stock worth $1.5 billion for a company whose revenues were only $100 million and whose profits were a mere $10 million—150 times earnings!

"Growing up in Rochester as I did," recalled Rock, "I was familiar with Haloid and Xerox. And from everything I heard about him, Joe Wilson was a fantastic business leader, but his chosen successor was not. What could I do, as chairman of a public company that we had started only recently when somebody makes you an amazing offer? McColough was in a terrific rush to do a deal, and he offered us a huge premium—50% above an already high market price! Later, as a new member of the Xerox board, I learned that since McColough had decided Xerox had to go into computers because IBM was going into copiers. Some strategic concept! I got off that board as soon as I possibly could."[4]

Within months of the SDS acquisition, the 1970 recession put the computer industry—particularly the *scientific* part of the computer industry where deferring equipment purchases for a year or so was relatively easy—into a serious downdraft. Xerox Data Systems, as the company was renamed, was particularly hard-hit by federal spending cuts: Its revenues dropped by one-third in 1970—from $125 million to $83 million—and profits completely disappeared.

It got even worse. XDS lost $500 million over the next few years and then closed down for a cumulative loss of $2 billion—in addition to the opportunity cost of tying up Xerox management in a failing acquisition and destroying Xerox's image as the can-do company

---

[4]McColough recalled Rock's departure differently: "His business was not meeting budgets, so I took Rock aside at one board meeting and told him he'd have to leave."

with great management. Large as these costs were, the largest cost never showed up on Xerox's books.

The failure with Xerox Data Systems caused even greater harm through its indirect consequences than through the direct consequences of evaporating $2 billion of corporate treasure. XDS people argued that you couldn't develop a great computer company in Rochester: Too many top-ranked high-tech people would not even consider such a small city with such a cold climate. Rude remarks were made—and heard—about Eastern "uptight suits" or West Coast "hippie weirdos." Even after XDS was closed down, the confrontation of cultures between West Coast scientist innovators and East Coast conservative industrialists would not be forgotten. In a few years, it would fester and re-emerge in a somewhat different context and do more harm to Xerox. In addition, the SDS failure made McColough "puck shy"' about technology.

W here Wilson had done careful, extensive homework and then pressed ahead with astute, bold decisions, McColough had not been well prepared, made real mistakes, and began to pull back. How costly this could be would be clear to Steve Jobs years later: "If Xerox had known what it had and had taken advantage of its real opportunities, it could have been as big as IBM *plus* Microsoft *plus* Xerox *combined*—and the largest high technology company in the world."

Years before, Joe Wilson had become deeply intrigued with the benefits to 3M of its corporate policy of encouraging its scientist-inventors to spend boldly on developing unusual new products. Wilson was excited about a corporate "skunk works" where creative scientists would devote themselves to searching for technological breakthroughs. When Jack Goldman joined Xerox with his dream of developing a modern technological equivalent of Bell Labs, his dream fit with Wilson's concept, and Goldman had the drive and the mandate to bring it all to fruition at Xerox's Palo Alto Research Center, known as PARC. As Goldman then put it: "I see Xerox as being in a class with Bell Labs in a few years, and Bell Labs is the elite of corporate research. We're going to show the world."

PARC gathered together a spectacular group of brilliantly talented and inventive technologists who, among many exciting advances, created the personal computer and the computer mouse. They were prescient and were moving wonderfully opposite to the trend at the time toward large-scale, centralized computing. Like XDS, PARC had an open, creative culture that was just as alien—and alienating—to the Rochester culture as Rochester was alien to PARC. The visible manifestations of the PARC culture—totally unconventional working hours, shoulder-length hair in pony tails, rings in ears, sandals and jeans—were totally different from the Ivy League, conservative, button-down corporate culture at headquarters. Just as had happened with XDS, the two cultures all too quickly became dismissive of each other—"hippie weirdos" with no respect for their employer's senior executives versus totally out of touch, uptight, anal "suits"—and soon could not and would not work together or even communicate together. They stayed separate. So the best ideas of PARC never got taken seriously by Xerox and never got to the market—at least, not for Xerox.

When Steve Jobs and others wanted to visit PARC, a security officer protested. However, she was ordered by the East Coast headquarters to show them around. Still protesting, she asked for and got a sign-off from headquarters. On the East Coast, Xerox executives did not understand Moore's Law about the falling costs of memory and saw the PC as an item of very limited interest, never imagining that the cost of a PC would drop, as it did in just four years, from $12,000 to $3,000.

Understanding as he did that Xerox would be facing increasingly large challenges to sustain the humane climate and the practice of caring for each individual that Xerox was becoming known for, Wilson worried: "Already we see signs of losing it. We're trying to indoctrinate new people, but twenty thousand employees around the Western Hemisphere isn't like a thousand in Rochester."

Once asked if he had doubts about being able to sustain the company culture, Wilson nodded in recognition of the seriousness of the question: "It's an everlasting battle, which we may or may not win."

Wilson would not live to see the failure of XDS, nor the failure of PARC. Nor would he witness the destruction of the inspirational, empowering, entrepreneurial culture he had so carefully nurtured at Xerox; nor the loss in R&D and new product initiatives to the Japanese; nor the loss in integrity that would lead to junk bond ratings, a long-term collapse in share value capped by heavy fines for fraudulent accounting; nor the adverse changes that would come in labor relations that would lead to a bitter strike. But he did see the early stages and must have been very deeply disturbed.

But there was nothing he could see to do to stop it without harming Peter McColough as CEO. So, as always, he gave his support to the man with the direct responsibility.

There were other problems. Joe Wilson had not developed a strong board of directors—perhaps because of the troubles with Gilbert Mosher; perhaps because the company's board had been a place to park executives who were not keeping up; perhaps because he didn't want to take the time and energy to win support from a board after already winning it from his managers; perhaps because he used the annual planning conferences as an alternative "review board"; and probably also because he would have found it boring to go through the whole process of reviewing key plans and decisions with an outside group of directors.

Another reason was simple: Wilson knew how to use outside experts to get advice and did so quite regularly so he did not really need a strong board. While Wilson may well have been planning to make it strong and effective, the Xerox board of directors of the mid-1960s was as weak as it had always been. McColough apparently took advantage of this weakness: Instead of engaging directors in serious issues and decisions, he filled board meetings with reports

on financial measures in a format dominated by one-way presentations. And he filled the board with celebrities. (When the idea of
acquiring Crum & Forster, the insurance conglomerate, was presented—in just one half-hour without any prior briefings to the
Board—only Harvard Business School professor Kenneth Andrews
spoke against it as merely a blatant financial deal with no strategic
merit. William Simon, Vernon Jordan, and Robert Strauss all voted
for it.)

On September 19, 1968, Chet Carlson had a few hours between
a philanthropic conference and a dinner. Noticing a movie
he'd heard favorable reports on, he went in and took an aisle seat.
Watching the movie, *He Who Rides a Tiger*, at the Festival Theater on
West 57th Street in Manhattan, Carlson had a heart attack and died.
He was 62.[5] The day before, while his wife, Dorris, waited in the
entrance to the Sherry Netherlands Hotel on Fifth Avenue, Carlson
had seen a man selling helium-filled balloons across the street at the
entrance to Central Park, crossed over to buy one balloon—and let
it go. Asked why, Carlson replied, "To set it free—to let it soar over
those high buildings."

Carlson's technology dream—brilliant as it was and so very
timely—came true and made him the fortune he generously gave
away. He became one of the nation's best known inventors because
his brilliant invention interconnected with Joe Wilson's extraordinary entrepreneurial leadership. Carlson and Wilson profoundly
changed each other's lives. As was typical of Joe Wilson, he repeti-

[5]From Secretary General U Thant came this tribute: "To know Chester Carlson
was to like him, to love him and respect him. He was generally known as the
inventor of xerography, and although it was an extraordinary achievement in the
technological and scientific field, I respected him more as a man of exceptional
moral stature and as a humanist. His concern for the future of the human situation
was genuine, and his dedication to the principles of the United Nations was profound. He belonged to that rare breed of leaders who generate in our hearts faith
in man and hope for the future."

tively took occasions to celebrate Carlson and his essential contributions to the successes of Xerox and xerography.

"All progress depends on the unreasonable man," Wilson said, citing George Bernard Shaw, "because reasonable men accept the world as it is while unreasonable men persist in adapting the world to them. Chester Carlson was splendidly unreasonable."

Governor Nelson Rockefeller called Wilson very early one morning. Rockefeller was upset—and with good reason. He was calling to make a last ditch appeal. "Joe! You cannot leave New York!" Having a high-profile corporation like Xerox move to another state—particularly to nearby Connecticut where several other "New York" companies had already moved to avoid New York State taxes—was a serious political problem for Rockefeller. To him, Xerox *was* Joe Wilson. But Xerox was not Wilson's company anymore. Now it was McColough's company. So Wilson could only give one response, "Governor, you'll have to discuss that with Peter McColough. He's the CEO now."

Outwardly calm and self-disciplined, Wilson was, of course, deeply upset by this decision. As a native Rochesterian, he had always felt a special bond with his home city. Within the prior year he had promised a City Club audience: "I give you my word. Xerox will *never* leave Rochester!" And now his own choice as CEO was pulling out! His disappointment was profound. Wilson knew if he openly opposed the move, he would undermine his successor CEO. So once again, he maintained his remarkable, but customary, self-discipline and said nothing publicly. One telling measure of Wilson's distress: The move out of Rochester was the only corporate action that ever caused him to visit with each of his children to discuss the decision.

McColough's decision to move Xerox headquarters to Stamford illustrates J.P. Morgan's sardonic view that "for every major business decision, there are *two* reasons: One is a very good reason. The other is the *real* reason." The good reasons were easy: Get closer to New

York City and the nation's financial community; be closer to major airports; and be easier for customers and suppliers to get to. McColough offered another high-minded explanation that Wilson and others must have found even less plausible, since many other major corporations with their headquarters in outlying cities had convenience offices in Manhattan: "After I'd been CEO for two years, I had become increasingly aware of the problems of being headquartered in Rochester. We had large operations on the West Coast, and a big international business, and the people in these operations felt they were missing out on promotions compared to those in the operating divisions in Webster and Rochester who had informal access to senior management just by getting on the elevator. I wanted to be in a neutral area—but not a major city—and be near major airports because we had a lot of people flying to Europe and Latin America."

Joe Wilson couldn't have disagreed more, but true to his code, he kept silent while McColough, conveniently taking liberties in interpreting Wilson's disciplined silence, could say, "Joe understood my view and didn't disagree."

The *real* reasons for moving were personal and parochial. As a newly installed CEO, McColough was very aware of and sensitive to people at all levels of the corporation reaching out to Wilson for guidance, for judgment, and for decision. So long as Xerox was in Rochester, it would *always* be Joe Wilson's company—and McColough would be under Wilson's shadow inside Xerox and in the outside world. So McColough decided he had to move away from Joe Wilson's Rochester. The move to Stamford, Connecticut, was made in September 1969.

A special company "shuttle" plane flew back and forth from Rochester to White Plains, making five round trips every day. While only 168 people were actually moved to Stamford and some senior executives, like Kent Damon, refused to go, the personal disruptions caused by the move were many, often large, and simultaneous. Homes that cost $200,000 in Rochester could cost $500,000—

2½ times as much—to replicate near Stamford. Not only were a large number of Rochester's "finer" homes suddenly all for sale—too many for the local market to absorb without major price reductions—large new mortgages, with comparably higher monthly payments, were required to buy homes in Stamford. Xerox underwrote part of the annual costs, but workers with modest $50,000 homes in Rochester could not afford to buy *any* homes in Stamford and were obliged to move into apartments. Several moved into one rather drab apartment complex and sarcastic comments were soon heard about "Attica on the Hudson."

As the corporation was changing—moving farther and farther away physically and spiritually from the enterprise that Joe Wilson had devoted his career to developing—the joy of engagement he had always felt at Xerox was fading. When Don Clark, the superb product manager of the triumphant 914 said to Wilson, "I don't enjoy making decisions the way I always used to," Wilson replied: "I feel the same way. It's just not the same."

Colleagues observed that discussions with Wilson were just as thoughtful and probing, but they were "just conversations" and often, nothing much happened as a result. The familiar focus and drive were no longer there. Consulting psychologist Paul Brower observed: "Joe is coming to the end of his career. He doesn't have the same interest, the same commitment."

Shortly after moving to Stamford, McColough's company went silent on the man who had for so many years been its leader and spokesman. All attention would now focus on the company's new management and its future: There were to be no celebrations of past successes or Joe Wilson. His name was never mentioned. Soon the name and personality of Joe Wilson would fade from memory. And as more and more young people—who had not known him—became part of the crowd, Wilson's name and the reasons for his fame faded, too. By the end of the century, students at the University of Rochester's business school would not, when asked, even recognize the name Joe Wilson.

The impact on Rochester was equally damaging. The quality of life in any city, as Wilson had understood so well, depends on the commitment of volunteer leaders who bring vision and energy to its cultural and civic institutions. All the major organizations that had benefited from having Xerox executives in key leadership roles suddenly lost most of them. Finding capable, knowledgeable replacements from the company was not possible because the word had gone out: "Don't bother anymore with all that extracurricular stuff; current management does not care."

Changing from Rochester to Stamford, disruptive and damaging as it was, was not the greatest nor the gravest change for Xerox. The larger change began with what seemed a sensible answer to a problem that worried McColough. As one of the top executives at the time recalled: "Peter saw a real problem at Xerox: There was no age distribution in our management or our key professionals. We were all the same age. He also came to believe we were cut from the same cloth. So McColough brought us into a room one day and spoke very candidly to us: 'You're all my friends, and you've come a long way. But to go forward, we're going to need new talent with more experience in managing a very large, global corporation because Xerox is now a very large, global corporation and none of us has ever learned how to run a very large, global corporation.'"

McColough hired recruiters to bring in experienced multinational corporate executives and put them into top executive positions *over* the team Wilson had recruited and nurtured. Executives were hired, primarily from Ford and GE, who were skillful in financial controls and cost-cutting. McColough urged them on: "During the past decade, we had to make a choice: go for growth *or* manage for cost-efficiency. If we had chosen the latter, we would have sales of $300 million instead of a billion, so [in the past] we chose to go for growth. Now, we can bring cost disciplines to this larger company and increase our profitability to even higher levels."

Unfortunately, McColough's imported executives did not work well together. Ford ways conflicted with GE methods and GE people fought against Ford people as different "tribal" cultures competed with each other for dominance at Xerox. The focus changed quickly from long-term to short-term, from people to numbers, from value to costs, from inspiring potentials to hard facts, and from positive reward to negative threats. Corporate politics became rampant and often vicious. The collegial and entrepreneurial culture Joe Wilson had worked so long and hard to nurture was the first thing to go. Even the language changed. As Jack Goldman recalled hearing in his very first meeting with McColough: "It's your head on the block, not mine. If you don't get the results I expect, your head is in the noose—and I'll be the hangman."

PARC, which Wilson had envisioned as a highly creative research and development center, was not getting McColough's attention. Without a CEO's direct patronage and involvement, the innovative changes such a group might conceive and develop would never get the corporate cooperation needed to convert them into successful products.

Japanese competitors were gaining market share at the lower end of the product line and price range, but McColough seemed determined both to hold Xerox pricing high to maximize current profits and to concentrate on the high-margin, top-end copier-duplicators. Longer term, this made it all too easy for competitors to get established and was a major strategic mistake—and it got visibly worse and worse as Japanese competitors got stronger and stronger.

Changes at Xerox were shadowed by changes in Joe Wilson's outlook. To members of his family, Wilson seemed to be suffering from increasing depression. And as the months went by, Wilson's depression got visibly worse. There were many possible causes: the end of his years as CEO and builder of Xerox; the disappointment with Linowitz; his increasing distress about McColough's capabilities—about which he felt he could do little or nothing; *and* such personal matters as his continuing health worries and the empty nest at home as the Wilson children went away to school, got married, and changed the center of their orbit away from Clover Street. On a larger scale, Wilson was deeply concerned about the disturbing prospect that America—and the world—would not be able to achieve control over the great problems of poverty, racism, and the inadequacies in healthcare and education. During the summer of 1971, Wilson fell into a deeper depression. He even stopped going to the music concerts he had so loved.

To mark his 35th anniversary of supportive service to the City Club and its tradition of having outstanding speakers at noon on Saturdays, Wilson agreed to give a talk centered on his personal business philosophy. He had been giving some thought to writing a short book on the subject and this might be a good forum to try out some of his ideas. It wasn't. Only a dozen of his own friends came. The era of the City Club had passed. Even a talk by Joe Wilson of Xerox was not enough of a draw to attract a decent crowd.

30

AT THE ROCKEFELLERS'

"**G**reat news!" Joe Wilson told Peggy in November 1971. "Today I got my first totally clean electrocardiogram in years!"

As usual, Wilson had put in a long week with meetings and speeches in five different cities, concluding with Friday's investment committee meeting at the University of Rochester. On Saturday, he was at home on Clover Street, nursing a cold. Sunday, he worked out on his stationary bike while Peggy attended Mass.

Monday morning, Wilson flew in Xerox's corporate jet—The 914—from Rochester to the White Plains airport, just 20 minutes from the Stamford headquarters, where he met with Peter McColough to discuss another orderly change in the Xerox senior management structure. McColough explained that Archie McCardle would be advancing to President and COO and McColough as CEO would move to Chairman. This would displace Wilson, so the question was what title should he then be using? Wilson said he thought it important that his new title be chosen with the understanding that it would not get changed anytime soon. McColough agreed and they settled on Chairman of the Executive Committee. Neither man recognizing the ironic inversion: Joe Wilson was "succeeding" Sol Linowitz.

After spending the night in the Xerox apartment in Manhattan's Pierre Hotel, Wilson went by limousine to the Xerox monthly management meeting in the Bankers Trust Tower on Park Avenue at 48th Street. He had arranged with McColough that he would be leaving just before noon for a luncheon with Governor Rockefeller at the Rockefellers' triplex on Fifth Avenue for a meeting of the Governor's Club, a political fund-raising group that Wilson had recently agreed to chair. He would then return for the Board of Directors meeting that same afternoon. As a courtesy to Wilson, McColough arranged to have the morning meeting end a few minutes early so there would be plenty of time to get to the Governor's apartment 20 blocks to the north on Fifth Avenue.

As the morning session was breaking up, Wilson took Jack Goldman aside for a brief exchange. Goldman was on the verge of terminating for cause a 20-year veteran, and Wilson wanted to be sure that the traditional caring for individuals at Xerox would govern—even when the man's problems involved drinking and drugs and inappropriate behavior in the labs. "Do what you have to do, Jack, but please remember, in the past, he did a lot for this company."

"I understand, Joe. We'll do it right."

"Thank you, Jack."

Reaching out, Wilson warmly shook hands with Goldman, and stepped into the elevator. Coming off the elevator where it stopped at the mezzanine floor, he walked down the stairs to the ground level, out through the revolving door, down a few more steps to the sidewalk, and into the waiting limousine.

The limousine drove over to Madison Avenue and up to 68th Street, west one block to Fifth Avenue, and Governor Rockefeller's apartment building. Going into the building, Wilson gave his name to the concierge. "You are expected, Mr. Wilson."

Wilson entered the elevator and stood quietly near the back until it stopped at the vestibule to the governor's apartment. As the doors opened, the Rockefeller butler recognized him: "Good afternoon, Mr. Wilson. The governor is expecting you, sir."

Tasteful, of course, the Rockefeller apartment was slightly overweight with paintings and sculptures by a galaxy of leading artists of the nineteenth and twentieth centuries. Even though the individual works had long been in Rockefeller's private collection, many had been included in art books so they seemed familiar.

Wilson was dressed as usual in a conservative, dark suit with a striped tie, and wore dark, horn-rimmed glasses. He was friendly and personable, but still somewhat shy and inclined to listen and defer to others. While he was one of the best-known people there— after the Rockefellers, perhaps *the* best-known—Wilson blended, as usual, quite comfortably into the crowd.

After 20 minutes of pleasantries, Governor Rockefeller called everyone to come into the dining room for lunch. Putting his arm around his principal guest's shoulder, he guided Wilson to the center of the long dining table, saying: "Joe, won't you sit here— between Happy and me." All the guests took their seats and began to eat and chat.

Mrs. Rockefeller turned from the guest on her right to talk with Joe Wilson and saw that he had slid back in his chair. Her first thought was that he must be reaching down to get his glasses off the floor.

Then she realized that he was unconscious.

One of the waiters was an off-duty policeman. He tried CPR right away, but it was no use. Joe Wilson was gone.

Dr. Karl G. Klinger was called and Joseph Chamberlain Wilson was pronounced dead at 1:30 PM.

On Tuesday, November 23, 1971, the *New York Times* ran a detailed obituary and this unusually long editorial:

Joe Wilson had the qualities of greatness—courage, vision, leadership, humanity, eloquence, energy, dedication,

inspiration. The story of his daring development of xerography is well known but ever fascinating. It transformed the little Haloid Company into the giant and ever-expanding Xerox Corporation, was a major factor in Rochester's post-war boom, and made wealthy men and women of those bold enough to follow his lead.

But for Joseph Wilson, business success and fortune were simply means to achieving broader humanitarian goals. He constantly reminded Xerox employees and shareholders of the social responsibilities of business and backed up his words, despite some criticism, with corporate and personal contributions. He saw to it that Xerox pioneered in employing and otherwise assisting blacks struggling for business success. Mr. Wilson strengthened the University of Rochester and all of education immensely. His favorite message to the many scientific people with whom he associated was their obligation to harness technology to serve mankind's welfare.

Joseph Wilson loved his native Rochester and New York State, and he channeled much of his philanthropy—both known and unrecorded—to their benefit. He made Xerox Square a distinguished Rochester landmark and resisted as much as possible the lure of other areas, both personally and corporately.

Perhaps the greatest of Mr. Wilson's contributions was his own deep involvement in public affairs. He grappled with the sternest of community challenges. He had the ability to inspire the best energy and thinking of those who worked with him in volunteer enterprises, and he cut to the core of problems with incisive questions. He was disappointed when others failed to share his zeal to assist those who suffered from poverty, ill-health, discrimination, bad housing or insufficient education. Joseph Wilson took advantage of his retirement from active leadership of Xerox to strengthen his active participation in planning for change, better health education and other progressive movements.

He walked with the lowly as comfortably as with the mighty; he loved both humanity and humans. He was humble and vibrant and confident and scholarly and witty and optimistic and ever questing for new solutions to old problems.

(Copyright © 2006 by the New York Times Co. Reprinted with permission.)

AFTERWORD

Wilson was, in retrospect, astonishingly able to develop and hold steadfastly onto an inspiring yet abstract vision and to advance repetitively toward fulfilling and realizing that vision in specific, pragmatic ways; to take well-reasoned, deliberate risks with people, technology, finance, and new ways of marketing; to inspire and encourage or confront and discipline groups or individual peoples; and to balance and harmonize the long-term interests of shareholders, workers, and customers. He varied his tactics to keep advancing toward the long-term objectives he so clearly understood through both extensive study of philosophy, history, and literature and intensive consideration of specific people, problems, and innovation.

His persistence, stamina, and tenacity were balanced by his grace under pressure, engaging personal manner, and genuine caring for others. In retrospect, it is intriguing to consider how far ahead of his time Joe Wilson was in addressing gender and racial injustice, in improving labor-management relationships, and in understanding and articulating the role of corporations and individual business leaders in addressing the failures of our society.

As he so clearly understood, the real test of private enterprise is in an organization's ability to both earn profits through creative solutions to economic problems and to use its strengths—financial, managerial, and reputation—to provide leadership in solving social problems. In his own career, Joe Wilson demonstrated how similar and interconnected the roles of leadership are in private and social enterprise.

An American entrepreneur, Joe Wilson embraced the responsibilities of true leadership and devoted himself to an entrepreneurial grand strategy of very large dimensions that is worthy of careful study and sure to provide inspiration.

Over an unusually privileged professional career, I have worked closely as a consultant or advisor with a remarkably large number of leaders of successful organizations in Europe, North America, and Asia—particularly in finance and education. I believe that Joe Wilson represents the values, skills, and aspirations that great leaders care most about as they strive to develop the effectiveness and successes of their organization in achieving professional fulfillment for insiders and superior value for clients and customer service—secure in the knowledge that most workers prefer to be challenged and given opportunities to do their very best, knowing they and their work are truly valued while clients and customers always prefer to receive superior value and personable service. This is why our best organizational leaders are enablers and inspirers who are known to be Servant Leaders.

In professional organizations—hospitals, law firms, consultancies, healthcare institutions, investment managers, universities, etc.—particularly in the larger ones, there is an unrelenting competition between the perceived hard "realities" of the profit discipline versus the softer, but higher order professional values. At the best business organizations, there is a continuous striving for professionalism and the richer rewards for careers that come with success in pursuit of a holistic mission through consciously humane and enduring values.

Understanding that greater emphasis on the value factors of professionalism: respect, and caring for individuals; setting higher standards for the quality and consistency of work product; maintaining high ethical standards; developing new and improved products and services; and assuring clients always receive the best the organization is capable of delivering because that assurance is so important to the insiders who understand what it can mean to the client or customer is the real responsibility of great leadership.

Great leaders know that we enjoy doing our very best, particularly when it is for a worthy and meaningful cause or purpose.

People, with very few exceptions, like to do their best work—and like to be recognized and appreciated for doing their best. Joe Wilson understood this phenomenon and he responded to the will to excel by relating directly with people as individuals, by working with the union to develop positive working relationships, by thinking carefully with each executive about their "contract" with the company, and by treating all workers with respect.

Wilson's concepts and commitments ran counter to the then-contemporary drive for cost efficiency and assembly-line work that could neither understand nor accommodate the individual's nor the team's creativity and pride in workmanship. Joe Wilson recognized people as most wish to be recognized—with respect and as individuals—and this approach enabled him to connect and engage with many people.

If you don't understand who you truly are, positions of power—whether business, political, military, religious, or social—can prove very expensive ways to find out. They are expensive to the individual and expensive to others. Joe Wilson understood who he was and what he wanted to accomplish, and he had the self-discipline to stay focused on his chosen objective. Wilson's effectiveness as a leader centered on his aiming at achieving high values and his making pragmatic, disciplined commitments to achieving those goals by engaging other people.

Perhaps because he respected people as individuals, Wilson was unusually interested in fairness and was far ahead of his times on constructive labor relations, race relations, gender fairness, job opportunities, and welfare reform—and on many individual situations where justice was inadequate. And Wilson was not content to deal fairly with issues and cases presented to him; he actively sought out opportunities to do better.

He was exceptionally bright, remarkably rational, and unusually well connected to a wide array of information, ideas, and concepts through his extensive reading and persistent learning through others. His Emotional Intelligence was very high. His sustained concentration on his tasks and responsibilities was covered over with a modesty in manner that made it easy for others to feel connection and trust. And he was unusually worthy of trust. Consistent in what he said and did because he knew who he was and what he intended to accomplish, he lived by a set of values that others appreciated and aspired to live by.

Because his way of rendering service to organizations was "universal"—do research, set challenging goals, develop an effective strategy, build an organization, and commit to sustained effort—he developed and applied them in each of his undertakings in Xerox, at the University of Rochester, in Rochester as a community, and in national "social enterprise."

Time is treated differently by great leaders. Most obviously, the time into the future that they consider relevant is longer. Their colleagues are frequently surprised by how very far ahead they think about aspirations, strategies, resources, and people. They are also unusually able to commit long hours over many months and years, apparently without tiring. Alternatively, they are unusually capable of making time to care for others within their organization. Their interactions with colleagues are relational, not transactional, and they really do think "We," not "I" or "me."

Vision—visualizing and developing an inspiring purpose and realistic destiny for an organization—is taken very seriously. They see it as a real responsibility: a congenial blend of confidence and genuine doubt; the ability to have a clear sense of direction and purpose and, simultaneously be open to different views and different ways and means to achieving desired ends.

Integrity is so much more than not doing wrong: Business and personal ethics mean always doing right—to the highest possible level—not just in response to issues presented, but by actively looking for issues and then flooding the system with affirmative actions on core values.

Joe Wilson changed my life. We never met and I saw him only once, in 1965 across a crowded room. Wilson gave a 20-minute talk about business leadership and his work at Xerox, then one of America's most successful technology-based growth companies. His straightforward and high-minded explanation of the tasks, responsibilities, and rewards of real leadership in business raised and clarified my own aspirations for a career in leadership. As a recent graduate of Harvard Business School, seeking a meaningful direction in the early years of my career, I found Joe Wilson inspiring. He showed the way.

Wilson's message rang true for me then and still does today. I felt then and feel now a true connection. Over the next several years, I made a particular point of reading the numerous studies of Xerox written for institutional investors, Xerox's annual reports, and Wilson's always thoughtful speeches. I strove to understand the underlying sources of his leadership effectiveness.

Joe Wilson led Xerox through more years of uninterrupted growth at a more rapid pace than achieved by *any* other company. He developed an abandoned technology into a new kind of copier that revolutionized office work and made our economy more productive. In addition to transforming the business of his company, Wilson converted his company's labor relations from adversarial to collegial; set a new high standard in corporate graphics and enlightened advertising; created a new concept of business service; taught, through Xerox's example, how corporations could be effective engines for dealing with social problems by creating opportunities; and demonstrated how to develop innovative corporate strategies. (Yes, there is an exception to every rule: Joe Wilson was poor at athletics—consistently and throughout his life.)

Joe Wilson's example went far beyond his splendid business career. He devoted his entire life to creative and effective leadership in public service. He made time to gather the relevant information. He formulated astute strategies and engaged numerous others in concerted action. And when appropriate, he used the profitability of Xerox and his own increasing wealth to lead the process of social change, both in his home city and on a national scale in education, racial justice, and welfare reform.

After several years of extensive research for this biography and more than 30 years of strategy consulting with many of the most capable business leaders around the world, it is clear to me that Joe Wilson of Xerox gives all who aspire to a higher standard of leadership careers in business a truly exemplary and inspirational example. Joe Wilson's example was particularly important in my 30 years as managing partner of Greenwich Associates, as we went from a tiny, starry-eyed start-up to worldwide leadership in strategy consulting for professional financial service organizations, eventually serving the leaders in all 135 financial service markets around the world. Exciting as our progress over these 30 years seemed to us, it was candidly insignificant in comparison to the progression Joe Wilson achieved with Xerox and in public service, particularly to the University of Rochester.

I feel doubly blessed: first, to have been inspired by Joe Wilson many years ago at the beginning of my own career, and more recently to have that inspiration reaffirmed through many hours of discussions with those who knew him best through their work together many years ago at Xerox.

Joe Wilson was the kind of modest, principled, articulate, and inspiring leader Americans most enjoy admiring. Wilson's Xerox was the kind of dynamic, innovative, stylish growth company Americans most admire. Wilson thought deeply about leadership in business management and exemplified entrepreneurial *and* societal leadership and he worked very hard to make good things happen. For young business professionals like me, Joe Wilson was a model of a new kind of effective business leader, and I confidently adapted to my own life the example he made so convincing and accessible.

Nearly 40 years ago, Phil Bower stopped by my very small office on the 54th floor of 30 Rockefeller Plaza, where I was working on investments at Rockefeller Brothers, Inc., starting at the very bottom of the totem pole. "Charley, there's gonna be a presentation at the Analysts' next week by a company that might be interesting, so maybe you should go."

Over the next week, I read up on Xerox, an unusually interesting and exciting company, and learned how Joe Wilson had transformed his company from a tiny upstate New York photographic paper supplier into a major international corporation. I learned how it was creating its own rapid growth through pioneering technological innovations that were transforming the tasks of office work everywhere, and increasing sales one *hundred* fold—from less than $10 million to more than $1 billion—in just 20 years. Joe Wilson's Xerox was changing the lives of many people: thousands of workers at Xerox, hundreds of thousands of investors, and millions of office workers around the world *and* was reaching out to new fields in communication and education and setting an inspiring example of business integrity and social responsibility.

On January 27, 1965, I took the Sixth Avenue subway from Rockefeller Center to the Wall Street station, walked three blocks to 16 William Street, and took the elevator to the 18th floor meeting room of The New York Society of Security Analysts. The organization met in a large room where notoriously ordinary meals were usually served to motley crowds of skeptical analysts in their 20s and 30s. But that cold January evening, the room was filled with strikingly well-dressed men with nicely tanned faces who were well into their 50s and 60s. They were nearly festive as they greeted each other and bantered good-naturedly, their voices pitched half an octave lower than the usual, much younger crowd's. Even the quality of the food served was different: not baked, rubber chicken, but freshly grilled shell steaks; not fruit cup, but shrimp cocktail; not Jell-o, but a fine chocolate mousse.

The *bonhomie* of the occasion was understandable. In the four years since Wilson's last meeting with this group of investment professionals, Xerox's earnings had increased ten-fold. Xerox's earnings had risen more than 50% during the preceding nine months, by 100% over the previous year, and by a magnificent 300% over the prior five years. Xerox was *the* big winner in the personal accounts of most of the dinner crowd, and it had been the big winner for the accounts of their grateful customers—which made this gathering winners all over again. As Winston Churchill so aptly observed, "People like winning very much!" Wall Street is certainly no exception. Xerox had made everyone in that room a big winner, and they liked that very much.

Xerox was increasingly widely recognized as the exemplary modern American company, and Joe Wilson epitomized the contemporary high-minded business leader who, with tenacity to purpose, empowered young executives to help realize his inspiring vision with his engaging personal modesty and refreshing sophistication. Joe Wilson led his dynamic company in solving society's problems through creative technology and marketing innovations in several ways:

- The 914 and 813 copiers were revolutionizing office work, and more major new products were on their way.
- Through Rank-Xerox and Fuji-Xerox, Wilson's company was expanding internationally and in doing so, its profits were soaring.
- Education, with its seemingly limitless needs *and* opportunities, was Xerox's chosen territory for future growth of the company that was already transforming communication.
- Social responsibility—at a time when few accepted and some bluntly denied any major role for corporations in bettering society—was taken seriously and undertaken effectively.
- Joe Wilson—with conservative good looks and Ivy League suits that reminded many of JFK—had inherited a small upstate company with very uncertain prospects and, by finding, developing, and capitalizing upon a major new technology had, in a storybook adventure in enterprise, converted tiny Haloid into mighty Xerox.

Wilson was clearly comfortable with the significant connections he found between his business pragmatism and the rich canon of Western civilization in which he was unusually well-read and well informed. His explorations of the works of great thinkers and his well-reasoned concept of leadership linked his humbly inspiring core values and character to the tasks and responsibilities that came his way *and* those he sought out. Through his integration of gracefully articulated concepts and disciplined pragmatism, he made his core values the culture of his company and a universal beacon for all who aspire to leadership in the true public interest in business, government, or social enterprise.

Those who are prone to believe that leadership or management can be reduced to the simplistic and formulaic recipes of most popular books on these subjects will be disappointed. Effective leadership and management must always adapt to specific situations and particular individuals. That's why great leaders like Joe Wilson are both constant to purpose and imaginatively adaptive to circumstance. In my continuing consultations on strategy and its implementation with the leaders of nearly 200 major finance service organizations around the world, I see both success and failure determined by leaders' understanding or not understanding this reality that Joe Wilson understood so unusually well.

Wilson spoke about the kind of business leadership and management he believed were needed by the world we were going to live in. He also addressed how his company intended to earn increasing profits by meeting some of mankind's major needs and solving some of society's great problems. Through his own commitment and success, Wilson implicitly invited *and* challenged each of his listeners to consider new ways of understanding the role of the corporation in changing people's lives for the better.

The more I studied what he said and did, the more I believed with Wilson that three other measures of success were at least as important as profits:

- Providing opportunities for personal growth and professional fulfillment to those devoting their careers to the organization
- Achieving consistent fulfillment—or better—of clients' expectations

- Actively volunteering to help develop effective educational and social service organizations in the community—broadly delivered

Since success in each of these measures adds strength to the others, who would be willing to subordinate the three *qualitative* dimensions of life and living to the one *quantitative* dimension of profit maximization?

Years ago, I anticipated the pleasure of reading a major biography of this remarkable man who, by his thoughtful speeches and confirming action, redefined modern business leadership in America. No biography came, so I tried to encourage several business historians to write the Joe Wilson story, but while they recognized Wilson's biography should be done, no one seemed quite ready to try, at least partly because after Wilson's era, Xerox had fallen on difficult times. My determination to do what I could about Joe Wilson's biography hardened when I learned that when an audience of graduate students at the University of Rochester's business school were asked, "Who can tell us something about Joe Wilson?" no hands were raised. No one knew. Young men and women planning professional careers in business leadership and studying at his own university in his own home city did not know the inspiring story of Joe Wilson of Xerox.

As my service to Greenwich Associates came to a close, the idea that perhaps I should write Joe Wilson's biography myself began to gather momentum. After all, I'd been a major beneficiary of his example: He had given me something I treasured—a different way of conceiving leadership. So, believing Joe Wilson's story is truly an All-American story that would inspire young business leaders if made available to them, I wanted to fulfill a personal feeling of obligation to say thank you to the man who pointed the way for me to a more fulfilling way to make both a life and a living. Soon, the decision was obvious: Go!

Getting to know about Joe Wilson through the last several years of research has been an inspiring and affirming experience. This very bright and thoughtful man led his colleagues in a long and great adventure in technological enterprise while absorbing the burden of his own health problems and his disappointments in the behavior of others. He endured the profound stress familiar to great entrepreneurial leaders as they sustain their strong commitment to a still-dawning vision. With persistent drive and determination, Joe Wilson nurtured and led an organization to achieve results far beyond the resources available when he first made that commitment. As Wilson so often said, "If we have but one life to lead, pitch this one high!"

Joe Wilson was right for himself and his company in his particular times, yet his aspirations and expectations for modern organizational leadership are universal. That's why the man I never met is such a great example for business professionals intent on making something special of their lives and careers—and why he influenced me so much and to my very great benefit.

Charles D. Ellis
New Haven, Connecticut
April, 2006

JOE WILSON:
IN HIS OWN WORDS

His personal mission statement (always carried in his wallet)

"To be a whole man; to attain serenity: through the creation of a family life of uncommon richness; through leadership of a business which brings happiness to its workers, serves well its customers and brings prosperity to its owners; and by aiding a society, threatened by fratricidal division, to gain unity."

Leadership must have soul

"Leaders must have souls which have been enriched. There is another tempering need, the love and understanding of beauty in the broadest sense, the comprehension of art and literature, the appreciation of philosophy and ethics, of order and aesthetics, of the rich variety of man's character, of bravery, of weakness, of lofty aspirations. The best of them must have, on the one hand, the resources of the artist whose penetrating perception allows him to master and interpret phenomena he does not fully comprehend; and yet, on the other, he must strive constantly for the facts the scientist wants and use his method of precision."

On organizations and people

"Organized human endeavor can be lifted an order of magnitude through leadership if it is inspiring. The springs of inspiration lie deep in the knowledge of all that is worst and best in men and in the wholehearted acceptance of that worst and best. To lead well is to know people and to know, above all, that they are always people."

More important than the balance sheet, always

"To set high goals, to have almost unattainable aspirations, to imbue people with the belief that they can be achieved—these are as important as the balance sheet, perhaps more so."

Give me your imagination and creativity

"We are a company which pays a premium on imagination, on the use of creativity, on the use of brains to think of new ideas. We don't want to do things that same old way; we suspect the same old way. Therefore, as you come here, I hope you come with an attitude that changes will be a way of life for you. You will not be doing things tomorrow the way you are doing them today. And if you do, we will feel that some way or other the momentum that has taken years and years to build up, is perhaps slowing down. Therefore, we're seeking people who are willing to accept risk, who are willing to try new ideas, who have new ideas of their own, who are not afraid to change what they are doing, from one day to the next, or one year to the next, who welcome new challenges, who welcome new people, who welcome new positions. And if you're that sort of person you'll be very welcome here at Xerox."

Innovation is the first principle of success

"We believe first in innovation—throughout the company. We want to create new services that have not been rendered before and secure a profit from them. Our best rewards have come from things of this sort, like the 914—unheard of at the time it was introduced, but now one of the most successful products in America. This is the first principle."

On the importance of character

"There is another quality—of the spirit—which is equally meaningful. Call it esprit, call it enthusiasm, call it striving for excellence, call it willingness to change, to create, to innovate—

or call it courage to risk. Call it many things but it adds up to character."

Business as ten words of poetry (which Wilson artfully "misses by a unit")

"The head of a business works with people, and all other phases of his task pale in significance compared to this need to know human beings, to understand the complexity of their characters and motives, to persuade them of sound judgments, and above all to inspire in them the desire to lift their joint efforts to planes above those which their individual capacities could achieve. Think of that line of Browning's, 'This high man, aiming at a million, misses by a unit.' In ten words, it distills an essence of business leadership, and it comes from nineteenth-century English poetry."

Social progress

"Business leaders—because they will direct the new technologies—will be held accountable in larger part for the total quality of society, for the kind of life the people live throughout much of the world. We therefore cannot give lip service to social progress. We must be committed to it, work for it and achieve it . . . else we shall lose our power to be free."

On morality in business

"The happiest development, however, amid all indications of maturing thought about the relationship between business and society, is that gain is no longer thought to be the sole motivating force of businessmen. The man who selects business as a career is no longer, of necessity, assumed deficient in spiritual sensitivity nor atrophied in his development as a whole man. The kind of escape from responsibility prescribed by Adam Smith is now considered by many businessmen as unrealistic, a concept of the utmost sterility.

"The significance of this change cannot be overemphasized. When businessmen were believed bound to selfishness, they could not be entrusted with great power without great risk. As long as business activities were thought to be outside morality, businessmen inevitably were kept aloof from social involvement. The change in thinking about business' responsibilities clears the way for true understanding by both public and businessmen of the real problems confronting society, and, hopefully, for cooperative action to help solve them."

The challenge ahead

"Alfred North Whitehead once said that 'a great society is a society in which its men of business think greatly of their functions.' Perhaps businessmen have never been called upon more urgently to bear witness to that statement as at the present time, for the interest of business and the interest of society have never been more closely joined. The hot and dangerous core of the challenge to the free world lies in the disparity between the material well-being of Americans and that of almost two-thirds of the rest of the human race."

Expand your vision

"It seems beyond belief that anyone could contest the view that the businessman, who wields a vast amount of economic, and therefore social power, must expand his vision beyond the limits of making maximum profit, the traditional definition of his primary function, to encompass many of society's harassing problems which wash the edges of his island. In the last few years, the idea of corporate responsibility has gained broader acceptance. In its employee benefit programs and carefully administered programs of financial support for educational, cultural, and charitable organizations, business has extended its influence over a whole range of human endeavor."

On sound business judgment

"Every businessman who must make the final decision lives at times in a kind of impenetrable loneliness where judgment and its consequences loom large and awful because they focus so tightly on one being. Then the price of power seems high. But more often comes the ecstasy of common aspiration and effort, of the well-joined movement of the group toward valuable objectives through an imaginative, creative process over which no man has control but which must be studied with insight and acted upon with vigor, else others suffer or gain. So great a swing from solitude to community sometimes brings strain to the most resilient personality.

"This is a role that calls for a scholar's willingness to study, analyze, and synthesize, to project bravely, to hypothesize with boldness and wisdom, and then to act from intellectual premises. Those who scoff at the businessman do not understand the good ones and the satisfying richness of their job's demands upon them, just as many businessmen who shrug off the academician do not appreciate the seminal contribution the true lover of knowledge makes to a free society."

ACKNOWLEDGMENTS

Although research for this biography has encountered roadblocks, considerable aid has been provided along the way. In the third of a century since Wilson died, so have several of his closest colleagues. For others, personal recollections are less clear and sometimes bend to conform to conclusions already formed. Peggy Wilson, suffering from Alzheimer's, spent a day in the late 1970s burning all of the family papers. The corporate records of Xerox Corporation are not accessible because of various law suits.

Still, fortune has smiled on this project and help has come from several important sources. Carol Loomis generously provided access to *Fortune's* files and Jon Lovelace arranged to open the historical research files of Capital Group Companies. Ann Neal of Xerox volunteered to guide a search through historical photographs and alerted Xerox alums around the world to the project, inviting submissions of specific memories and experiences. She also made many helpful suggestions on early drafts. Harold Tanner, hearing of my hope to write a biography of Joe Wilson, introduced me to Sol Linowitz, who said he could only help if the Wilson family was in favor of the project. He recommended that I make contact with Chris Wilson, Joe and Peggy Wilson's youngest daughter. Chris invited me to visit with her in Rochester. Gracious and direct, she explained that she really wanted to have her Dad's biography written. After two hours of serious discussion, she decided that I would do—as far as she was concerned—but she suggested that I meet at least some of her siblings because she didn't want to decide alone. An evening in Connecticut, a luncheon in Boston, and a return to Rochester resulted in a favorable consensus. Chris Wilson has consistently encouraged this project and opened doors to many of the individuals who have contributed so much to bring this adventure to fulfillment. Her sisters Diedre Garten, Kathy Roby, and Joan Dahlby have been both patient and warmly encouraging while helping with family insights and wise counsel. Sol Linowitz interviewed with me several times, and his book *The Making of a Public Man* has been helpful, as have John Dessauer's *My Years at Xerox*, Blake McKelvey's privately published *Joe Wilson*, and David Owen's biography of Chester Carlson, *Copies in Seconds*. Erik Pell's *From Dream to Riches*, which details in a careful way the remarkable development of xerography—and the story of those who made it happen—has been particularly helpful. His patient critique of drafts of this book have given me delightful lessons in rigor and kindness.

Along the way, one of my pleasures has been to learn what a remarkable leader and enjoyable person Joe Wilson really was. Another pleasure, through interviews—often long and often several—has been getting to know so many people who would and did gladly give time and effort because they care about the Joe Wilson story being accurately told. Bill Asher, Bob Barker, Merritt Chandler, Minister Franklin Florence, Jack Goldman, Bob Gundlach, Jon Holman, Mike Jensen, David Kearns, Tony Kobayashi, Peter McColough, Ken Rind, Bill Simonds, Robert Sproull, Ernie Stowell, Al Swett, Oscar Tang, and Abe Zarem all gave generously of their time and expertise in often lengthy interviews. Gloria Chapman graciously identified numerous imperfections and provided equally numerous improvements and additions for which I'm very grateful. Hal Bogdonoff, working with a cumbersome device to aid his reading, critiqued and edited—line-by-line—an advanced draft, proving once again the validity of Einstein's view that "My best friend is he who frees me from error!" He critiqued a late draft too, sustaining his generosity.

Special thanks for their remarkable generosity of time during visit after visit—followed by warm encouragement and thoughtful critique—will always go to Erik Pell, John Glavin, Al Swett, David

Curtin, and Horace Becker. Out of their affection for the Joe Wilson they knew and admired, they devoted hours and hours of time to teaching me the history of xerography and Xerox. They illuminated the frustrating struggles to convert little Haloid from a low-volume, job-shop assembler to a modern, high-volume, continuous-process manufacturer of complex, precision equipment, even as a new technology was for the first time being made operational. They patiently corrected errors while encouraging me with their friendship. They are the godfathers of this biography.

Professor John Gaddis, one of the great teacher-scholars of Yale College, generously invited me to join his Yale College senior seminar in biography where we read a 500-page biography each week and discussed the different techniques used to capture the nature of lives led. I enjoyed the Yale tradition of great scholar-teachers working closely with gifted students. John and his wife Toni Dorfmann several times gave me encouraging guidance on ways to improve and strengthen the story. Lorraine Siggins and Braxton McKee, with their understanding of psychology, provided me with helpful insights.

My friends from prior times were helpful in several ways. Howard "Pete" Calhoun was the key Arthur D. Little researcher retained by IBM to estimate copier demand. Jim Weinberg introduced me to his Harvard Business School classmate, Peter McColough. John Pepper introduced me to Tony Kobayashi, his fellow director of Xerox. Stewart Greenfield introduced me to Jack Goldman and Abe Zarem, who both joined in helping with their insights and understanding.

The daunting task of gathering documents and periodical literature was brought under control by the spirited work in the summer of 2001 of two delightful Yale College history majors who were also leaders of the *Yale Daily News*: Tim Cooper and Michael Horn. They plumbed the Internet, dug into the archives of Yale's Sterling Library and the New York Public Library, and made numerous trips to Rochester. Together, we interviewed retired Xerox executives and shared hypotheses while studying documents and exploring every pathway toward understanding—always striving to get the story right. They returned to the project in its later stages, generously and skillfully meeting my request to be "tough on task" as editors.

Significant suggestions for clarifying meaning through macro-restructuring, as well as specific examples and even sentences came at an ideal time from Joel Podolny, the unusually capable and inspiring Dean of Yale's School of Management. He understood from his research and teaching not only what Joe Wilson accomplished, but also the great importance of his principled leadership for the United States' and the world's business community. Leadership such as Joe Wilson's unites an organization's development and respect for individuals with a long-term investor's discipline in finance and creative entrepreneurship. The objectives are to achieve both profit and important societal purposes, just as Joe Wilson did.

Michelle Koss, with consistent good humor and cheerful tolerance for revised revisions ad infinitum did all the typing. She encouraged confidence that an end, eventually, was sure to come.

My beloved wife and best friend, Linda Koch Lorimer, always gave me patient encouragement and insightful critique in a pleasing and productive combination.

Charles D. Ellis
New Haven, Connecticut
April, 2006

INDEX